Webcasting

How to Broadcast to Your Customers Over the Net

Jessica Keyes
New Art, Inc.
New York, New York

McGraw-Hill

New York San Francisco Washington, D.C. Auckland Bogotá
Caracas Lisbon London Madrid Mexico City Milan
Montreal New Delhi San Juan Singapore
Sydney Tokyo Toronto

McGraw-Hill
A Division of The McGraw·Hill Companies

Copyright © 1997 by The McGraw-Hill Companies, Inc. All rights reserved. Printed in the United States of America. Except as permitted under the United States Copyright Act of 1976, no part of this publication may be reproduced or distributed in any form or by any means, or stored in a data base or retrieval system, without the prior written permission of the publisher.

2 3 4 5 6 7 8 9 0   DOC/DOC   9 0 2 1 0 9 8 7

ISBN 0-07-034581-3

The sponsoring editor for this book was Scott Grillo, the editing supervisor was Bernard Onken, and the production supervisor was Pamela A. Pelton. It was set in Century Schoolbook by Jessica Keyes.

Printed and bound by R. R. Donnelley & Sons Company.

McGraw-Hill books are available at special quantity discounts to use as premiums and sales promotions, or for use in corporate training programs. For more information, please write to the Director of Special Sales, McGraw-Hill, 11 West 19th Street, New York, NY 10011. Or contact your local bookstore.

> Information contained in this work has been obtained by The McGraw-Hill Companies, Inc. ("McGraw-Hill") from sources believed to be reliable. However, neither McGraw-Hill nor its authors guarantee the accuracy or completeness of any information published herein and neither McGraw-Hill nor its authors shall be responsible for any errors, omissions, or damages arising out of use of this information. This work is published with the understanding that McGraw-Hill and its authors are supplying information but are not attempting to render engineering or other professional services. If such services are required, the assistance of an appropriate professional should be sought.

 This book is printed on recycled, acid-free paper containing a minimum of 50% recycled, de-inked fiber.

Contents

Preface	ix
Chapter 1. The New Media	**1**
Introduction	
The Webcasted World	3
The Video Connection	7
When Media Collide	7
Webcasting in a Nutshell	11
What All This Means is Now Push Can Come to Shove	13
Chapter 2. Webcasting Success Stories	**15**
The Proof is in the Pudding	15
Wimbelton	15
Ultra-Throb Online	17
Financial Times Television	18
ITV Net	18
Worldwide TV	19
Sci-Fi Channel	21
Film Scouts	23
Virtual Film Festival	25
3WB World Wide Web Broadcasting	26
University Video Communications	27
You Don't Know Jack Show	28
Brainworks Net	29
Hewlett-Packard's Distance Learning System	30
Chapter 3. Unicast, Broadcast, Multicast and the Mbone	**35**
Introduction	35

Unicast, Broadcast and Multicast ... 36
How IP Multicasting Works ... 38
Multicast Design Considerations ... 41
Multicast Extensions to OSPF (RFC 1584) ... 43
Intel Intercast ... 45
Convergence of the Analog TV and Digital PC ... 45
Intel Internet Technology: New Opportunities for Software Developers ... 46
Examples of the Intercast Medium ... 47
How Intel Intercast Works ... 47
Intercast Industry Group ... 50
The Mbone (For Those Who Like to Do It Themselves) ... 51
Mbone Hardware and Software ... 53
How Do You Join the Mbone ... 55
How Do You Find Out About Mbone Events ... 57
Downloadable Mbone Tools ... 59
Problems With the Mbone ... 60
Notes and Online Sources About Mbone ... 61

Chapter 4. Microsoft's View of Webcasting ... 65

NetShow ... 65
An Introduction to Multimedia on the Internet ... 66
How NetShow Works ... 68
Using NetShow ... 2
The Fun Is In Developing the Content ... 75
The NetShow Live Server ... 84
NetMeeting ... 85
Surround Video ... 92
The New Microsoft Network ... 95
Resources ... 97

Chapter 5. Using RealAudio ... 99

Recording Audio Files ... 101
Starting the Encoding Process ... 104
Web Site Configuration ... 106
Using the RealAudio Plug-Ins ... 110
Programming the Plug-in ... 110
Starting a RealAudio Clip from HTML ... 115
Producing RealAudio Events ... 116
Synchronized Multimedia ... 120
Using Frames ... 121
Making Quality RealAudio Recordings ... 122
The RealAudio Server ... 127
Performance Issues ... 134
Encoding Audio ... 136
RealAudio encoder platforms ... 136
RealAudio Live ... 138

Bandwidth Negotiation	139
RealAudio Service Providers	140

Chapter 6. Using VDOLive — 141

First, An Example	141
The VDOnet Technology	147
How Does VDOLive Work	149
The VDOLive Player	150
The VDOLive Server	150
The Video Server Log	152
Using VDOLive Tools	153
VDO Capture: Capturing Video	154
VDO Clip: The Compression Tool	156
The HTML Connection	164
How to Create Embedded (Plug-in) Video	166
Buying VDOLive	169

Chapter 7. Webcasting with Netscape — 171

CoolTalk	171
CoolTalk Chat	175
CoolTalk Whiteboard	175
LiveMedia	179
Netscape Media Server	180
LiveAudio	189
Coding Examples	192
Live3D	196
Netscape Multimedia Plug-ins	201

Chapter 8. More Webcasting Tools — 207

VivoActive	208
VivoActive Producer	209
Steps for Adding Vivo Video to a Web Site	210
Vosaic	214
Xing StreamWorks	216
XingMPEG Encode	218
StreamWorks Transmitter	219
InterVU	220
HTML Coding	223
Tools for Encoding MPEG	225
ClearVideo Decoder	226
Quasi-webcasting Products	226
CU-SeeMe	227
Voxware	229
Macromedia Shockwave	231
Chatting and Collaboration on the Internet	234

Chapter 9. The Telecom Connection — 237

- Television as Precursor to the Information Revolution — 238
- The Wired World — 242
- The Wired Home — 244
- Building the GII — 246
- The Universal Box — 249
- The Internet — 251
- The Case for Internet Access Via Cable TV — 252
- ECnet — 253
- Hawaii Public Schools — 254
- How to Set Up A Community Ethernet to Internet Network — 255

Chapter 10. Audio and Video Production Values — 257

- Guidelines for Digital Video — 257
- Broadcast-Quality Software — 259
- Vivo's Recommendations for Video and Audio Capture — 260
- Audio Considerations — 261
- Digital Editing - The Key to Digital Production — 262
- Applications and Design Considerations in Using Audio in Webcasting — 265
- Speech — 265
- Music — 265
- Sound Effects — 265
- Narration — 265
- Developing the Speech — 266
- Selecting Music — 267
- Selecting Sound Effects — 267
- General Guidelines — 268
- Audio Hints — 269
- Digital and Audio Resources — 273
- Digital Video — 273
- Media Add-in Boards — 286
- Sound — 287
- Animation — 296
- Photographic — 300
- Graphics — 301
- Media Clips — 307

Index — 311
Author Bio — 316

Preface

Imagine a TV show that downloads Web pages while you're watching. Or how about a PC that downloads the movie of the week while you're surfing the 'Net? The first breakthrough is the idea behind Intercast, an Intel-based TV standard that will allow broadcasters to send data via the TV signal's vertical blanking interval right into your computer. The second breakthrough is ready for sale at your local Wiz. Gateway's Dimension PC, complete with 31 inch monitor cum TV set, has a chip built into the unit that lets you display both TV as well as Web images.

CNN, NBC and Viacom are all experimenting with the broadcast of Intercast data. Then there's @Home (pronounced at home) which offers a whopping 10 megabits per second access — over six times faster than a T-1 line. Webcasting is here to stay.

Webcasting. What is it? From a purely syntactic point of view webcasting must have something to do with casting a web. And so it does. The convergence of broadcasting and the Internet has cast a web over the denizens of the Internet, drawing them ever deeper into the murky culture of the online world. And like a spider's web, once entrapped, you can never break free.

Not that you'd want to (sociologists' dire predictions aside)! In just a few short years, the Web has become the world's town square, a common community center, so to speak, where views, thoughts and ideas find a fair, public and free forum. In a world where democracy is the exception rather than the rule, and in a democracy which is representative rather than direct, the voice of the individual has not been heard for a millennia. Now, the collectivity of the Web can break down these barriers. And for the first time, we can talk not country to country, country to person, or organization to person, but person to person.

But person to person does not necessarily mean text-based e-mail or chat. We are a visual species and make good use of our five senses. When Marc Andressen put a graphical face on the Internet, he opened the floodgates for transmission of three dimensionality as well.

In the short three years since the graphical Web has been in place, thousands of organizations and millions of individuals have built home pages. For the most part, text was the focal point of their efforts, although the obligatory graphic or even animated graphic adorned these early pages. But then there came audio. And video. Today the Web is on the threshold of, if not replacing traditional broadcast media, then joining broadcast media in its role of disseminating the news as well as general information.

But along with this vast opportunity is danger. Danger that the webcasted Web will be little more fair or impartial than today's very yellow and biased journalism. Make no mistake about it. Although webcasting techniques (techniques later chapters in this book will explain in detail) provide the ability for any organization, large or small, or even any well-financed individual, to "grow their own", the chief purveyors of this new twist on the Internet are most likely to be the NBC's, CBS's and ABC's — with a little touch of CNN and just maybe the Sci-Fi channel.

And there are problems with traditional media. It comes as no secret that newspapers and magazines are very much biased. Not too long ago, the TV news program Dateline came under fierce attack for rigging a car explosion. Their motives were innocent enough — to expose a safety hazard. But their methodology was anything but. As a result the Dateline disaster has become synonymous with what's wrong with journalism today.

Howard Rosenberg of the Los Angeles Times called the fiasco an "electronic Titanic — an unprecedented disaster in the annals of network news and perhaps the biggest TV scam since the Quiz Scandals." What Dateline had the audacity to do was to stage a crash test that was rigged to get a particular outcome. They purposely concealed from the public's view the hidden rockets, the over-filled tank and the loose-gas tank that precipitated the crash. And if many thought the Dateline scandal was a freak or bizarre departure from accepted network standards, they were wrong. Both CBS and ABC had previously run the same sorts of grossly misleading crash videos and simulations, while also withholding the same sorts of material facts about the tests. But perhaps the most serious of misjudgments on NBC's part was in trusting "experts" who were deeply involved in litigating against the target of the expose.

A 1993 issue of the National Review devotes the majority of its publication to one salient topic, "The Decline of American Journalism". Although a publication with a bias admittedly right of center, the forty-odd pages it devotes to this topic are rare in its self-exposure. The essence of what this series of articles said was that journalists themselves are biased. And that they write through the haze of this bias. In other words, since most journalists are quite liberal in their political stance articles about pro-liberal causes are written about supportively while articles about conservative topics are written about less so — if at all. Those astute readers who have noticed the seeming embrace of the PC (politically correct) movement by the press will understand immediately what I'm referring to. How else can one explain the dozens of magazine lead stories and TV specials on AIDS. Granted it's a most dreadful scourge, but if the truth be known many more women are diagnosed with breast cancer than people diagnosed with AIDS on a monthly basis. How else can you explain the press's seeming fascination with people like Donald Trump or JFK, Jr. when most of us have no interest in these people whatsoever. The press rarely write stories that reflect our interests and needs.

Criticism of the press is not limited the right of center publications. A literature search in the public library on the subject turns up these gems:

> *Junk stories are slowly eroding public's faith in the media. The press is being used as dupes for lawyers and other charlatans who want to implicate public figures. Seeking to satisfy what they perceive to be the tastes of the American public, the press is printing first and asking questions later. Mark DiIonno. The Sporting News. April 20, 1992.*
>
> *The centrist bias of the U.S. media. Neither left nor right, but biased just the same. Jeff Cohen. Utne Reader. Sept-Oct, 1990.*

Given the press's predilection for half-truths and half-research, does anyone honestly think that broadcast news on the Web will be any different? Or will we wind up with a hodge-podge of disconnected pieces of information. Barry Diller, former head of Fox, Paramount Pictures, and QVC, and now chairman of Silver King Communications has decried the concept of "information without knowledge." As he puts it, "It used to be that there was a cadence, a rhythm to things. It would take a reasonable length of time for an event not only to get known, but to play out — for the consequences and the analysis and the understanding to incubate. Today, everything is available instantly. It's all about being on the scene, in real time. The problem is, getting to the scene quicker doesn't make us smarter. Information is not synonymous with knowledge. One is about facts, the other about understanding."

Of course webcasting opens the barn door for people other than the traditional media to air their views online. This "new media", as it is being called, brings to the table its own set of problems. Norman Pearlstine, editor-in-chief of Time Warner Inc. notes that, "There are larger and larger numbers of players in the new media for whom journalism isn't a particular interest. I hardly ever hear discussion of the public interest when I'm at gatherings of people in new media."

Let the Chips Fall

Although in its infancy, webcasting capabilities on the Web have the capability of changing the way we perceive information. Today information is disseminated in one of a variety of venues which include print, radio and television. Although there are many cable stations, radio stations and the number of magazines is perennially creeping upwards, information moves from the few media outlets to the many consumers of that information — in other words information is broadcast, with an emphasis on the word broad.

Webcasting is a many to many operation. There are many consumers of Web-based information content and there can be many purveyors of that content. For the most part, these new media content providers (except for, as I already mentioned, the traditional broadcast media) will target special interests. In other words, webcasting can be described as narrowcasting.

This book was written for the many who want a roadmap to the brave new world of webcasting. In it you'll find a plethora of "hands-on" information which will show you exactly how you too can join the growing legion of webcasters. In chapter one we'll delve into the definition of webcasting and find out just what makes it tick. In chapter two we'll explore some excellent examples of the best of the best of webcasting sites on the 'Net today. In chapter three we'll get real technical and learn about unicasting, multicasting and that old Mbone.

In chapters four through seven you'll find mini-tutorials on products from the "biggies" —- Microsoft, RealAudio, VDOnet and Netscape. These products include chat, collaborative application sharing, and video and audio streaming. In chapter eight we'll cover a wide spectrum of competitive products including Macromedia, of Director fame. In chapter nine we'll discuss the telecom issues you need to understand if you are to successfully webcast over the Internet. And finally, in chapter 10, we'll explore production tips and techniques for delivering quality audio and video over the 'Net.

A home on the Internet is what you need to get started. This book provides you with an excellent education in the art and science of video, audio and content production along with the tutorials you'll need to bone up on covering the intricacies of telecommunications, compression, simulcasting, and video conferencing.

Good luck and "quiet on the set!"

Notes:

1) Olson, Walter. "*It Didn't Start With Dateline NBC*". National Review. June 21, 1993.
2) National Review. June 21, 1993.
3) Oppenheimer, Todd. *Reality Bytes*.Columbia Journalism Review, September 1996. P. 42.

Webcasting

Chapter 1

The New Media

Introduction

Unless you've been hiding under a rock, the Internet is probably the hottest topic in town. You can't open a newspaper, turn on the TV or the radio without WebSpeak coming right at you. We're the wired generation. We're tuned in and turned on. We use it for school, to shop and to conduct our financial transactions. And the more prurient among us use it as a low-res Playboy substitute.

There are anywhere from 27 million to 50 million hardy souls, depending on the flavor of statistics you're quoting, webcrawling on any given day. Although the initial mix of crawlers was decidedly academic and government, the advent of graphical browsers such as Netscape opened the doors for the rest of us to crawl right in and log on.

The new webcrawler can be anyone. From the business person who needs to look something up to his son who uses it for homework. A doctor in a remote area may use the Internet to get assistance from a teaching hospital in the city. And her patients may use it to purchase that special something that just can't be found in town. What all these webcrawlers have in common is opportunity. An opportunity to expand one's horizons beyond the geographic and physical borders we now operate within.

It's a vast opportunity for business as well. Yahoo, one of the original Web directories, lists over 10,000 corporate sites in their directory. But that's only the tip of the iceberg:

- ActivMedia measured the 1995 growth rate of Web business marketers at an astounding 1800%
- Hambrecht & Quist forecasts Internet-related sales soaring to $14.5 billion in the year 2000, just around the corner

- A Nielsen Media study finds an astonishing 63% of 'Net surfers are business related
- The Internet Society announced that the number of hosts on the Internet has passed the 3.8 million mark
- Lycos has indexed over 1.53 million Web pages with possibly thousands being added daily
- Bluestone reports that the number of business home pages rose from a mere 30 in early 1993 to more than 50,000 by the end of 1995
- Hambrecht & Quist forecasts that Internet equipment sales will grow from $500 million in 1995 to $2.5 billion in 2000; network services will escalate from $300 million to $5 billion; software from $250 million to $4 billion; consulting/integration services will increase from $250 million to close to $3 billion
- The Internet Engineering Task Force has indicated that it is fast reaching the capacity of .com registrations with over 200,000 commercial names registered (80% of these are legal entities)
- Nielsen Media's CommerceNet funded study of Internet usage found that 37% of 'Net surfers were professional, 12% technical and 14% administrative/managerial. They also found that 66% of the 4200 respondents accessed the Internet through work and spent an average of 5 hours and 28 minutes online.

What came first the chicken or the egg? This is actually quite a meaningful question if you replace chicken with *technology* and egg with *need*. So what comes first? The technology or the need for the technology?

Well, both actually. There have been many cases when technology was introduced into the marketplace where there was actually no real need for it — until it was introduced that is. And then suddenly everyone began using it. These are the "market shapers." Visicalc, the first automated spreadsheet, was a market shaper. Nobody asked for it. But when it was introduced it jumped into the marketplace like gangbusters — and ultimately changed the way we think about computers. Essentially, a market shaper is a piece of software, or hardware, that is pivotal in changing the face of business.

On the other hand, the introduction of the word processor was not a pivotal event in the history of business computing. For years before the introduction of the first word processor, the typewriter industry had been successfully making and selling millions of souped-up typewriters. These typewriters were electronic, contained some memory and had built-in functionality such as spell checks. The PC-oriented word processor was nothing more than the next logical step in the technological advancement of typing. It wasn't dramatic. It didn't shape the industry. It was just a nice easy progression from mechanical typewriter to electronic word processor to PC word processor. So, as you can see, technology creeps through the door in two ways. One as an egg and the other as a chicken.

The most dramatic difference between today's PC and yesterday's is not in hardware but in ways the hardware is utilized. Networks now enable instantaneous access to global information. Innovative "groupware" software packages are now commonly used to ease collaboration and the pooling of knowledge. The PC has all but replaced the telephone as purveyor of messages – essentially turning the PC into a mini-post office. In the not too distant future, our e-mail facilities will even be more intelligent by providing the capabilities of organizing voice mail, faxes and e-mail, including messages sweetened with video clips.

David Ferris, a San Francisco consultant on messaging systems, accurately estimated that the average number of e-mail messages sent and received per person would increase from 20 a day to about 40 by the end of 1996. BIS Strategic Decisions of Norwell, Massachusetts, now predicts that by 1998 the number of LAN-based e-mail users will reach 38.9 million, or more than twice the total of 16.9 million users in 1993. And it won't be just the electronic transmission of text. As the memory capabilities of computers continue to increase users will be able to transmit graphics, animation and even video clips.

The past couple of years has seen the rise of, with the introduction of Lotus Notes (now owned by IBM), the groupware paradigm. Webcasting, the subject of this book, falls under this rubric. Groupware enables people in different locales to work together in real time. Groupware is actually a generic category under which several disciplines fall, the common denominator being providing the "ability to collaborate." The technologies of chat, conferencing, audio streaming and video streaming all fall under this umbrella. Webcasting is nothing more, and nothing less, than the art and science of "putting all of these technologies together."

The Webcasted World

The PC as broadcast medium is an apt description. We've grown accustomed to watching TV news where an anchor interviews one or more guests, perhaps thousands of miles apart. This is done with a camera crew at each location, some TV monitors and some satellite equipment for transmission of the actual broadcast. The same is being done on the PC.

Cuba Memorial Hospital, a typically small-town health facility, in a typically small western New York town, has seen the technological future — and seized it! It's a choice that will enable them to save even more lives in their bucolic community. Already being utilized as a tool to connect its patients with some of the top specialists in the country, Cuba is now expanding telemedicine to its emergency room. Health care professionals will now be able to turn on a video camera and computer, dial another hospital miles away, and seconds later a trauma specialist will appear on the screen. The off-site physician will then, with continued use of the camera and other high-tech tools, be able to observe and diagnose treatment for the emergency admittance. And later, via video conferencing, be available for consultations.

The virtual hospital has arrived! Without leaving their own community, patients can now consult some of the country's top specialists. Relying on a multitude of high-tech communications devices such as video cameras that can zoom in on things as microscopic as minute skin melanomas; electronic stethoscopes that magnify a heartbeat and transmit it hundreds, even thousands, of miles away through phone or cable lines; virtually instantaneous computer access to a patient's medical charts, and large-screen TVs that permit doctors to see and chat with patients and other medical professionals, the small-town hospital has dramatically increased its value to its patients.

Dr. Francis Tedesco, president of the Medical College of Georgia, a pioneer in this growing communications network, passionately champions telemedicine stating that doctors can look into the eyes, hear a heartbeat, and listen to the lungs.

According to Dr. Jane Preston, president of the American Telemedicine Association in Austin, Texas, the ER is definitely going to be where this technology shines. And James Toler, co-director of the bioengineering center at Georgia Institute of Technology, adds that the ability to administer treatment to patients during that golden hour saves lives and results in less serious medical complications. Heart attack or stroke, natural disaster or vehicular accident victims; telemedicine will enable all to receive the quickest help possible.

Aside from a treatment tool, telemedicine has also produced benefits in terms of education. Many states have already approved programs allowing doctors to obtain continuing education credits working with a specialist on telemedicine systems.

Military uses are also conceivable in the near future. A backpack system for the military that would use two lipstick-size cameras inserted in a helmet has been designed to enable a medic to transmit information in actual-time from the battlefield. Doctors at military bases could then examine the wounded soldier and advise treatment and prepare for arrival at the hospital.

Dr. Jay Sanders of Massachusetts General Hospital and early booster and user of this technology (in the early 1970s he set up one of the first telemedicine systems between his hospital and Boston's Logan Airport) would like to see it employed in schools, as a teaching tool, and in peoples' home to enable doctors to make housecalls, whatever the time of day! A true believer he sees telemedicine as one of the factors that will radically change health care.

Other industries are making use of network broadcasting too. New York's Citibank is typical of those banks looking to cash in on the virtual business. Citibank recently made a giant leap toward virtual banking by making stock quotes and securities transactions available at its 1,800 proprietary automated teller machines (ATMs) nationwide. This service was inaugurated during the Fall of 1994 in New York, Chicago, Miami, San Francisco, and Washington.

Citibank's ATM users are able to see up to 10 stock quotations, buy and sell stocks or invest in money market funds simply by following the instructions on the screen. This is just the first of many virtual banking programs under development at Citibank. The bank is also improving its phone option with sophisticated screen phones and expanding its PC banking through software giveaways on the Internet.

In addition to the convenience offered their customers, there's the cost-saving benefits of this new technology. According to Mark Hardie, an analyst with the Tower Group, a bank technology consultancy in Wellesley, Massachusetts, electronic transactions are more economical than those processed by personnel. And the high operational costs of branch offices can definitely be lessened.

IBM video conferencing kiosks are offering the $150 billion Royal Bank of Canada in Toronto the chance to centralize its intelligence and services. According to Dennis Graham, manager of advanced concept networks for Royal Bank, these kiosks will definitely make more sense than having licensed, experienced salespeople stranded in seldom-visited branch offices.

Allowing the bank to situate their experts in one central location, lessening these employees' downtime and increasing their availability to a wider range of customers via the video conferencing kiosks, this new technology has definitely improved their customer service and management of personnel.

Another financial institution that has forayed into the world of virtual business is Huntington Bancshares, Inc. of Columbus, Ohio. This $16.5 billion dollar institution is currently converting their branch offices to accommodate these new customer-intensive technologies. A move that is pleasing — allowing the bank to expand without building or leasing new office space — the bank's financial managers as well.

To make automated check cashing services possible, Huntington has hooked-up with AT&T Global Information Solutions to add imaging technology to its teller machines. More detailed transactions, such as opening deposit accounts, are handled separately through interactive video conferencing ter-

Figure 1-1. Videoconferencing is a form of webcasting.

minals or telebanking. The reason, according to Jan Tyler, research and development manager at Huntington, is the desire to keep ATM lines and transactions short.

The key driver behind the virtual business is video conferencing which allows groups, over long geographic distances, not only to share a common PC blackboard, but to see and hear each other.

Danvers, Massachusetts-based PictureTel is one enterprising organization that is marketing such a technology. LIVE Share operates using affordable dial-up digital lines. A small video camera is mounted to the top of the PC which transmits the individual's image while audio is transmitted through a PictureTel telephone as shown in figure 1-1. Software enables users on both ends of the connection to share a PC session. So I can be in New York and a staff member can be in San Diego, and both of us can pour over a spreadsheet in real-time, talking with and seeing each other the entire time.

Not to be outdone, a very user-friendly desktop video conferencing product has been made available through a joint venture by AT&T and Intel Corp. This company, formed in the summer of 1994, links Intel's ProShare video conferencing equipment and AT&T's Worldworx networking services. The joint product, produced to operate over digital phone lines, includes software and a reasonably priced video camera and headset and will be priced between $999 and $1,500. AT&T's Worldworx network service will manage ProShare calls for between 50 cents and $1 per minute.

Amy Pearl runs the Enterprise Communication Initiative (ECI) at Mountain View-based Sun Microsystems. ECI is a cross-functional collaboration between Sun's MIS department, Sun's training organization, Sun Laboratories and SunSoft. Pearl believes that the advent of e-mail has not replaced the need for interactive, or synchronous, communication, even in computers. For example, people have found simple text-based interactive "talk" programs useful for as long as computers have supported multiple users.

Video conferencing is a technology that has been emerging over the past thirty years, motivated by how much of our face-to-face communication is visual, or nonverbal. For example, there have been efforts to augment telephones to include transmission of visual images. Recently the Computer Supported Cooperative Work (CSCW) community has been exploring the use of computer controlled analog audio and video transmission to support group work. Recent advances in media compression technology along with shrinking component size and cost have made digital video feasible. Unlike analog video, digital video can take advantage of the growing number of digital communication networks, including phone (e.g., ISDN) and institutional networks (e.g., LANs and WANs).

Sun funded a project called Videoconf to explore just these issues. Like the PictureTel system it enables users on multiple ends of a geographic perspective to share information as well as see and hear each other. Although Sun is very much a vendor, Videoconf was an internal project. Given the company's size and its diversity, video conferencing was seen to be a way to simultaneously decrease costs and improve productivity.

According to Sarah Dickinson, an analyst with Personal Technology Research, a Waltham, Massachusetts consultancy, desktop video products — including hardware and software for voice, data, and digital video services — will reach about $2.1 billion in revenue by the year 1998.

Of course a hop, skip and a jump from video conferencing is the whole idea of the use of digital video in business.

The Video Connection

One need only peruse the trades, by using your intelligent agent software, of course, to find numerous articles on the coming boom in video.

A video camera that connects to mobile computers via a PCMCIA card was released in November 1994 by the Scottish company VLSI Vision Ltd. The company sees as their target market such on-the-go professionals as real estate agents, site inspectors and graphic designers.

Named PC Card Camera by VSLI Vision, the device consists of a handheld camera and mounting apparatus, PCMCIA Type II interface card with cable and documentation. Camera exposure can be set either automatically or manually and optional lenses are available. To enable the camera to capture still-image and motion-video, VLSI Vision has created VVL Snap, a still-image and motion-video application that runs under Microsoft Windows.

The collected images are displayed on the computer in real-time enabling the user to precisely control what is being captured. Then, for ease of integration into other applications, these images are stored as TIF files. Alister Minty, product group manager for VLSI Vision sees the PC Card Camera being utilized in presentations, document imaging, real-estate applications and conferencing.

Though business applications for video are still in the very beginning stages some companies are already using this new technology. For example, NBC News is using the Oracle Media Serve to log video clips.

This is the side road but the main path chosen by many companies for video servers is training. As vast libraries of interactive courseware continue to be accrued by corporations they are beginning to stress the existing standard LANs. Bruce Yon, multimedia analyst at Dataquest of San Jose, California, states that the ever-increasing amount of software being installed within organizations is surpassing the ability of businesses to absorb servers or CD-ROM jukeboxes. Intranet-based video servers enable employees to train themselves at their PCs as their time allows instead of completing a whole course or jamming the network.

Video Servers have definitely found a home in manufacturing. Jeff Capeci, advanced manufacturing engineer at defense contractor Nordon Systems Inc., says his company is using the technology to help educate their workers to perform certain manufacturing processes, feeding the video instruction live to their terminal for convenient review. Video servers are a hot topic in the electronic commerce arena as well. Stamford, Connecticut-based OmniBox is marketing a video server capable of 100 to 1 compression that delivers content to a

TV or a PC. The future, it seems, is really here.

When Media Collide

Leigh Buchanan, who writes for *WebMaster Magazine*, has renamed NBC from the National Broadcasting Corporation to "Now Begins Convergence."

It's a good idea. As mentioned in the introduction, the conventional media are moving into the online world in a big way. Convinced that broadcast-only news is going the way of the dodo bird, the company that launched the very first radio station over 70 years ago is now betting the farm on convergence.

To succeed in the era of the Information Superhighway, some believe we will need to create mega-companies that embrace — and control — as many of the converging technologies as possible. Others say that the small high-tech venture companies, particularly software firms, will lead us into the convergence era.

While most experts agree that consolidation is inevitable in the communications industry, no one large company can create the intense focus and agility needed to compete successfully across the breadth of the Information Superhighway. And no small firm will be able to generate the intellectual and financial capital necessary to control a segment of the highway in the same way that Microsoft and Intel did in their respective industries. An alternative way to achieve the benefits of both large company scale and small company flexibility is by creating joint ventures with partners who have complementary

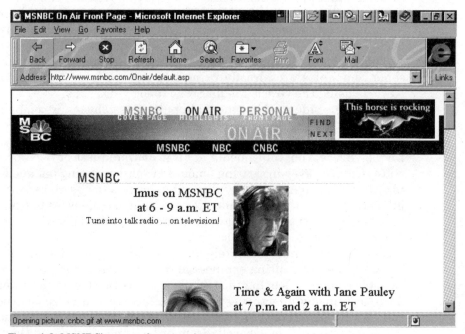

Figure 1-2. MSNBC's new webcast environment.

technologies.

NBC is giving it that old cheerleader try, however. In 1991 it spent $150 million to buy the Financial News Network as part of its launch of CNBC. And 1996's launch of MSNBC, the all-news cable-online hybrid is the progeny of its long term alliance with Microsoft Corp.

In spite of technical problems, criticism from the press and the public, MSNBC makes an excellent example of what webcasting really is. It's not a rehash of news and video from it's cable counterpart and it's not just a marketing and promotional Web site for NBC and Microsoft. Rather, it is a unique amalgam of the best of both the broadcasting and Internet arenas. It is a full-fledged news effort, staffed with both journalists and technologists, who work as a team to exploit the best features of the webcasting environment.

NBC often collects more material (audio, video and images) than it can use in its half-hour nightly newscast or weekly hour long news magazines such as Dateline and Meet the Press. This excess broadcast material, much of it background and analysis, is customarily excised from the broadcast due to network time constraints. What better venue, thought Executive Producer Allison Davis, then to use it on MSNBC.

This she did with background information on the topic at hand, for example Bosnia, that includes history, geography as well as the biographies of the major players. Davis is of the opinion that, "when you have gone through the site and absorbed what's in it, you can better understand what you see night after night on the news."

But MSNBC isn't all serious news. They've also created complementary content such as an online honesty quiz that accompanied a week-long series called, "Lie, Cheat and Steal."

While MSNBC does typify the very high end of webcasting, which is something that many readers of this book may aspire to but never reach, nonetheless its introduction does provide some insight into what makes a webcast successful.

MSNBC is no mere digital extension of its cable counterpart. Journalists and technologists work as a team to exploit what is unique about the medium rather than repurposing broadcast content and/or using the site as a marketing medium. It is properly funded. Microsoft paid NBC $220 million for a half stake in the venture and both companies will invest many millions more in the next five years.

Producer Davis insisted that the effort be a journalistic effort and not a marketing enterprise; therefore, MSNBC Online has staffed up with a combination of journalistically savvy technologists and technologically savvy journalists. In other words, everyone concerned understands both sides of the business. Interestingly, one of the job requirements is that everyone, even content providers, must learn HTML.

Online honesty quizzes, backgrounders on a geographic "hotspot" are the kinds of capabilities that are the "core" of the Microsoft/NBC alliance. Says Martin Yudkovitz, president of NBC Interactive Media, "We are not playing this game for what it is today. We are playing this game for what we believe it will become: a video-oriented, mass-market information vehicle."

While MSNBC may be the flagship of NBC's online empire, it's not the only ship in the Internet fleet. NBC.com and SuperNet, a Microsoft Network (go word = nbc) product, figure in the equation as well. Where NBC.com is essentially a TV guide for the network as shown in figure 1-3, SuperNet utilizes a more sophisticated level of technology.

But there's a lot more up NBC's sleeve. For several years, Desktop Video has been delivering coverage of corporate announcements, congressional testimony and CEO interviews to the desktop. Soon, customers will be able to retrieve that same information from a Web site directly from NBC – or from one of the Internet Service Providers it will license the product to. So, if a CEO from Bankers Trust sees an interesting broadcast from, say Citibank, he or she can copy the video clip to the corporate intranet for company-wide viewing.

NBC also plans to license this software to its affiliates who, according to Michael Wheeler, president of Desktop Video, "can put up their six o'clock newscast on their Web sites so people who missed it can get in at 9 or 10 o'clock to pull up the big story."

NBC's ultimate goal is intercast, a technology that embeds data into video signals. Intercast would allow the network to send HTML pages along with its

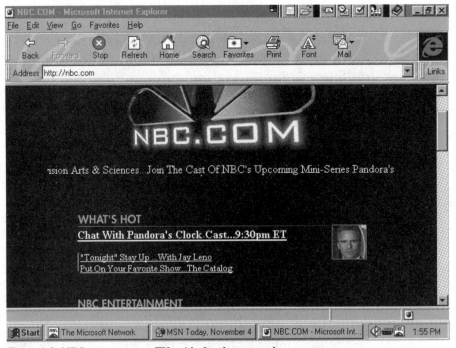

Figure 1-3. NBC.com acts as a TV guide for the network.

regular programming. Both the television show and the associated HTML-encoded information travel the same route as a normal television signal. So if an anchor is discussing events in Bosnia in the main TV window, the viewer can scroll through Bosnia information in a small window-in-window (which, of course, can be enlarged for easier viewing).

Ultimately, Yudkovitz is right on target when he says that NBC's strategy is to play the Web game for what it ultimately will become – a video-oriented, mass-market information vehicle.

There's a lot of other exciting developments just over the horizon that's going to make webcasting as ubiquitous as delivery of text is now. @Home (http://www.home.net/) is getting ready to roll out 10 megabits per second access by connecting directly through your favorite cable company. That's over six times faster than a T1 line. @Home, based in Palo Alto and headed by former *San Francisco Examiner* publisher Will Hearst, is funded by leading venture capital firm Kleiner, Perkins, Caufield & Byers. Distribution will be via cable giant TCI. An early '96 consumer test market in Sunnyvale follows with a national roll-out to millions of Web users over the next few years. Cable modem prices will probably start around $500 and drop to a few hundred as it takes off. Oracle (http://www.oracle.com) plans to launch a similar service next year called Oracle TV, targeted to the corporate market.

However, @Home is not quite ready and neither is your cable company. So today we have to be quite clever to be able to deliver webcast content over the Internet. Clever as a company called Brainworks.net (http://brainworks.net/) which is starting up an interactive multimedia video network to deliver streaming MPEG video to the Web. The company says that you'll be able to see and interact with an "Open Camera Forum" offering PBS-level quality multimedia programming, with feeds from multiple sites. Or you'll access webcasts at any time from a knowledge bank.

Ultimately, that's what this book is about — the tools and techniques of webcasting. But before we kick off, let's consider the multitude of issues surrounding the delivery of webcast content over the Internet.

Webcasting in a Nutshell

To view most multimedia or webcasted content using a network, the files must first be completely downloaded to a local hard drive and then displayed or played. The network's role is to retrieve the file, so that all the information resides locally. The user's online experience is a combination of click, wait, and view. Most people connected to the Internet have extremely slow connections at the rate of about 2K per second (i.e. 28.8 modems). If the multimedia file that is being downloaded is 100K in size, users have to wait at least 50 seconds before they are able to see anything (100K divided by 2K/second). Most multimedia content files are much larger than 100K and therefore the wait is usually much longer.

Streaming works differently. Streaming transfers the beginning of a file, then starts playing it while continuously transmitting more data. In effect, streaming allows a viewer to watch and listen to the beginning of the multimedia content, while the middle is being sent. While playing back the middle section the end is transmitted and then the end plays. Of course, the data isn't really broken up into sections it just continues to be downloaded as it is played back. Streaming technology enables developers to reduce the waiting and create an online experience of click and view, with little or no wait.

Depending on the content, streaming can significantly improve the user's experience. Multimedia content that might have taken minutes to download in its entirety can now begin playback within just a few seconds and play for several minutes while later pieces of the content are being streamed.

Much has been said about how slow the Internet is and about how long users have to wait before they are able to view their favorite Web sites. There are several reasons for this, but the most common is lack of bandwidth. Bandwidth refers to the capacity of a connection between two machines or devices connected to the network to transfer data. Different types of connections have different bandwidths (capacities) or speeds associated with them. The Internet is made up of many different connections, but it is important to remember that the smallest connection in the path through which data flows sets the maximum rate at which data can be transferred.

A 14.4 modem that can transfer data at approximately 1K per second is considered to be very, very slow, while a T1 line that can achieve average rates as high as 70-80K per second is considered very fast. However, it is important to realize that a single-speed CD-ROM can transfer data at 150K per second. So, even a fast Internet connection is still slower than the slowest of CD-ROM drives. This assumes that the data that is being transferred has not been compressed using a data compression scheme.

Data compression is a technique by which the actual size of a data object is reduced. Using an algorithm, the original data is transformed into a new format that represents the same data but that uses fewer bytes. There are several different schemes for reducing the amount of data, but they all fall into two distinct categories : lossless and lossy.

Lossless data compression means that although the data size is reduced, it is possible to create an identical version of the original data. *Lossy* compression means that it is impossible to ever restore an identical version to the original data. Compressing data that is going to be transferred over a network makes it possible to effectively increase the bandwidth available at a given connection speed.

For example, if it were possible to compress all data with an algorithm that yielded a 10:1 compression ratio (10 bytes of data are compressed into 1 byte) then it would be possible to effectively increase throughput by a multiple of ten. So, a 28.8 modem that could receive 2K per second of uncompressed data could receive a theoretical 20K per second of data. Of course, only 2K of data is actually transmitted, but the recipient could then decompress the data and get a reasonable representation of the original 20K. Actual bandwidth has not changed, but the effective rate at which data is transferred has increased.

Compression helps reduce the amount of data that actually needs to be transferred. However, when creating content for online delivery with a "streaming" system, the most important factor is the rate at which data is used by the content. Streaming algorithms, then, are the real secret behind webcasting.

Just a few short years ago it would have been impossible to even consider providing webcasting content over the Internet, the problems of bandwidth and compression being seemingly insurmountable. As we will read in Chapter 3, the academic community was beginning to experiment with the Mbone, an experimental multicast environment, but this was, and still is, considered to be insufficient to meet the growing needs and demands of the commercial community. Fortunately, the companies profiled in this book came to the rescue.

Netscape, Microsoft, RealAudio, VDOnet, Narrative, Macromedia and others saw an opportunity to provide state-of-the-art webcasting facilities for the non-academic among us. It's good that they did because they provided a set of tools and facilities that makes it downright easy to turn today's rather flat 2-D Web pages into exciting and unique experiences for your viewers.

What All This Means Is Now Push Can Come to Shove

Marketeers of the world unite! The Internet now has a set of technologies that will finally permit you to get your message across to a particular target audience. Actually *push your message across* is more like it since the technology used is a client-side form of webcasting where a permanent *receiver* sits on a PC with the user either instructing it to automatically or manually call the *sending* Web site. The goal? To gather tailored-to-the-user news and other information such as stock quotes. The marketing message usually comes along for the ride.

The grand-daddy of push technology is PointCast (www.pointcast.com) with Marimba (www.marimba.com), a Wall Street darling pioneered by yet more refugees from Sun's Java group, coming in a close second. But these two entrepreneuring firms won't be alone in this market for long. As this book was going to press both Netscape and Microsoft announced that they too are entering the arena.

For push marketing to succeed you've got to have two things. On one hand, you've got to have the content. PointCast is a good example. PointCast calls themselves the Internet news network that appears instantly on your computer. Headlines move dynamically across the screen, the colors pop and all you have to do is keep your eyes open. Effortless. No surfing required.

PointCast broadcasts national and international news, stock information, industry updates, weather from around the globe, sports scores and more from sources like CNN, CNNfn, Time, People and Money Magazines, Reuters, PR Newswire, BusinessWire, Sportsticker and Accuweather! Advertiser supported, the best thing about PointCast is that it's completely customizable. Interested in news in your particular industry? How about your own personalized stock ticker. Receive just the news and information you care about.

The second thing you need is the technology to push out both content and one or more marketing messages. That's where companies like PointCast, Marimba and soon-to-be Netscape and Microsoft come in. They're the ones that will supply the client/server software that will permit you to build the receiving and sending model I described above.

But of course, all this content and marketing is just so much data without a visually exciting way to present it. That's where the techniques in this book come in. For webcasting is to push marketing much like broadcasting is to advertising.

Let's take a good look at what some webcasters are doing online with an eye on just how they accomplished their technological feats. Turn the page to Chapter two.

Chapter

2

Webcasting Success Stories

The Proof is in the Pudding

Webcasting means many things to many people. On the high end is Intercast, briefly mentioned in the last chapter as NBC's penultimate goal to simultaneously transmit television and content over the same wire. On the low end is any system that combines computers with audiovisual components to broadcast a particular message using the trusty PC as a receiver. This message may be something as simple as transmitting a canned speech, conference or tutorial over long distances to real-time broadcasting.

In this chapter we'll examine a wide variety of webcasting examples. For each, we'll describe the technology as well as provide "rules of thumb" that you can use to copy its success.

Wimbeldon

IBM developed the Wimbeldon site (http://www.wimbledon.org), shown in figure 2-1, which was webcasted "live" during Wimbledon games. Using Live Bamba, a new IBM Research protocol for Web-based sound transmission, IBM provides a good example of a low-end webcasting site.

A tickertape window provided real-time updates on key events thanks to a Java applet. The most interesting component of the site, however, was the pages that listed the matches included in the various "draws" of the tournament which included point-by-point updates of matches in progress.

A NetCam page, shown in figure 2-2, provided links to online cameras grabbing still images of play. Print news items describing matches and other happenings were updated regularly. The draws for the various competitions were displayed in a scrollable tree chart.

16   Chapter Two

Figure 2-1. www.wimbeldon.org's webcasting site.

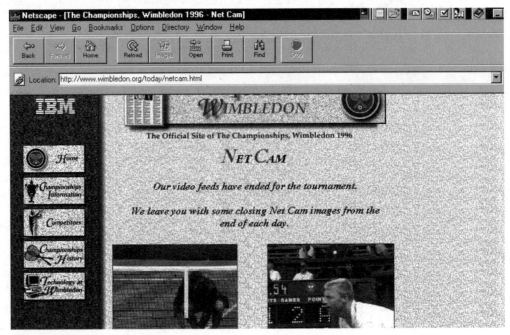

Figure 2-2.Wimbeldon's NetCam.

A variety of static components backed up the real-time information. Image Of The Day is a link to a high-res photo of players or spectators in action. Players' names are hyperlinked to their bios and photos. Interactivity options are also included, such as providing the opportunity to e-mail questions to favorite players.

Ultra-Throb Online

One of the many music purchasing sites on the Web (see figure 2-3) (http://www.ultronic.com/sug1.1.html), Sonic uses RealAudio to let customers try before they buy.

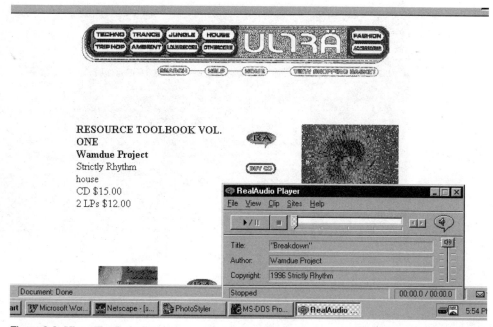

Figure 2-3. Ultra Throb Online.

This site was actually rather simple to create. The hard work was in creating the sound clips. After that was done, and encoded with RealAudio to maximize compression rates while sacrificing minimum quality, the HTML coding was quickly achieved as shown below:

```
<a href="http://www.ultronic.com/sounds/sug1a.ram">
<img border=0 src="img/a.gif" hspace=10></a>
```

Financial Times Television

Financial Times Television uses RealAudio (http://www.FT-Television.com) to provide transcripts of interviews as well as a streamed RealAudio feed of the whole show as shown in figure 2-4. Again, a simple matter to encode this within the HTML:

```
<A HREF="../../sound/a251096d.ram">Listen to Power Broking</A>
```

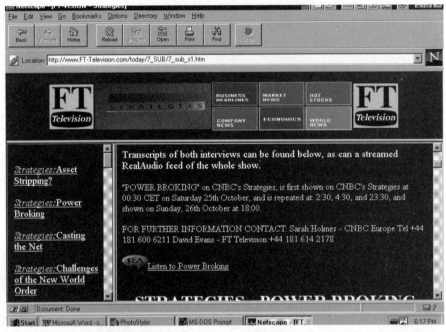

Figure 2-4. The Financial Times.

The Financial Times has learned the real secret of webcasting — provide a lot of content. Webcasting does not mean providing a paltry one or two video or audio clips. It means providing a veritable library of information.

ITV Net

This site (http://www.itv.net) uses streaming video feeds from live events. This 24-hour webcasting station uses Xing Technologies StreamWorks (see Chapter 8) to broadcast a wide variety of sports films, documentaries and live events from around the world. Figure 2-5 shows the broadcast of the making of a 50 minute sci-fi movie called Starlight.

Since most of the webcast work was in making the movie, the only thing the content developer needed to do was to add a line of code to the HTML as follows:

```
<A HREF="star.xdm">Tune-in and watch Starlight.</A>
```

Calling star.xdm starts playing the movie. The end-user is provided a viewing area as well as playback controls which can be used to stop and start the film. The size of the viewing area and the nature of the playback controller is controlled by the content developer at the point in time he or she compresses the video into the Streamworks format.

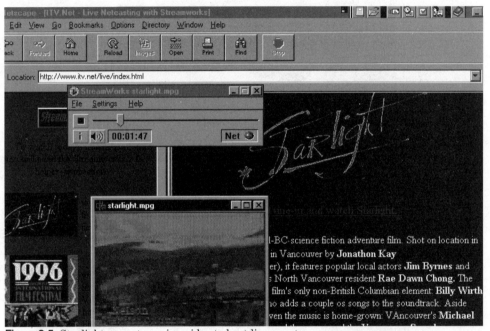

Figure 2-5. Starlight uses streaming video to host live events.

Worldwide TV

This site (http://www.worldwidetv.com) bills itself as the Internet "superstation" as shown in figure 2-6. Clicking on the Computer Broadcast Network (TCBN) icon gets some pretty exciting stuff, as shown in figure 2-7.

This fabulous image of what looks like a broadcasting station's control room is really an image map. Click on any of the TV screens and you'll wind up in an area that has streaming video.

This site makes use of the VDOLive Player (see Chapter 6). Clicking on PM News I get the display seen in figure 2-8. This is a rather nice way to handle videocast material.

Figure 2-6. The Internet's First Superstation.

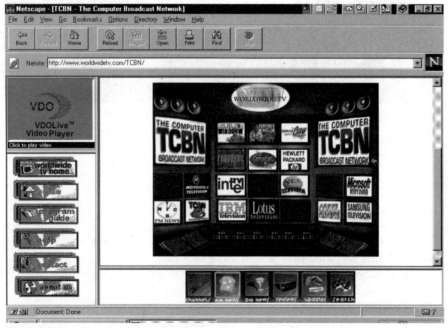

Figure 2-7. The Computer Broadcast Network.

Note that the screen is divided into four sections, with the right hand side describing the videocast, the bottom frames providing menus and the top right frame displaying the actual webcast.

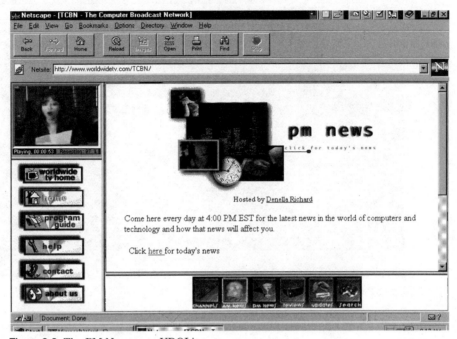

Figure 2-8. The PM News uses VDOLive.

The HTML tag to run a VDO clip is:

```
<EMBED SRC="../vdo/pmweekend.vdo" WIDTH=160 HEIGHT=128 STRETCH=TRUE
AUTOSTART=TRUE>
```

Notice the width and height parameters, the fact that the clip starts automatically without the end-user clicking on a control and, in fact, that no controllers are present at all. While this may look great, this site has one flaw. There is no way for the end-user to stop the video. He or she wouldn't necessarily know that a right click of the mouse button displays a menu where the video can be stopped — or restarted.

The Sci-Fi Channel

Figure 2-9 shows what real creativity can do. Those of you who have the Sci-Fi channel know that these folks understand good programming, so it shouldn't surprise you that they have a decidedly novel approach to programming their Web site (http://www.scifi.com) as well.

22   Chapter Two

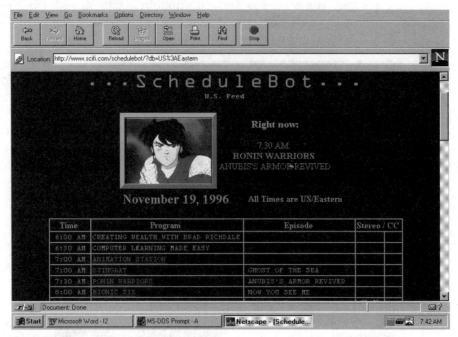

Figure 2-9. The creative Sci-Fi channel site.

The Sci-Fi channel has a lot of programming so it's natural that they would want to use their Web site to provide a list of what's on the channel on a daily basis. Their ScheduleBot page not only provides a comprehensive listing of programming, it "grabs" a real-time clip of that program and displays it on the Web page.

The code to perform this feat of magic is:

```
<a href="/screengrab/startcaption.cgi">
<img src="/screengrab/theClip.gif?848408507"
height="120" width="160" border=0 alt=" [SCREENGRAB] "></a>
```

This feat isn't as magical as it sounds, and although I'm not privy to exactly how the Sci-Fi channel created this real-time programming feed, I can take a good guess. At the end of Chapter 10 are a bunch of utilities that will let you capture clips (still and moving) of anything on television. One of these utilities is CameraMan by Motion Works USA. This utility has been programmed to capture clips on a continuous basis. Since I've never used CameraMan personally, I don't know whether the utility itself lets you do this or the Sci-Fi channel had to write a program to "call" CameraMan when it wanted a screen capture to be taken.

The programmers among you will notice that the code above calls a CGI (common gateway interface) program called startcaption.cgi. This program, which could have been written in C, Perl or any one of a number of programming languages, takes the screen capture and converts it to a GIF file on the fly and then passes the name it creates (in this case, 848408507) to the Web page which then displays it.

At most, the Sci-Fi channel had to write two original programs for this task: 1) a program to call a CameraMan type of utility continuously and pass the screen clips to a Web server; and 2) a program or Perl script to convert the clip to a GIF file, create a name for it and then pass it to the Web page.

Film Scouts

I've included this Web page, not because it's using advanced webcasting techniques but, because the overall design is an excellent example of what good graphics can do to enhance a webcast.

Film Scouts (http://www.filmscouts.com), as seen in figure 2-10, uses a movie theater motif to "set the stage", so to speak. Clicking on Admit One gets you inside of a theater, as shown in figure 2-11.

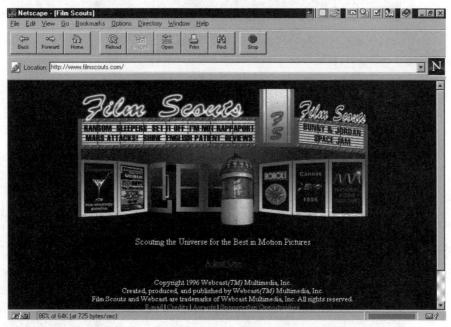

Figure 2-10. Film Scouts uses a movie theater motif.

Clicking on Screening Room gets you a seat, as shown in figure 2-12, and clicking on Call the Projectionist gets you a film clip as shown in figure 2-13.

The webcasting method chosen was a poor choice, however. QuickTime movies are not streaming video. A small .6 megabyte file took about 2 minutes to fully download, while a 7.6 megabyte trailer took almost an hour.

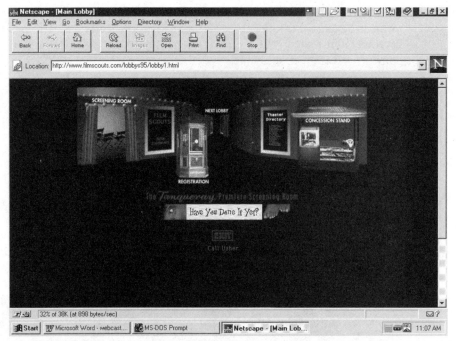

Figure 2-11. Inside the virtual theater.

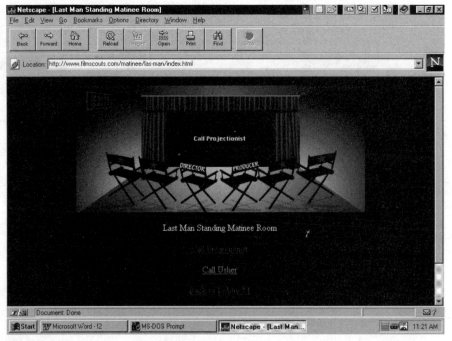

Figure 2-12. Calling the projectionist.

Figure 2-13. The film clip.

The Virtual Film Festival

The Virtual Film Festival (http://www.virtualfilm.com/) site is also a good example of how a site should be structured. Figure 2-14 shows how, on one page, both QuickTime movies and RealAudio sound are used to give the site visitor a sense of the Film Festival.

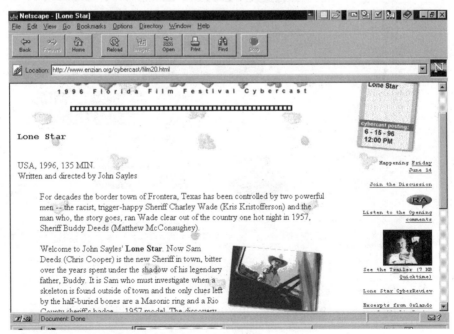

Figure 2-14. QuickTime and RealAudio on one page.

The HTML tag to display the QuickTime movie is:

`<a href="http://www.enzian.org/cybercast/video/opening.mov">`.

The HTML tag to play the RealAudio sound is:

`<a href="http://www.enzian.org/cybercast/audio/opening.ram">`.

3WB World Wide Web Broadcasting

As shown in figure 2-15, this site (http://www.3wb.com) uses a lot of graphics to lure the end-user into a choice of four news or radio stations. Each of these images is an imagemap. I selected IBNN, the Internet Business News Radio.

Clicking on the LIVE button to the right of the program name initiated a XingTech Streamworks streaming audio file of surprising good quality.

Figure 2-15. World Wide Web Broadcasting.

The code to call the Streamworks audiofile is as follows:

`http://www.3wb.com/targets/ibr.xdm`

University Video Communications

UVC (http://www.uvc.com/gbell/promo.html), which videotapes important lectures in the scientific, academic and technical communities, has begun experimenting with webcasting. Figure 2-16 demonstrates UVC's use of Netscape's LiveAudio product to webcast a lecture by Gordon Bell on the subject of the Internet.

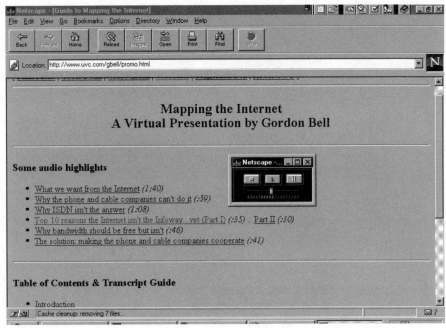

Figure 2-16. A webcasted lecture by Gordon Bell.

What I liked about this site is the way UVC meticulously "cut up" Bell's lecture into manageable audio units as follows:

What we want from the Internet (1:40)
Why the phone and cable companies can't do it (:59)
Why ISDN isn't the answer (1:08)
Top 10 reasons the Internet isn't the Infoway...yet
    (Part I) (:35)
    (Part II) (:30)
Why bandwidth should be free but isn't (:46)
The solution: making the phone and cable companies cooperate (:41)

Along with making the audio easier to handle, this methodology expedites the end-users' access to the specific information he or she is interested in. The code to accomplish this is as follows:

```
<h3> Some audio highlights </h3>
<ul><li><a href="/sound/gbell29.au">
What we want from the Internet</a> <em>(1:40)</em>
<li><a href="/sound/gbell35.au">
Why the phone and cable companies can't do it</a> <em>(:59)</em>
<li><a href="/sound/gbell29a.au">
Why ISDN isn't the answer</a> <em>(1:08)</em>
<li><a href="/sound/gbell31.au">
Top 10 reasons the Internet isn't the Infoway...yet (Part I)</a>
<em>(:35)</em>
<li><a href="/sound/gbell32.au">Part II</a> <em>(:30)</em>
<li><a href="/sound/gbell40.au">
Why bandwidth should be free but isn't</a> <em>(:46)</em>
<li><a href="/sound/gbell37.au">
The solution: making the phone and cable companies cooperate</a>
<em>(:41)</em>
</ul>
```

The You Don't Know Jack Show

http://www.jacknetshow.com is the place to go if you want to see webcasting in its customized form (see figure 2-17). *You Don't Know Jack* is the online ver-

Figure 2-17. The You Don't Know Jack Show.

sion of the award-winning, irreverent pop-culture quiz show party game now showing on beZerk (http://www.bezerk.com).

The netshow is no webpage! Complete with real studio audio sound effects, seamless game play and wisecracking humor just like the CD-ROM game, it sports new episodes available weekly. The questions are hilarious combinations of pop-culture with classic trivia.

Played just like Jeopardy, complete with sponsors, as shown in figure 2-18,

Figure 2-18. Webcasting can be financed by advertisers.

and money prizes, the Jacknet Show takes over complete control of your PC.

This site uses a customized version of Streamworks called Jellyvision to turn your PC into a private TV entertainment system.

Brainworks Net

Figure 2-19. The Brainworks remote control.

This VDO-enabled site (http://brainworks.net/) uses remote control imagery as shown in figure 2-19. When you press any of the buttons on the remote control, a VDOlive movie begins to play.

The remote control image is described by a client-side imagemap in the HTML as shown below:

```
<map name="remot5">
<area shape="rect" coords="42,130,166,147" href="bella.htm" target="main">
<area shape="rect" coords="38,157,158,177" href="roadwar.htm" target="main">
<area shape="rect" coords="39,183,107,201" href="bike.htm" target="main">
<area shape="rect" coords="40,209,103,227" href="wind.htm" target="main">
<area shape="rect" coords="40,235,110,254" href="water.htm" target="main">
<area shape="rect" coords="40,262,136,291" href="dee.htm" target="main">
<area shape="rect" coords="26,53,63,94" href="index.htm" target="_top">
<area shape="default" nohref>
</map>
```

Each remote control button points to a separate HTML file. And each of these HTML files points to an separate VDO file as shown below:

```
<EMBED src="vdo/bella.vdo" autostart=true loop=true stretch=true width=290 height=225>
```

Again, this site demonstrates that a multitude of content is what webcasting is all about.

Hewlett-Packard's Distance Learning System

The rest of this chapter will examine in detail an exciting internal use of webcasting — distance learning. Hewlett Packard is a world class technology company that used its technological know-how to solve a common dilemma: How do you train thousands of widely dispersed employees? The answer, according to Ken Gerlach, a HP marketing programs manager, is Distance Learning.

In the Virtual Classroom that a Distance Learning (DL) system creates, specially designed hardware and software enable real-time interaction between an instructor at a host site, and students who may be located at multiple, global remote sites. It employs two-way interactive telecommunications and electronic devices to teach from a distance.

There are various delivery technologies for DL to choose from: satellite, fiber optic, cable, codecs over telephone lines and microwave. Computer response units, scanners, facsimile machines, CD-Rom, videodisc and radio are also utilized. For purposes of focusing on larger numbers of students and widely dispersed receiving sites, satellite delivery best serves the objective.

Transmission, via traditional, analog satellite signals, broadcasts audio and video to multiple receiving sites with return audio and two-way data communication supported over conventional land phone lines. High quality audio is paramount in learning environments — speech delivered without excessive reverberation, noise, feedback, distortion or returning echo characteristic of a satellite transmission delay are important considerations.

Video compression eliminates the redundant part of the analog signal, taking the analog video transmission and converting it to digital. With digital, there is no degradation of signal as it is retransmitted; and an additional benefit is that it requires significantly less bandwidth. Advances in digital compression will lower transmission costs but more importantly will double or triple channel capacity (number of channels than can be sent over any transmission medium).

A total distance learning solution (production, video, audio and control system) is pulled together from various suppliers. A full integration of components requires expertise in audio, video, data and control. This integration has been a barrier to market acceptance because users do not have all the necessary expertise. Outside services are usually required for hardware/software installation and test, design, production training and prototyping of the specific training/educational programming.

Let's consider the various configurations of communication technology available and how they are applied.

Synchronous mode:
1 way audio   Radio program
2 way audio   Telephone conferences, radio
                        talk show
1 way audio/1 way video Television program and video
                        distribution

Asynchronous or virtual classroom:
2 way audio/2 way video Video conferencing with
                        compressed digital over
                        telephone lines

The most economic and effective for training environments is:
2 way audio/1 way video DL transmitted over a high
                        quality analog satellite to
                        multiple sites over a vast area.

The virtual classroom simulates the feeling of a large number of students being in one classroom together even though they are physically dispersed. Technology is applied seamlessly and is the most transparent to learners and instructors where the TV-quality image is maintained and the two-way questioning/answering process is unimpeded. Interaction is supported through computer-assisted response devices and communication technologies that enhance further feedback.

For simplicity, DL configurations include a host site, mode of signal transmission and receiving sites.

Host site: The program originates from the host site where the session is broadcast from a studio classroom. This teleclassroom would include a lectern/console where an instructor has the ability to either take complete control of the console features or have the production crew handle them. The lectern is equipped with a computer-based console that facilitates interaction between the instructor and students at remote sites through voice or electronic question and answer.

The broadcasting facility, or uplink, is equipped with a control room where a technician has duplicate controls to assist the instructor if needed. It may also include a director's console, various special effects generators including VideoShow, stillstore, animation, chromakey (for displaying and annotating one image in combination with another), and camera and sound system controls. Video editing and duplicating equipment could also be included in this facility.

Transmission chain: The first mile of communication link between the studio and satellite uplink usually consists of cable, fiber optics, microwave, laser or telephone land line. The program signal is delivered to an uplink antenna or dish, then transmitted to a geosynchronous satellite in a fixed position 22,300 miles above the equator. Satellites have transponders (video channels) that receive and retransmit the video signal. If a broadcast is encrypted, the encoder or scrambler would be co-located with the uplink and each receiver location would need a decoder to unscramble a broadcast.

Receive sites: A satellite downlink receives and decodes the satellite signal into channels. Equipment configurations may include satellite dish, low-noise block converter, satellite video receiver, decoder for encrypted, scrambled code to maintain confidentiality and security, connectors, power supply and video display.

Interactivity: distinguishes DL from one-way, passive instructional television. Interactivity allows each student to participate with the instructor and with each other, giving students a sense of being connected with the remote class members and facilitating their active involvement. Interaction is accomplished via telephone, two-way audio, video, two-way electronic text and/or graphics interactivity. Interactive Response Units (IRUs) or keypad devices, allow remote and local students to interact electronically with the instructor and among themselves during live classes. With IRUs, students can receive quick and meaningful feedback and actively participate when directly linked with the instructor. Instructors also receive immediate feedback from compiled student responses to numerical or multiple choice questions via the interactive keypad system, and are able to immediately assess the students' comprehension of the material, modifying the content, rate or presentation style in real-time. A database can be used to gather all the transactions for later evaluation and analysis.

There are production staff who can aid the instructor and insure that the technology does not inhibit the process. The instructor is then free to concentrate on content and leave the production to the experts who might include:

Administrator: schedules the facilities and satellite time, organizes timely distribution of materials to all remote sites.

Remote Site (field) Coordinator: communicates directly with each receiving site coordinator. Reserves room and equipment, sets up a room for satellite signal receiving, troubleshoots technical problems, arranges participants' question procedure and follows up with student evaluations.

Producer: oversees the entire production. Conducts initial meeting to define what is needed and to advise the instructor on techniques, resources, media and production methods. The producer facilitates the process and makes sure the instructor's teaching aides, (i.e. live product demonstrations, videotapes) are properly integrated into the class.

Director: works with instructor and directs the crew during rehearsal and broadcast to plan and select best way to "shoot" the program, timing and pacing, camera angles, placement of graphics.

Additional crew (when necessary): videotape recorder operator, additional camera operator, character generator/graphics operator, production assistant.

Televised teaching requires skills different from traditional teaching. Instructors need to familiarize themselves with the studio environment, the control room and computer console, and learn new teaching skills for telecourses. An array of electronic educational tools including stored graphics, animation, videotape (roll-ins), drawing tablets and remote cameras will need to be mastered so they can be effortlessly incorporated in the program.

Since timing is critical, there must be detailed organization of the class and explicit pre-planning of the presentation. A script should be developed to insure broadcast time constraints are adhered to, and procedures established for course administration (i.e.student questions and distribution/retrieval of materials). New presentation skills, suited to the medium, need to be fostered such as responding to camera movement, cueing and speaking directly to the camera in an unhurried fashion occasionally varying the tone of voice. Select clothing with bright and bold colors, avoid plaids, stripes and patterns that cause video interference. Orchestrate frequent interaction with students through predefined questioning strategies that stimulate discussion. Practice and rehearse to perfect timing and transitions, and to become comfortable with the technological tools. This is an extremely important objective — the instructor should be comfortable enough to easily focus on the student and use the technology to modify the course pacing or content to meet students' needs.

Now that you've had a taste of what's possible in a webcasting environment, go on to Chapter 3 to discover the differences between unicast and broadcast. In this chapter, you'll also discover that webcasting, in the guise of the Mbone, has been around for longer than you thought.

Chapter

3

Unicast, Broadcast, Multicast and the Mbone

Introduction

Running video and audio applications over the same network as text sounds appealing but experienced net managers know better. Voice and video are time-sensitive, and packet technologies like TCP/IP can't guarantee that the traffic will get where it needs to go without being jumbled and jerky. The big issues in webcasting over packet nets are bandwidth and burstiness. Audio and video applications generate lots of bits, and the traffic has to be "streamed," or transmitted continuously rather than in bursts. That's in contrast to conventional data types (such as text, files, and graphics), which are able to withstand short and inconsistent periods of delay between packet transmissions. What's needed, then, is a network capable of transporting both streaming and bursty data.

A suite of protocols from the IETF (Internet Engineering Task Force) makes it possible for IP networks to carry voice and video in addition to the bursty LAN traffic that's already traveling across the cable. Where multicasting minimizes bandwidth, RTP (real-time transport protocol) delivers real-time traffic with timing information for reconstruction of webcast information. Finally, RSVP (resource reservation protocol) lets network managers reserve a slice of network bandwidth and assign priorities to various traffic types. Essentially, the IETF protocols make it possible, for the first time, to offer voice, video and data in a single application.

This chapter provides an overview into the technical aspects of webcasting over the Internet. It's not meant to be an in-depth discussion (see the references at the end of the chapter for more information). Rather, it's to introduce the reader to the technical constraints that webcasting operates under.

Unicast, Broadcast and Multicast

The bulk of the traffic on today's networks is unicast: A separate copy of the data is sent from the source to each client that requests it. Networks also support broadcasting. When data is broadcast, a single copy of the data is sent to all clients on the network. When the same data needs to be sent to only a portion of the clients on the network, both of these methods waste network bandwidth. Unicast wastes bandwidth by sending multiple copies of the data. Broadcast wastes bandwidth by sending the data to the whole network whether or not the data is wanted. Broadcasting can also slow the performance of client machines needlessly. Each client must process the broadcast data whether the broadcast is of interest or not.

Multicasting takes the strengths of both of these approaches and avoids their weaknesses. Rather than sending a separate stream of packets going to each intended user (unicasting) or transmitting all packets to everyone (broadcasting), it involves the simultaneous transmission of traffic to a designated

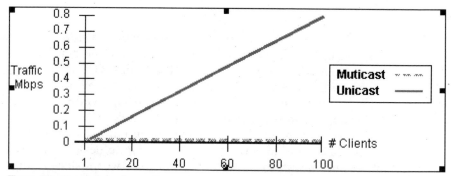

Figure 3-1. Network load per client.

subnet of network users. In other words, multicasting sends a single copy of the data to those clients who request it. Multiple copies of data are not sent across the network, nor is data sent to clients who do not want it. Multicasting allows the deployment of multimedia applications on the network while minimizing their demand for bandwidth. Figure 3-1 compares the network load per client when unicasting an 8 Kbps PCM audio stream and multicasting the stream and shows how a multicast saves bandwidth.

Today, the most widely known and used multicast enabled network is the Internet Multicast Backbone, or Mbone. The Mbone (Virtual Multicast Backbone On the interNEt) is a virtual network consisting of those portions of the Internet, sometimes called multicast islands, in which multicasting has been enabled. Multicasts that must travel across areas of the Internet that are not yet multicast enabled are sent as unicasts until they reach the next multicast enabled island. This process is referred to as tunneling and is shown in figure 3-2.

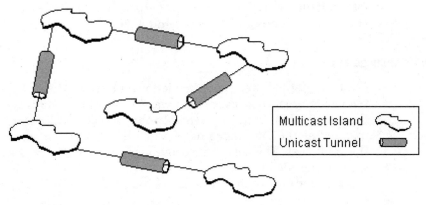

Figure 3-2. Multicast islands and tunnels.

The Mbone has been in place since 1992 and has grown to more than 2000 subnets. It has been used to multicast live audio and video showing Internet Engineering Task Force conferences, NASA astronauts working in space, and the Rolling Stones in concert. The Mbone has successfully demonstrated the practicality and utility of using multicasting to send multimedia across the network.

The Mbone is actually a virtual network, a network that runs on top of the Internet, which allows multicast packets to travel through the same routers that are set up to handle only unicast traffic. Essentially, the multicast packets are hidden inside of the unicast packets in a process called tunneling. When these hidden multicast packets reach a router that understands the multicast packets (i.e. the right software is running on the workstation), the packets are processed for what they really are.

The hardware for multicasting, chiefly multicast enabled routers and their software, has reached a point where corporations can take advantage of multicasting on their own LANs and WANs. However, be forewarned that you need a considerable amount of compute power to handle a multicast. Most of the software to run a multicast on the Mbone is for high-end UNIX workstations such as those from Sun, Digital and Silicon Graphics. Another hurdle is the bandwidth. A multicast video stream of 1 to 4 frames per second eats about 128 kbps of bandwidth and only delivers a grainy picture (by comparison, TV-quality video scans at about 24 frames per second). You'll need a minimum of 128 kbps which is about the speed of an ISDN line. The most effective telecom link is a T-1 or faster.

Still, the technology is of benefit in any scenario where several (or hundreds or thousands) of individuals need the same information. Because such information can be multicast live, multicasting is the ideal method to communicate up-to-date information to a wide audience. For example, sales trends for the week could be presented to all regional sales managers via multicast. Events such as product introductions or important press conferences could also be multicast. Multicasts can also support bi-directional communication allowing, for example, individuals in widely dispersed locations to set up a live conference that includes audio, video, and a whiteboard.

How IP Multicasting Works

Multicasting follows a push model of communications. That is, like a radio or television broadcast, those who want to receive a multicast tune their sets to the station they want to receive. In the case of multicasting, the user is simply instructing the computer's network card to listen to a particular IP address for the multicast. The computer originating the multicast does not need to know who has decided to receive it.

Multicasting, as shown in figure 3-3, requires the following mechanisms:

• Clients must have a way to learn when a multicast of interest is available.
• Clients must have a way to signal that they want to receive the multicast.
• The network must have a way to efficiently route data to those clients who want to receive it.

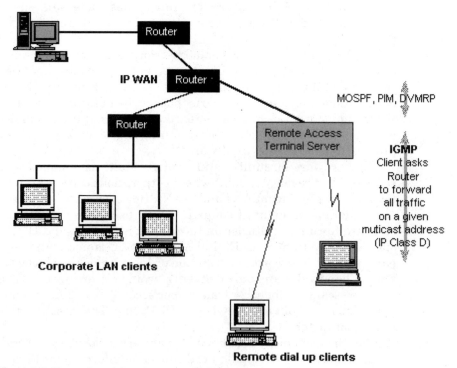

Figure 3-3. Network multicasting.

Multicasts are announced in advance so that clients know when a multicast is available. On the Mbone, multicasts are announced using the Session

Description Protocol (SDP). This protocol supplies clients with all the information they need to receive a multicast including its name and description, the times it is active, the type of media (audio, video, text and so on) that it uses, and the IP addresses, ports, and protocol it uses. The announcement information is multicast to a well-known IP address and port where clients running the session directory tool receive this information.

In addition to SDP, there are other ways that multicasts can be announced. For example, on the corporate intranet, multicasts can be advertised using Web pages. Controls embedded in the Web page can then receive the multicast data.

To signal that they want to receive a multicast, clients join the group to whom the multicast is directed. The Internet Group Management Protocol (IGMP) handles this task. IGMP enables users to sign up for multicast sessions and allows these multicast groups to be managed dynamically, in a distributed fashion.

Multicast groups provide several advantages. Groups are dynamic, clients can join or leave at any time. No elaborate scheme is required to create or disband a group. When a group has no members, it ceases to exist on the network.

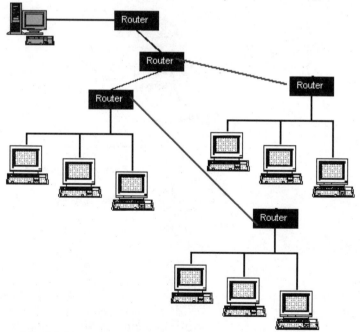

Figure 3-3a. Multicast groups are scaleable.

Groups also scale upward easily because as more clients join a multicast, it becomes more likely that the multicast is already being routed close to them.

When a client joins a group, it initiates two processes: First, an IGMP message is sent to the client's local router to inform the router that the client wants to receive data sent to the group. Second, the client sets its IP process and network card to receive the multicast on the group's address and port. Multicast addresses are Class D IP addresses ranging from 224.0.0.0 to 239.255.255.255. Class D IP addresses map automatically to IEEE-802 Ethernet multicast addresses, which simplifies the implementation of IP multicasting on Ethernet. When a client leaves a group and is the only one receiving the multicast on that particular subnetwork, the router stops sending data to the client's subnetwork, thereby freeing bandwidth on that portion of the network.

The bulk of the work that needs to be done to enable multicasting is performed by the network's routers and the protocols they run. A few years ago major router manufacturers began adding multicasting capability to their routers. Multicasting can be enabled on such routers by simply updating their software and adding memory.

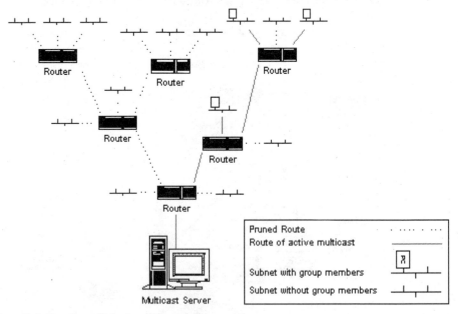

Figure 3-4. Creating efficient multicast delivery paths.

There are several multicast routing protocols in use today: Distance Vector Multicast Routing Protocol (DVMRP), Multicast Open Shortest Path First Protocol (MOSPF), and Protocol-Independent Multicast (PIM). The task of these protocols is to create efficient multicast delivery paths through the network as shown in figure 3-4. Multicast routing protocols use varying algorithms to achieve efficiency.

An efficient delivery path implies that multicast data travels only to those clients who want to receive it and takes the shortest path to those clients. If data travels elsewhere through the network, bandwidth goes to waste needlessly. You can visualize the network as a tree structure. The source of the multicast sends data through the branches of the tree. The routers are responsible for sending data down the correct branches to other routers and to the subnetworks where members of a group are waiting for data. Routers prune off branches where no one wants data and graft branches back to the tree when a client in a new subnetwork joins the group. Routers can also stop data from traveling to their own subnetworks when it is not wanted.

Where TCP (of the TCP/IP) handles the delivery of bursty data efficiently, it can't handle multicast and real-time data. RTP (real time transport protocol is defined in IETF RFC 1889) works alongside TCP, providing end-to-end delivery of video and audio-casting data. Feedback on reception quality and optional identification of the receivers of the multicast stream are provided by the real time transport control protocol (RTCP), which is an integral part of RTP.

To set up an RTP session, the application defines a particular pair of destination transport addresses (one network address plus a port pair for RTP and RTCP). The address pair is the same for all participants for IP multicast and different for each for individual unicasts.

RTP's viability and scalability have been proven on the Mbone, which handles videoconferencing, data conferencing and audio/video over a multicast subset of the Internet. The Mbone will be discussed, at length, later in this chapter.

Multicast Design Considerations

With a unicast design, applications can send one copy of each packet to each member of the multicast group. This technique is simple to implement, but it has significant scaling restrictions if the group is large. In addition, it requires extra bandwidth, because the same information has to be carried multiple times — even on shared links.

In a broadcast design, applications can send one copy of each packet and address it to a broadcast address. This technique is even simpler than unicast for the application to implement. However, if this technique is used, the network must either stop broadcasts at the LAN boundary (a technique that is frequently used to prevent broadcast storms) or send the broadcast everywhere. Sending the broadcast everywhere is a significant usage of network resources if only a small group actually needed to see the packets.

With a multicast design, applications can send one copy of each packet and address it to the group of computers that want to receive it. This technique addresses packets to a group of receivers rather than to a single receiver, and it depends on the network to forward the packets to only the networks that need to receive them.

Multicast can be implemented at both the data-link layer and the network layer. Ethernet and FDDI, for example, support unicast, multicast, and broadcast addresses. An individual computer can listen to a unicast address, several multicast addresses, and the broadcast address. Token Ring also supports the concept of multicast addressing but uses a different technique. Token Rings have functional addresses that can be used to address groups of receivers. If the scope of an application is limited to a single LAN, using a data-link layer multicast technique is sufficient. However, many multipoint applications are valuable precisely because they are not limited to a single LAN.

When a multipoint application is extended to an internet consisting of different media types, such as Ethernet, Token Ring, FDDI, ATM, Frame Relay, SMDS, and other networking technologies, it is best to implement multicast at the network layer.

There are several parameters that the network layer must define in order to support multicast communications:

Addressing. There must be a network-layer address that is used to communicate with a group of receivers rather than a single receiver. In addition, there must be a mechanism for mapping this address onto data-link layer multicast addresses where they exist.

Dynamic registration. There must be a mechanism for the computer to communicate to the network that it is a member of a particular group. Without this ability, the network cannot know which networks need to receive traffic for each group.

Multicast routing. The network must be able to build packet distribution trees that allow sources to send packets to all receivers. A primary goal of these packet distribution trees is to ensure that each packet exists only one time on any given network (that is, if there are multiple receivers on a given branch, there should only be one copy of the packets on that branch).

The Internet Engineering Task Force has been developing standards that address each of the issues described above:

Addressing. The IP address space is divided into four pieces: Class A, Class B, Class C, and Class D. Classes A, B, and C are used for unicast traffic. Class D is reserved for multicast traffic. Class D addresses are allocated dynamically.

Dynamic registration. RFC 1112 defines the Internet Group Membership Protocol (IGMP). IGMP specifies how the host should inform the network that it is a member of a particular multicast group.

Multicast routing. There are several standards available for routing IP Multicast traffic:

- RFC 1075 defines the Distance Vector Multicast Routing Protocol (DVMRP).
- RFC 1584 defines the Multicast Open Shortest Path First (MOSPF) protocol — an extension to OSPF that allows it to support IP Multicast.

• Two Internet standards-track drafts describe PIM — a multicast protocol that can be used in conjunction with all unicast IP routing protocols. These documents are entitled Protocol-Independent Multicast (PIM): Motivation and Architecture and Protocol-Independent Multicast: Protocol Specification.

DVMRP is the Distance Vector Multicast Routing Protocol; it is the routing protocol implemented by the mrouted program. An earlier version of DVMRP is specified in RFC-1075. However, the version implemented in mrouted is quite a bit different from what is specified in that RFC (different packet format, different tunnel format, additional packet types, and more). It maintains topological knowledge via a distance-vector routing protocol (like RIP, described in RFC-1058), upon which it implements a multicast forwarding algorithm called Truncated Reverse Path Broadcasting. DVMRP suffers from the well-known scaling problems of any distance-vector routing protocol.

DVMRP uses a technique known as Reverse Path Forwarding. When a router receives a packet, it floods the packet out of all paths except the one that leads back to the packet's source. Doing so allows a data stream to reach all LANs (possibly multiple times). If a router is attached to a set of LANs that do not want to receive a particular multicast group, the router can send a "prune" message back up the distribution tree to stop subsequent packets from traveling where there are no members.

DVMRP will periodically reflood in order to reach any new hosts that want to receive a particular group. There is a direct relationship between the time it takes for a new receiver to get the data stream and the frequency of flooding.

DVMRP implements its own unicast routing protocol in order to determine which interface leads back to the source of the data stream. This unicast routing protocol is very like RIP and is based purely on hop counts. As a result, the path that the multicast traffic follows may not be the same as the path that the unicast traffic follows.

DVMRP has significant scaling problems because of the necessity to flood frequently. This limitation is exacerbated by the fact that early implementations of DVMRP did not implement pruning.

DVMRP has been used to build the Mbone — a multicast backbone across the public Internet — by building tunnels between DVMRP-capable machines. The Mbone is used widely in the research community to transmit the proceedings of various conferences and to permit desktop conferencing.

Multicast Extensions to OSPF (RFC 1584)

Multicast OSPF (MOSPF) was defined as an extension to the OSPF unicast routing protocol. OSPF works by having each router in a network understand all of the available links in the network. Each OSPF router calculates routes from itself to all possible destinations.

MOSPF works by including multicast information in OSPF link state advertisements. An MOSPF router learns which multicast groups are active on which LANs.

MOSPF builds a distribution tree for each source/group pair and computes a tree for active sources sending to the group. The tree state is cached, and trees must be recomputed when a link state change occurs or when the cache times out.

MOSPF works only in internetworks that are using OSPF and is best suited for environments that have relatively few source/group pairs active at any given time. It will work less well in environments that have many active sources or environments that have unstable links.

Protocol-Independent Multicast (PIM) works with all existing unicast routing protocols. PIM supports two different types of multipoint traffic distribution patterns: dense and sparse.

Dense mode is most useful when:
• Senders and receivers are in close proximity to one another.
• There are few senders and many receivers.
• The volume of multicast traffic is high.
• The stream of multicast traffic is constant.

Dense-mode PIM uses Reverse Path Forwarding and looks a lot like DVMRP. The most significant difference between DVMRP and dense-mode PIM is that PIM works with whatever unicast protocol is being used; PIM does not require any particular unicast protocol.

Sparse multicast is most useful when:
• There are few receivers in a group.
• Senders and receivers are separated by WAN links.
• The type of traffic is intermittent.

Sparse-mode PIM is optimized for environments where there are many multipoint data streams. Each data stream goes to a relatively small number of the LANs in the internetwork. For these types of groups, Reverse Path Forwarding techniques waste bandwidth. Sparse-mode PIM works by defining a Rendezvous Point. When a sender wants to send data, it first sends to the Rendezvous Point. When a receiver wants to receive data, it registers with the Rendezvous Point. Once the data stream begins to flow from sender to Rendezvous Point to receiver, the routers in the path will optimize the path automatically to remove any unnecessary hops. Sparse-mode PIM assumes that no hosts want the multicast traffic unless they specifically ask for it.

PIM is able to simultaneously support dense mode for some multipoint groups and sparse mode for others.

Intel Intercast

The Intercast medium, while still in the beta stages, offers people a more productive way to experience television programming, while taking advantage of popular and familiar content. The Intercast medium combines the digital power of the PC, the global interactivity of the Internet, and the rich programming of television. Using television transmission — either over-the-air, cable or satellite — to powerful PCs, the Intercast medium delivers an interactive information and entertainment experience. The vertical blanking interval (VBI) signal which delivers the Web pages is not available in all areas. Be sure to confirm VBI availability with your local Cable operator.

Intel Intercast (http://www.intel.com) technology allows content providers to create new interactive content — text, graphics, video or data — around their existing programming, and deliver this content simultaneously with the TV signal to a PC equipped with Intel Intercast technology.

Intercast content is created with HTML. This means the new interactive content broadcast with the television signal appears to the user as Web pages, exactly as if he or she were using the actual World Wide Web. These broadcast Web pages can also include embedded hyperlinks to related information on the actual Internet. Using a telephone modem and any direct Internet connection, PCs with Intel Intercast technology can use the hyperlinks to move transparently between television and Internet sites related to the television program.

Users of these Intel Intercast technology-enabled PCs can watch TV on one part of the screen and, in another part of the screen, seamlessly interact with Web pages containing information, graphics or video about the TV program which "pop up" as the program proceeds. These Web pages may have been broadcast to the user's hard disk, or accessed on the broader Internet through a modem connection. A PC's fast bus and graphics — for displaying TV digitally — and its high resolution screen — for displaying both TV and associated Web pages — makes possible a rich presentation that would be impossible on a TV set.

Combining the power of the PC with existing consumer behavior, namely, watching TV, greatly increases the navigability of the Internet. The hyperlinks serve as navigational pointers to help individuals find additional content of interest to them. Using television programming as a context for both broadcast Web pages and hyperlinked World Wide Web sites, consumers will be able to create and experience their own personal Web of information.

The Convergence of the Analog TV and Digital PC

The arrival of the digital world is much anticipated, but the fact remains that high bandwidth communication today is still dominated by analog delivery. In order to realize the benefits of digital television, information, communication, and entertainment, we must start by building a bridge between these two worlds — analog and digital. The Intercast medium is the first realistic step toward convergence of the analog language of the television and the digital language of the PC.

The vast digital storage capability of the PC amplifies the power of the Intercast medium. Intercast content received by the PC is cached, or intelligently stored, on the PC's hard drive. Using just a small percentage of today's hard drive capacity, hundreds or even thousands of pages of information can be stored. In this mode, the user interactively browses the cached pages, as if they were being retrieved from the Internet itself. Access is at the speed of hard drive access, not the speed of a modem, and costs nothing.

Intel Intercast technology is highly scaleable, allowing it to take advantage of faster communication lines to the home, faster PCs, and future forms of broadcast digital video. Intel Intercast technology is the architectural basis for the first bridge between television and the Internet. It is the first step toward digital, interactive video, made possible by the capabilities of powerful PCs.

Intel Intercast Technology: New Opportunities for Software Developers

New applications and uses result when the power of the CPU is applied to video and audio from television or elsewhere. The PC captures, compresses, and stores television in real time, creating a source of nonlinear, interactive entertainment in the user's home without the need for video servers. In this way, the medium is more interactive for the user, who is now able to control the experience through the power of the PC. This model opens up possibilities for software developers, who can develop applications for increasingly powerful home PCs.

With the addition of a camcorder, the PC becomes a source of video for video conferencing, or a vehicle for editing home videos. An open architecture will allow development of software applications that take advantage of live video and data. An open, widely available platform is important for software development to be commercially viable.

The Intercast medium brings together leaders from the broadcast, cable, and PC industries. These leaders believe that the application of digital technology can transform the analog medium of television with the power of PC interactivity, while preserving the shared experience paradigm that has made television so central to society. Content and transport providers, software and hardware developers, and OEMs support the Intercast medium.

All the information third-party developers need — Application Programming Interfaces (APIs), hardware specifications — to create custom applications for the Intercast medium will be made widely available by Intel in the near future.

Television content providers will take a leadership role in creating new Intercast content to accompany their regular programming. Delivery of TV, live video, and real-time information to home PCs will create new opportunities for cable operators as well. OEMs will offer home PCs equipped to receive Intercast content. Software developers will play an important role in creating compelling applications that make use of the Intercast medium. Finally, hardware developers will ensure that Intercast technology is available to the broadest audience possible.

Examples of the Intercast Medium

When special events occur, such as the Kobe earthquake, Intercast medium users could view supplementary information about the latest developments, rescue efforts or historic earthquakes.

Sending a "scoreboard" with the broadcast of a basketball game would let users access the current score at their convenience. Networks could send statistics, still snapshots or video clips to users watching the game.

Music fans could click on a button to bring up a list of other titles on the release. An "info" button might point to an Internet music shopping service, where the user could purchase the CD. A "tickets" button could display a list of a performer's upcoming concert tour dates.

On a shopping channel, graphics and text descriptions of all the items in a shopping segment could be shown in the information window while the shopping host concentrates on a single item in the television window.

How Intel Intercast Works

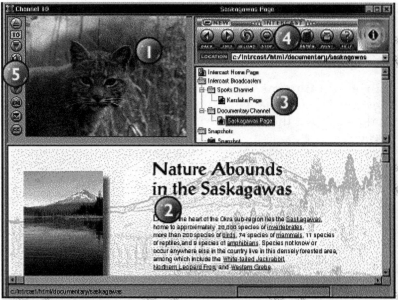

Figure 3-5. How Intercast works.

As one of the founding members of the Intercast Industry Group, Intel developed Intercast technology, including the hardware, much of the required software, and the technology that helps content providers input Web pages into their broadcast signal. Other members of the group provide content and develop products including PCs and add-in cards that use this new technology. Members include top media companies, cable operators, broadband communications equipment suppliers, computer manufacturers, and computer hardware and software vendors. Figure 3-5 diagrams how Intel Intercast works:

1. Program Window. Televised broadcasts run here. Resizing the window enables you to watch full-screen. Smaller window sizes provide progressively more room for viewing accompanying Web pages.

2. Intel Intercast Viewer. This browser window displays both broadcast and Internet HTML pages. Broadcasted pages accompany television programs. Internet Web pages require a direct connection to the Internet. Hypertext links on broadcasted pages guide you to the appropriate sites on the Internet's World Wide Web.

3. HTML Index. This is an index of all the downloaded HTML pages. Pages are cached and saved on your hard disk as they are received on the Intercast signal. Pages are arranged in folders you open by clicking on the appropriate icon. Whenever a new page is received, a green NEW button flashes at the top of the screen and the page's name is added to your index.

4. Browser Navigation Buttons. Using these buttons, you can navigate the World Wide Web, bookmark favorite sites and print Web pages. There's even a Location window to key in URLs. Intel Intercast technology includes the pictured browser, but other vendors may also develop browsers that are compatible.

5. Program Buttons. These buttons are similar to those you'd find on a TV. They enable you to change channels, raise or lower the volume, and view closed captioning. Use the snapshot button to capture video images right off the screen.

Intercast content is received in the same way you receive TV now — whether it is through a conventional TV antenna, cable, or C-band satellite dish. Any way your television set receives analog television, your Intel Intercast technology-enabled PC can also use. New PCs incorporating Intel Intercast Technology include: the AST Advantage Multimedia PC and Quantex Microsystems VM-1 Series PC. CompUSA has integrated a Pentium processor-based Compaq Presario home computer with special Intercast hardware and software from Intel. Intel Intercast technology add-in boards are available as well. Hauppauge Computer Works WinCast/TV receiver is an add-in board that will upgrade most Pentium processor based PCs for Intercast programming reception. This product is available at CompUSA as well.

Working prototype systems are currently being tested in Portland, Oregon, metro-area households. In addition, on October 10th, 1995, KGW, a Portland NBC affiliate, successfully completed the first live transmission of broadcast video and Web pages to an Intercast-enabled PC.

The Intercast medium is not meant to displace TV or to compete with interactive TV or even dumb Web terminals. Depending on the program, and individual preferences, some content will be better-suited to the Intercast medium, and some will be better-suited to the interactive TV model. The fundamental difference between the Intercast medium and other "Web terminal" or "Web TV" products is the unique capabilities made possible by the digital power of a high-performance PC. With the Intercast medium, the user — not a video server — controls the interactive experience. The hard disk of a high-performance PC can store hundreds or even thousands of broadcast Web pages, making this information available at any time for the user to manipulate. The high-resolution graphics of a PC are unmatched by conventional TV monitors. Pentium processor-based PCs enable a level of integration of the Internet and television impossible on a conventional TV set.

In order to receive the full benefits of the Intercast medium, the user will need to purchase an Intel Intercast technology-enabled high performance PC. These PCs take advantage of the speed of the PCI bus which results in cost-effective video delivery and display.

High performance PCs enabled with Intel Intercast technology also become video-capable platforms for a wide range of applications. Video input from a camcorder could be turned into a .AVI file, or video from a camcorder could be compressed for a video phone application. Intercast content from broadcasters cannot be recorded on most home VCRs however, as most of the high speed associated data is lost in the recording process on consumer-grade VCRs. Of course, you can use your PC to capture and cache Web pages, and your VCR to record video.

The Intercast Web browser can also receive Web pages broadcast to your hard disk using Intel Intercast technology. These broadcast Web pages will be cached and retrieved from your hard drive. When you follow a link from a broadcast Web page out of the cache to the Web, the browser will connect you to your regular Internet service provider. At that point, it functions like any other Web browser.

A standard PC modem (28,000 bps recommended) is used for back-channel transactions. Intercast uses one-way broadcast communications to receive the TV programming and related Web pages. Embedded in these broadcast Web pages are hyperlinks to additional Web pages. The user simply clicks on that page's title, which is displayed in the Media Library section of the viewing screen. To request a page located on the World Wide Web, a user clicks on a hyperlink if provided, or types in the URL address of the Web site.

To request a Web page which has not been broadcast to a user's hard drive via the Intercast medium, the user will need to go online with an Internet Service Provider via a modem "back-channel."

For example, a television advertiser may send down three "pages" of information related to their ad along with the television commercial. The Intel Intercast technology user can browse these three pages at their leisure. The advertiser may also embed within these pages a hyperlink back to the advertiser's Web site on the Internet. By clicking on this hyperlink, the user will be connected to the advertiser's Web site via the modem back-channel.

Each broadcaster will broadcast Web pages with content about their particular programming. The user receiving these broadcast pages on an Intel Intercast technology-equipped PC will be able to interact with these pages or store them for later use on their PC. When transactions occur between the user and the advertiser or broadcaster, such as purchasing an item or participating in a viewer poll, the telephone modem back-channel is used.

It is expected that Intercast content will be delivered along with the regular television signal, similar to today's economic model for TV. Some content will be free or advertiser-subsidized, some will be included as part of basic cable services, and other content will be offered as a premium service.

The Intercast Industry Group

The IIG is composed of America Online, Asymetrix, Comcast, En Technology, Gateway 2000, Intel Corporation, NBC, Netscape Communications Corporation, Packard Bell, Turner Broadcasting's CNN Interactive, QVC, Viacom and WGBH Educational Foundation as well as many associate companies. The proposed charter of the group is to develop and promote the Intercast medium. They share the common goal of developing technology, PC platforms, software applications and content for broad market deployment. Their goal is to create an industry-accepted, open medium which will spawn industry-wide implementations.

The initial IIG members will be companies that have joined together to take a leadership position in defining and developing the Intercast medium. The goal is for the Intercast medium to become an open, generally-accepted industry approach supported by all PC manufacturers and broadcast companies. If your company is interested in joining, please write to:

The Intercast Industry Group
PO Box 10266
Portland, OR 97210

The member companies will develop product and content that supports the Intercast medium. The IIG plans to build awareness of the link between Intercast content and Intel Intercast technology through press and marketing campaigns. The IIG hopes to ensure its success by broadening the array of products and services that can take advantage of this new medium.

The Mbone (For Those Who Like to "Do It Themselves")

The Mbone is an outgrowth of the first two IETF "audiocast" experiments in which live audio and video were multicast from the IETF meeting site to destinations around the world. It's a collection of Internet routers that support the Internet Protocol (IP) multicast routing protocol. A network within a network, the Mbone can carry live audio and video on the Internet.

Currently there are about 2000 Mbone-using sites, and the Mbone itself is doubling in size every six months or so. Some observers expect the originally experimental multicasting features to percolate Internet-wide by the turn of the century. The software itself is free and available for downloading.

So why doesn't everyone use the Mbone for easy videoconferencing and easy listening? Possibly because you need a heavy-duty UNIX workstation as well as a T-1 line to get started on video. A mere 56-kbps line will do if all you're after is audio. But Mbone eats bandwidth: An Internet backbone line that can handle millions of ordinary computer transactions, like e-mail, can carry only about 100 Mbone sessions.

It all started in March 1992 when the first audiocast on the Internet took place from the Internet Engineering Task Force (IETF) meeting in San Diego. At that event 20 sites listened to the audiocast. Two years later, at the IETF meeting in Seattle, about 567 hosts in 15 countries tuned in to the two parallel broadcasting channels (audio and video) and also talked back (audio) and joined the discussions! The networking community now takes it for granted that the IETF meetings will be distributed via Mbone. Mbone has also been used to distribute experimental data from a robot at the bottom of the Sea of Cortez as well as a late Saturday night feature movie. The Discovery of Television Among the Bees by David Blair was also shown on the Mbone.

Several elements came together to make this possible. Many UNIX workstations now have built-in audio devices and sufficient processing power to decompress and display video in a window. That provided a platform for the development of conferencing application programs to packetize the real-time media for transmission across the Internet. IP multicast — the ability to deliver an IP packet to multiple destinations — allowed efficient distribution to a large number of participants.

The idea behind Mbone is to construct a semi-permanent IP multicast testbed to carry the IETF transmissions and support continued experimentation between meetings. This is a cooperative, volunteer effort.

The Mbone is a virtual network. It is layered on top of portions of the physical Internet to support routing of IP multicast packets since that function has not yet been integrated into production routers. The network is composed of islands as shown in figure 3-6 that can directly support IP multicast, such as multicast LANs like Ethernet, linked by virtual point-to-point links called "tunnels." The tunnel endpoints are typically workstation-class machines having operating system support for IP multicast and running the "mrouted" multicast routing daemon.

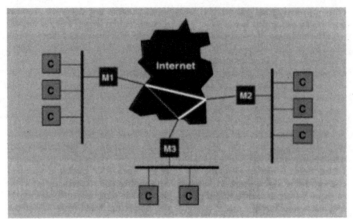

Figure 3-6. Mbone topology — islands, tunnels, mrouted.

The Mbone topology, always under construction, is a combination of mesh and star: the backbone and regional (r mid-level) networks will be linked by a mesh of tunnels among mrouted machines located primarily at interconnection points of the backbones and regionals. Some redundant tunnels may be configured with higher metrics for robustness. Then each regional network will have a star hierarchy hanging off its node of the mesh to fan out and connect to all the customer networks that want to participate.

Between continents there will probably be only one or two tunnels, preferably terminating at the closest point on the Mbone mesh. In the US, this may be on the Ethernets at the two FIXes (Federal Internet eXchanges) in California and Maryland. Since the FIXes are fairly busy, it will be important to minimize the number of tunnels that cross them. This may be accomplished using IP multicast directly (rather than tunnels) to connect several multicast routers on the FIX Ethernet.

There is no "network provider" of the Mbone. In the spirit of the Internet, Mbone is loosely coordinated via a mailing list. When end-users want to connect to Mbone, they are encouraged to contact their network provider. If that network provider is not participating in Mbone and, for some reason does not want to, a tunnel can be arranged to another point in Mbone.

From time to time, there have been major overhauls of the topology as Mbone has grown. Usually this has been prompted by an upcoming IETF meeting. These meetings put a big strain on Mbone. The IETF multicast traffic has been about 100 to 300 kb per second with spikes up to 500 kb per second. The Mbone is organized and coordinated by volunteers through a series of e-mail lists. The goal is to avoid loading any one individual with the responsibility of designing and managing the whole topology, though perhaps it will be necessary to periodically review the topology to see if corrections are required.

The intent is that when a new regional network wants to join in, they will make a request on the appropriate Mbone list, then the participants at "close" nodes will answer and cooperate in setting up the ends of the appropriate tunnels. To keep fanout down, sometimes this might mean breaking an existing tunnel and inserting a new node, so three sites will have to work together to set up the tunnels.

To know which nodes are "close" will require knowledge of both the Mbone logical map and the underlying physical network topology. This means understanding the physical T-3 NSFnet backbone topology map combined with the network providers' own knowledge of their local topology.

Within a regional network, the network's own staff can independently manage the tunnel fanout hierarchy in conjunction with end-user participants. New end-user networks should contact the network provider directly, rather than the Mbone list, to get connected.

Each network-provider participant in the Mbone provides one or more IP multicast routers to connect with tunnels to other participants and to customers. The multicast routers are typically separate from a network's production routers since most production routers don't yet support IP multicast. Most sites use workstations running the mrouted program.

It is best if the workstations can be dedicated to the multicast routing function to avoid interference from other activities and so there will be no qualms about installing kernel patches or new code releases on short notice. Since most Mbone nodes other than endpoints will have at least three tunnels, and each tunnel carries a separate (unicast) copy of each packet, it is also useful, though not required, to have multiple network interfaces on the workstation so it can be installed parallel to the unicast router.

Mbone Hardware and Software

The most convenient platform is a Sun SPARCstation simply because that is the machine used for mrouted development. An older machine (such as a SPARC-1 or IPC) will provide satisfactory performance as long as the tunnel fanout is kept in the 5-10 range. The platforms for which software is available:

Machines	Operating Systems	Network Interfaces
Sun SPARC	SunOS 4.1.1,2,3	ie, le, lo
Vax or Microvax	4.3+ or 4.3-tahoe	de, qe, lo
Decstation 3100,5000	Ultrix 3.1c, 4.1, 4.2a	ln, se, lo
Silicon Graphics	All ship with multicast	

The IP multicast software is available by anonymous FTP from the vmtp-ip directory on host gregorio.stanford.edu. Here's a snapshot of the files:

```
ipmulti-pmax31c.tar
ipmulti-sunos41x.tar.Z (Binaries & patches for SunOS)
ipmulticast-ultrix4.1.patch
ipmulticast-ultrix4.2a-binary.tar
ipmulticast-ultrix4.2a.patch
ipmulticast.README
ipmulticast.tar.Z (Sources for BSD)
```

You don't need kernel sources to add multicast support. Included in the distributions are files (sources or binaries, depending upon the system) to modify your BSD, SunOS, or Ultrix kernel to support IP multicast, including the mrouted program and special multicast versions of ping and netstat.

Silicon Graphics includes IP multicast as a standard part of their operating system. The mrouted executable and ip_mroute kernel module are not installed by default; you must install the eoe2.sw.ipgate subsystem and "autoconfig" the kernel to be able to act as a multicast router.

Documentation on the IP multicast software is included in the distribution on gregorio.stanford.edu (ipmulticast.README). RFC1112 specifies the "Host Extensions for IP Multicasting."

Multicast routing algorithms are described in the paper *Multicast Routing in Internetworks and Extended LANs* by S. Deering, in the Proceedings of the ACM SIGCOMM 1988 Conference.

A postscript map of the Mbone is available on parcftp.xerox.com:

```
/pub/net-research/mbone-map-{big,small}.ps
```

The person supporting a network's participation in the Mbone should have the skills of a network engineer, but a fairly small percentage of that person's time should be required. Activities requiring this skill level would be choosing a topology for multicast distribution within the provider's network and analyzing traffic flow when performance problems are identified. To set up and run an mrouted machine will require the knowledge to build and install operating system kernels.

Part of the resources that should be committed to participate would be for operations staff to be aware of the role of the multicast routers and the nature of multicast traffic, and to be prepared to disable multicast forwarding if excessive traffic is found to be causing trouble. The potential problem is that any site hooked into the Mbone could transmit packets that cover the whole Mbone, so if it became popular as a "chat-line," all available bandwidth could be consumed. There are plans to implement multicast route pruning so that packets only flow over those links necessary to reach active receivers to reduce the traffic level. This problem should be manageable through the same measures we already depend upon for stable operation of the Internet, but Mbone participants should be aware of it.

How Do You Join Mbone

STEP 1: If you are an end-user site (e.g., an organization), please contact your network provider. If your network provider is not participating in the Mbone, you can arrange to connect to some nearby point that is on the Mbone, but it is far better to encourage your network provider to participate to avoid overloading links with duplicate tunnels to separate end nodes. Below is a list of some network providers who are participating in the Mbone, but this list is likely not to be complete.

AlterNet	ops@uunet.uu.net
CERFnet	mbone@cerf.net
CICNet	mbone@cic.net
CONCERT	mbone@concert.net
Cornell	swb@nr-tech.cit.cornell.edu
JvNCnet	multicast@jvnc.net
Los Nettos	prue@isi.edu
NCAR	mbone@ncar.ucar.edu
NCSAnet	mbone@cic.net
NEARnet	nearnet-eng@nic.near.net
OARnet	oarnet-mbone@oar.net
PSCnet	pscnet-admin@psc.edu
PSInet	mbone@nisc.psi.net
SESQUINET	sesqui-tech@sesqui.net
SDSCnet	mbone@sdsc.edu
SURAnet	multicast@sura.net
UNINETT	mbone-no@uninett.no

If you are a network povider, send a message to the -request address of the mailing list for your region to be added to that list for purposes of coordinating setup of tunnels, etc:

mbone-eu:	mbone-eu-request@sics.se	Europe
mbone-jp:	mbone-jp-request@wide.ad.jp	Japan
mbone-korea:	mbone-korea-request@mani.kaist.ac.kr	Korea
mbone-na:	mbone-na-request@isi.edu	North America
mbone-oz:	mbone-oz-request@internode.com.au	Australia
mbone:	mbone-request@isi.edu	other

These lists are primarily aimed at network providers who would be the top level of the Mbone organizational and topological hierarchy. The mailing list is also a hierarchy; mbone@isi.edu forwards to the regional lists, then those lists include expanders for network providers and other institutions. Mail of general interest should be sent to mbone@isi.edu, while regional topology questions should be sent to the appropriate regional list.

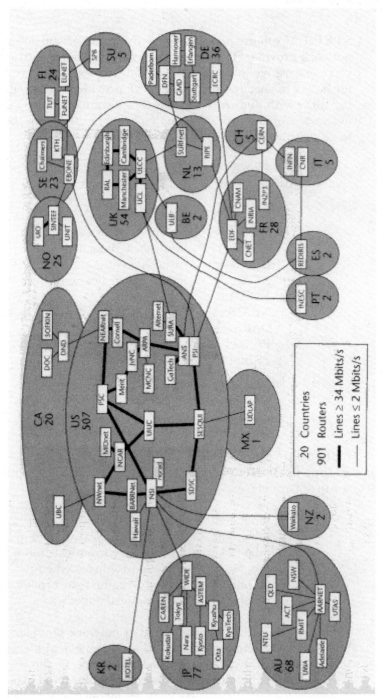

Figure 3-7. Participating Mbone subnets.

Individual networks may also want to set up their own lists for their customers to request connection of organizational mrouted machines to the network's mrouted machines. Some that have done so were listed above.

STEP 2: Set up an mrouted machine, build a kernel with IP multicast extensions added, and install the kernel and mrouted; or, install MOSPF software in a Proteon router.

STEP 3: Send a message to the Mbone list for your region asking to hook in, then coordinate with existing nodes to join the tunnel topology.

How Do You Find Out About Mbone Events

Many of the audio and video transmissions over the Mbone are advertised in "sd," the session directory tool as shown in figure 3-8. Session creators specify all the address parameters necessary to join the session, then sd multicasts the advertisement to be picked up by anyone else running sd. The audio and video

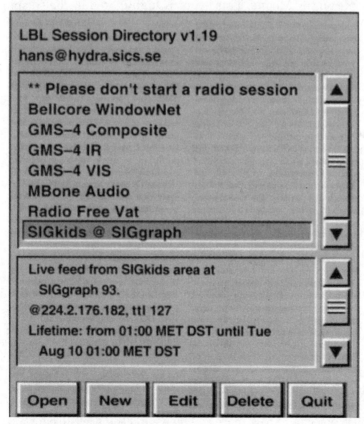

Figure 3-8. Sd, the session directory.

programs can be invoked with the right parameters by clicking a button in sd. From ftp.ee.lbl.gov, get the file sd.tar.Z or sgi-sd.tar.Z or dec-sd.tar.Z.

Schedules for IETF audio/videocasts and some other events are announced on the IETF mailing list (send a message to ietf-request@cnri.reston.va.us to join). Some events are also announced on the rem-conf mailing list, along with discussions of protocols for remote conferencing (send a message to rem-conf-request@es.net to join). Another place to find out about events is:

```
A HREF="http://www.cilea.it/Mbone/agenda.html
```

Sd offers a convenient way of announcing "sessions" that will take place on the Mbone. When creating a session, you specify the multicast address (an unused address is suggested by sd) and the various tools that are used. Other people can then just click "Open" and sd will start all the necessary tools with appropriate parameters.

When this snapshot in figure 3-8 was taken, the SIGGRAPH conference was taking place. As a special event at that conference, children were invited to talk with people on the Mbone. This event is highlighted in the sd snapshot. Going up in the list we have Radio Free Vat. This is the Mbone "radio" station where anyone on the Mbone can be the "disk jockey." Next up is Mbone Audio, which is the common chat channel of the Mbone. Everyone is free to join and start a discussion about any subject. The Global Mapping Satellite (GMS) sessions are pictures from a satellite above Hawaii. The pictures (composite, infrared or visual spectra) are sent out using imm (Image Multicast Client). Second to the top is the Bellcore WindowNet. If you tuned in to this session, you would see the outlook from a window at Bellcore. At the top we have a plea. As audio and video consumes a fair amount of bandwidth and Mbone is global, rebroadcasting your favorite local radio station onto Mbone will put a hard strain on many networks. Not shown in this particular snapshot, but a frequent and very popular guest on Mbone, are the Space Shuttle missions. The NASA select cable channel is broadcast onto the Mbone during the flights.

Currently there are three more-or-less permanent sessions going on in Mbone. There is one audio and video channel for free-for-all use and there is Radio Free Vat. In addition to the IETF meetings, which are transmitted three times per year, several major conferences and workshops are being transmitted onto the net, such as JENC93 and some IETF working group meetings.

Mbone in its present form should be viewed as one single resource. Only in a few places can it handle more than one video channel together with audio. The IETF tries to make two video and four audio channels but does not always accomplish this, even if the best "networkers" in the Internet put in their best efforts. So far, we have not had any major collisions of major events. The collisions that have occurred have been resolved after some brief discussions. Essentially it is first-announce-first-serve scheduling. As Mbone increases in popularity, one can expect more collisions and the pressure for a particular slot will increase.

Downloadable Mbone tools

The teleconferencing applications used on the Mbone are known as the Mbone tools. The most popular programs are Visual Audio Tool (vat), written by Van Jacobson and Steve McCanne at Lawrence Berkeley Laboratory (LBL), and the program Network Video (nv) from Ron Frederick at Xerox Palo Alto Research Center. The vat window, shown behind the nv windows in figure 3-9, presents a list of session participants, along with meters to indicate the microphone and speaker volume levels and sliders to adjust them. The audio stream is normally uncompressed 64 kbps pulse-code modulation (PCM), but vat also implements multiple software compression algorithms that can produce data rates as low as 9 kbps when required for transmission through slow lines.

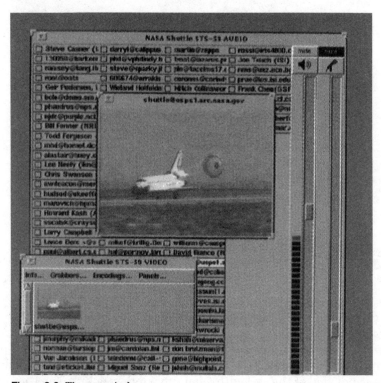

Figure 3-9. The vat window.

Other available tools include the audio tool Network Voice Terminal (nevot), written by Henning Schulzrinne at the University of Massachusetts, and the INRIA Videoconferencing System (ivs) video and audio program, written by Thierry Turletti and Christian Huitema from the French National Institute for Research in Computer Science and Control. The ivs tool uses a more complex video compression algorithm, a software implementation of the H.261 standard. Commercial conferencing products using IP multicast have also begun to emerge, including PictureWindow from Bolt Beranek and Newman, InPerson from Silicon Graphics, and ShowMe from Sun Microsystems.

Also useful for presentations or small-group interactions is the shared whiteboard tool (wb), from LBL (figure 3-10). It displays PostScript or text files on the shared drawing space; any of the participants can then add sketches and text annotations. All marks are distributed and displayed in near real time for each participant. Unlike the audio and video tools, wb implements reliable communication over the best-effort multicast IP service by allowing retransmission from any participant who possesses the missing data.

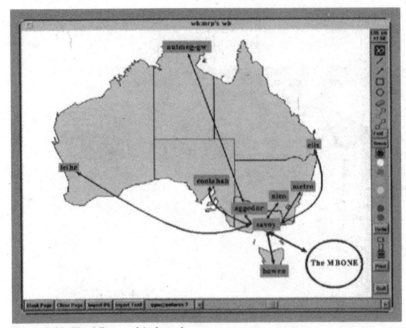

Figure 3-10. The Mbone whiteboard.

For private sessions following the telephone model, the Multimedia Conference Control tool (mmcc), developed at the University of Southern California's Information Sciences Institute, orchestrates point-to-point or multipoint teleconferences. The caller places a call and waits for an answer. Each callee is notified of the call with a pop-up window asking whether to receive the call. If a callee answers, the caller's mmcc distributes the session parameters to that participant's mmcc. Each mmcc then starts the underlying media tools and, at session completion, shuts them down.

Problems with the Mbone

Multicasting can be dangerous, but it also carries the promise of very useful applications. As an indication of this, Mbone usage is increasing very rapidly.

As a probably unintentional side effect, it has also brought out some bugs in some routers and hosts in the Internet. Before Mbone can be provided as a regular widespread service, some issues have to be addressed.

Some of these issues are still difficult research issues, like resource control and real-time traffic control. Other work is directed toward better management hooks and tools and incorporating multicasting in the Internet routers.

Using Mbone today, the sender has no control or implicit knowledge of who is listening out there. A receiver can just "tune in," like a radio. Some applications would want some kind of information about who is listening, for example by asking Mbone which hosts are currently in a particular multicast group. There are mechanisms in some applications for end-to-end control of who is listening (i.e., encryption) but there is so far no common architecture for this. When the going gets rough and a lot of packets are dropped, some applications would be helped by some feedback on the actual performance of the network. A video application could, for example, stop sending raw HDTV data when only 2% make it to the receivers and instead start sending slow-scan, heavily compressed pictures.

Some of the success of Mbone is dependent on the "courtesy" of TCP. When someone starts sending audio onto a fully loaded Internet link, it will cause packet losses for many of the connections that are running on that link. They are usually TCP connections and they will back off when packet losses occur. UDP-based audio does not have any such mechanism and will effectively take the bandwidth it needs.

On several occasions end-users have started a video session with a high time-to-live (TTL) and subsequently swamped the network with a continuous stream of 300 to 500 kb per second. These users have not been malicious. Sometimes the program has just been started with "-ttl 116" instead of "-ttl 16" with the effect that it reaches most parts of the Mbone instead of just the local part. At other times, the users have not really been aware of what "256 kb per second" really is netwise. Very few links in the Internet can handle that load without severely disturbing normal traffic. Usually, after the mistake has been pointed out, the users have stopped their transmissions. The problem is that with the new video and audio applications the mistakes have severe consequences and, with multicasting on the Mbone, the consequences are spread globally. It will take some time before the user community gets a feel for how much bandwidth video and audio takes.

Notes and Online sources about Mbone:

Information Sources:
http://www.best.com/prince/techinfo/MBone.html
http://hill.lut.ac.uk/DS-Archive/MTP.html
ftp.isi.edu as mbone/faq.txt (Questions and Answers)
http://www.research.att.com/mbone-faq.HTML (Q&A as html)
ftp://taurus.cs.nps.navy.mil/pub/mbmg/mbone.html (Mbone info)

ftp://genome-ftp.stanford.edu/pub/mbone/mbone-connect (connection info)
http://www.cilea.it/MBone/agenda.html (Mbone Session Agenda)
http://www.fokus.gmd.de/step/hgs/rtp/
(The Audio-Video Transport Working Group)
http://www.es.net/pub/mailing-lists/mail-archive/rem-conf
(Mailing list archive)
ftp://ftp.isi.edu/confctrl/mmcc (Multimedia Conference Control)
ftp://ftp.ee.lbl.gov/conferencing/sd (Session Directory)
ftp://ftp.ee.lbl.gov/conferencing/vat (Visual Audio Tool)
ftp://gaia.cs.umass.edu/pub/hgschulz/nevot (Network Voice Terminal)
ftp://parcftp.xerox.com/net-research/nv.tar.Z (Network Video)
http://zenon.inria.fr:8003/rodeo/personnel/Thierry.Turletti/ivs.html
(INRIA Videoconferencing System)
http://www-nrg.ee.lbl.gov/vic (Videoconferencing too)l
ftp://ftp.ee.lbl.gov/conferencing/wb (Whiteboard)
ftp://ftp.hawaii.edu/paccom/imm-3.3 IMM
ftp://nic.ddn.mil/rfc/rfc1301.txt.Z (Multicast Transport Protocol RFC 1301)
http://www.eit.com/software/mmphone/phoneform.html
(Multimedia Phone Service)
http://www.cl.cam.ac.uk/mbone/ (The JIPS Mbone Page)
ftp://agate.lut.ac.uk/pub/mbone (Mbone/IP Multicast Tools)
http://chocolate.pa.dec.com/mbone (Digital Mbone Page)
http://www.acm.uiuc.edu/signet/ SigNet Home Page

Version 3.8 of Mrouted and Version 3.5 of IP multicast OS kernel extensions are available at the following sites.

For SGI, ftp ftp.sgi.com
For Solaris, ftp ftp.uoregon.edu, and playground.sun.com
For DEC-Alpha running OSF1 V2.0, ftp chocolate.pa.dec.com
For FreeBSD 2.1/NetBSD, ftp ftp.parc.xerox.com
For HP/UX 9.05, ftp ftp.parc.xerox.com

Online Mailing Lists:

For MboneDeployment related issues, subscribe to:
mboned@ns.uoregon.edu

For all Mbone Engineering related issues, the following mailing sublists have been put into place:

Australia: mbone-oz-request@internode.com.au
Canada: canet-mbone-request@canet.ca
Japan: mbone-jp-request@wide.ad.jp
Korea: mbone-kr-request@cosmos.kaist.ac.kr

Singapore: mbone-sg-request@lincoln.technet.sg
UK: mbone-uk-request@cs.ucl.ac.uk
Europe: mbone-eu-request@sics.se
N. America: mbone-na-request@isi.edu
Other: mbone-na-request@isi.edu

For all Remote Conferencing related issues, subscribe to:
rem-conf-request@es.net

For all Conference Control related issues, subscribe to:
confctrl-request@isi.edu

For Radio multicasts on Mbone, subscribe to:
vat-radio-request@elxr.jpl.nasa.gov

For all IDMR related issues, subscribe to:
idmr-request@cs.ucl.ac.uk

For RSVP discussions, subscribe to:
rsvp-request@isi.edu

For Integrated Services issues, subscribe to:
int-serv-request@isi.edu

Mbone Tools:

The following tools are located at: http://www.mang.canterbury.ac.nz/

Sun OS 4.1.x Binaries
IP Multicast Extensions for BSD-Derived UNIX Systems (gzip 1.19 Mb)
    apps/ipmulti3.3-sunos413x.tar.gz
Session Directory v1.14 (gzip 964 Kb)
    apps/sd-1.14.tar.gz
Visual Audio Tool v3.4 (gzip 1.62 Mb)
    apps/sun/vat-3.4sun.tar.gz
Net Video Tool v3.3beta (gzip 640 Kb)
    apps/sun/nv-3.3bsun.tar.gz
Shared Whiteboard Tool 1.59 (gzip 1.12 Mb)
    apps/wb-1.59sun.tar.gz
IMM (JPEG Images) (gzip 761 Kb)
    apps/sun/imm-3.4sun.tar.gz
Video Conference Tool (IVS) (gzip 2.61 Mb)
    apps/sun/ivs_vfc-3.3sun.tar.gz
Video Conference (VIC) (gzip 3.44 Mb)
    apps/sun/vic-2.6sun.tar.gz

Network Voice Terminal (nevot) (gzip 3.65 Mb)
    apps/sun/nevot-3.25sun.tar.gz

Solaris 2.x Binaries

Session Directory v1.14 (gzip 964 Kb)
    apps/sd-1.14.tar.gz
Visual Audio Tool v3.4 (gzip 1.43 Mb)
    apps/sol/vat-3.4sol.tar.gz
Net Video Tool v3.3beta (gzip 471 Kb)
    apps/sol/nv-3.3bsol.tar.gz
Shared Whiteboard Tool 1.59 (gzip 1.12 Mb)
    apps/wb-1.59sun.tar.gz
IMM (JPEG Images) (gzip 323 Kb)
    apps/sol/imm-3.4sol.tar.gz
Video Conference Tool (IVS) (gzip 2.21 Mb)
    apps/sol/ivs_vfc-3.3sol.tar.gz
Video Conference (VIC) (gzip 1.81 Mb)
    apps/sol/vic-2.6sol.tar.gz

SGI (IRIX 5.x) Binaries

Session Directory v1.14 (gzip 861 Kb)
    apps/sgi/sd-1.14sgi.tar.Z
Visual Audio Tool v3.4 (gzip 1.07 Mb)
    apps/sgi/vat-3.4sgi.tar.Z
Net Video Tool v3.3beta (gzip 706 Kb)
    apps/sgi/nv-3.3bsgi.tar.Z
Shared Whiteboard Tool 1.59 (gzip 1.49 Mb)
    apps/sgi/wb-1.59sgi.tar.Z

Chapter

4

Microsoft's View of Webcasting

Microsoft has taken an aggressive stance on all things related to the Internet. Never to be outdone by any other *Netpreneur*, webcasting is a big part of its overall strategy. In this chapter we will review several of Microsoft's webcasting products.

NetShow

NetShow On-Demand is a streaming webcasting product which enables content producers to deliver content "after the fact," or non-real-time. Normally, when accessing networked multimedia content a user has to wait for the entire file to be transferred before they can use the information. Streaming allows a user to see or hear the information as it arrives without having to wait. NetShow also enables the content provider to generate productions in which audio, graphics, video, URLs and script commands can be synchronized based on a timeline.

NetShow Live uses IP Multicast to deliver a stream of live audio information to intranet users. IP Multicast is an open, standards-based way to distribute identical information to many users simultaneously. This contrasts with regular TCP/IP (IP unicast) where the same information may be sent to many clients, but the sender must transmit an individual copy to each user.

NetShow On-Demand (http://www.microsoft.com/netshow/), which is downloadable for free, is designed to provide streaming, synchronized presentation data, as well as high-quality audio and video data streams, to accompany data stored on corporate intranets or on the Internet. NetShow On-Demand allows the content provider to place rich multimedia content on a bandwidth-limited network, and allows the viewer to experience this content almost immediately, without suffering through prolonged download times. To understand the opportunities and potential uses that this technology creates, it is helpful to first take a brief look at the Internet/intranet phenomenon in general and at the challenges and limitations involved in implementing multimedia networked applications on the World Wide Web.

An Introduction to Multimedia on the Internet

The growth of the Internet has reached phenomenal proportions and is perhaps the most important platform shift to hit the computing industry since the introduction of the IBM personal computer in 1981. The World Wide Web is a key driving force in this growth and has become one of the largest repositories of information in the world. Establishing a World Wide Web presence on the Internet offers organizations the opportunity to expand communications with their customers, partners, and remote employees. Organizations of all sizes are finding that the Internet gives them invaluable exposure at a very manageable cost.

In short, the general growth of the Internet is a well-known phenomenon. Recitations of geometric growth abound, but the most explosive expansion will be the use of Internet technologies to improve communications within organizations. One such area is the use of intranets — Web technologies running on internal corporate or organizational local area networks. Audio and video content is becoming a fundamental part of the intranet and Internet experience. From the beginning, the World Wide Web has offered businesses and individuals the opportunity to distribute information in a more effective and compelling fashion, but Internet sites used only text because of limitations in Internet and client technologies. With the surge in capabilities of Internet World Wide Web browsers that support multimedia capabilities, Web site developers have responded with more multimedia-laden web pages, using text with images and graphics. Now many Web site developers are starting to use audio and video content to entice more people to visit their sites.

The same phenomenon is happening inside the firewalls of corporations, people are communicating more efficiently by using audio over their corporate intranets. Experts say that people learn better when information is communicated over a variety of media, and audio is one way companies can deliver information to enhance comprehension and improve the overall user experience.

Most of the audio and video content currently hosted on intranet and Internet sites is downloadable content. This means that the multimedia content must be copied to the user's PC before he or she can play it. The process of copying a file can take a long time. For example, a short 3.15 second audio clip can be 30 kilobytes in size, and it can take 40 seconds to download it over a 28.8 kilobit per second (kbps) connection. Video is significantly more expensive in terms of storage and download time. For example, a 1/4-screen 41.67 second video clip consumes 2.4 megabytes of storage and takes over 18 minutes to download over a 28.8 kbps connection.

This "download-then-play" approach has seriously limited the ability of Web content authors. For example, a company that wants to enhance their site with audio explaining a product or service must keep clips extremely short to avoid annoying customers with long download times. The same limitations apply to training applications. Long video-based training applications cannot be posted on the Web because downloads would take too long and hard disk space on trainee computers would be too limited.

On a related note, companies that want to deliver entertaining music or video clips must be concerned about intellectual property issues because once the clip is downloaded to the user's hard drive, its future use is out of their control. Also, Web-based advertising is often evaluated by the number of hits to the site per day; if a user downloads the content, there is no incentive to re-visit the site and be exposed to additional advertising.

There would be no multimedia field today without dramatic advances in data networking, compression, and computing technologies. Let's analyze the improvements in these three fields and see how they are synergistically related to the success of networked audio and video and to streaming media.

Dramatic progress has occurred over the last five years in compression algorithms and in their implementation. Compression is necessary for two reasons: to reduce the storage volumes of sounds, images, and video, and to limit the bit rate necessary to transmit them over the networks. The innovation in this technology has been incredible; JPEG, MPEG, and many other efforts have constantly improved the boundaries of compression technology, making it easier to use audio and video over networks.

Microsoft's strategy is to support multiple compression technologies and multiple codecs to suit the needs of the individual content provider and to allow optimization of the specific content being produced.

Another important innovation for facilitating networked audio and video is the ability for media to stream. Streaming is a significant improvement over the download-then-play approach to multimedia file distribution. Whereas most existing multimedia content on the Internet today is downloaded to the user's hard drive before playback, streaming allows content to be "spoon fed" to the client with little waiting before playback begins. Pieces of content arrive, are buffered briefly, play, and are discarded. The entire file is never actually stored on the user's computer.

This is significant for content providers because it allows them to deliver large content files without having to anticipate how much hard disk space is available on the client's PC. Content is maintained on the provider's site, and the user must re-visit the site to experience the content again. Users benefit by experiencing instant play; they don't have to suffer through the frustration of waiting for content to download to determine if it meets their needs or interests. In addition, they don't end up with unwanted media clips in their cache directory taking up valuable hard disk space.

How NetShow Works

Microsoft NetShow On-Demand is a software architecture that enables the streaming and playback of multimedia content over corporate networks using Microsoft's own NT Server, although Microsoft's recent agreement with Digital to port NetShow to the AlphaServer indicates the company's strategy toward portability and scalability. On the client side, NetShow On-Demand works with Microsoft Internet Explorer.

NetShow On-Demand provides an ActiveX control that developers and content providers can use to incorporate illustrated audio in their HTML pages and client applications. The ActiveX control is a programming interface that lets the developer manage multimedia streams using the control's properties, methods, and events. The control handles all video and audio rendering. Among other things, ActiveX facilitates pseudo-streaming playback of ActiveMovies, which are embedded AVI, QuickTime, MPEG or other files.

Illustrated audio is a term Microsoft uses to generically describe the content type that NetShow On-Demand software architecture stores and delivers. Illustrated audio is a new way of sharing ideas and information on narrow and mid-band networks; it synchronizes graphic images, such as video frames, still pictures, or Microsoft PowerPoint slides, with an audio track to create an interesting and effective interactive multimedia presentation, similar to an online slide show.

When working with video material, an author of illustrated audio can pick key frames to illustrate and augment the sound track, and thereby avoid the problems of random frames seen with slow-scan or reduced frame rate systems. If more bandwidth is available for video, the author can increase the number of frames per second, increase the size of the image, and increase the quality or sharpness of the individual images. It is this trade-off between the amount of bandwidth available on a given network and the demands for quality and performance that determine how content authors should develop their illustrated audio content.

Using NetShow On-Demand, a content provider can also enrich a site with AVI (Microsoft's own video standard) as well as Apple QuickTime content. NetShow On-Demand can also store and transmit audio-only WAV files.

Ultimately, NetShow On-Demand enables the content provider to enrich intranet/internet-based applications with audio, illustrated audio, and video content. Corporate, educational, retail, and government enterprises can turn networked mixed-media content into serious productivity tools for desktop and classroom training, distance learning, information delivery, customer support, corporate communications, work group collaboration, and more. This will improve the effectiveness of communications through an efficient usage of visual elements, and will improve the effectiveness of business operations through a more potent information delivery system.

Microsoft NetShow On-Demand is made up of server, client, and content authoring and encoding components. The server component allows customers to take a Windows NT Server and host illustrated audio and video content for fast, reliable, streaming delivery. The client software enables users equipped with conventional multimedia personal computers connected to a voice-grade telephone line or a corporate LAN to browse, select, and play illustrated audio and video content on demand, in real-time. In addition, NetShow On-Demand provides a set of tools for creating illustrated audio content and for enabling existing multimedia content (such as WAV, AVI, and QuickTime files) to stream from the server.

Microsoft NetShow On-Demand Server uses the Windows NT File System (NTFS) to store files meant for streaming via standard Win32 APIs. When the server receives a client request for data, it identifies the file requested and reads it to a buffer for transmission. The server is able to segment data in optimally sized pieces for network and client consumption, and can determine when a given file packet is timed for arrival at the client. The server schedules its workload, sending data packets to the client just in time for consumption.

Although data is streamed to the client in small pieces, the server reads large, contiguous pieces of the file to its buffer to conserve processor and disk resources. The server component also provides multiprocessor support; its disk and network operations are performed asynchronously to ensure that all processors are used.

Microsoft built NetShow On-Demand from the ground up to enable fast response on multiple bit rates, ranging from audio at 14.4 kbps to AVI at several megabytes per second (Mbps), and to maintain quality of content even in heavy load situations. The server accomplishes this by giving data operations (such as reading and sending data to current clients) priority over control requests (such as new requests for streaming media or "VCR" actions — stop, pause, and start — from a client currently streaming a file). For example, if the server is busy transmitting data and a stream request arrives from a new client, the server will complete its data operations before starting the new client request. If the server is very busy, the new request may be rejected or may time out. This ensures that currently scheduled clients do not experience degradation in service due to an influx of new control requests.

NetShow On-Demand scales from few to hundreds of simultaneous streams: the alpha release was tested up to 200 streams at 28.8 kilobits per second (kbps), and the current beta scaled to 1000 streams at 28.8, and more than 500 streams at 100 kbps. NetShow On-Demand currently supports NT striping, and future testing will include RAID devices.

NetShow On-Demand includes extensive LAN/WAN support on any IP network. Content streams are transported using UDP, and control streams are transported via TCP. To ensure optimum usability, network topology is independent. And firewall support will be included in the released version of the product.

With NetShow On-Demand Player, surfers can play audio (sound only), illustrated audio (synchronized sound and still images), and full-motion video files. When the user simply activates a link to a file, the player launches automatically and begins playing the file requested. Within just a few seconds, the content starts to play — with no download required. NetShow On-Demand Player enables the same functions as a regular VCR; the user can stop, pause and start content. This enables a user to control the flow of content as appropriate for his or her needs.

Application developers can incorporate the ability to play illustrated audio and video content within a standalone client player or as an integrated part of a Web-based application. This enables developers to integrate multimedia content into their Web pages, creating more interesting interactive applications. NetShow On-Demand provides a simple client SDK, which contains software and documentation that developers can use to add streaming support to Visual Basic and Visual C++ applications. The SDK includes an ActiveX control, reference documentation, and sample programs. The control is an easy-to-use programming interface that lets a developer manage multimedia streams using the control's properties, methods, and events. The control handles all video and audio rendering, simplifying programming tasks and making it easy to add support for multimedia streams to new applications.

One of Microsoft's major objectives when developing NetShow On-Demand was to make content creation easy. To this end, NetShow provides simple, starter tools to enable corporate content developers to prepare many popular content formats for streaming as illustrated audio. Files in WAV, AVI, QuickTime, PowerPoint, JPEG, GIF, and PNG formats can all be used to generate illustrated audio. In addition, content can incorporate calls to uniform resource locators (URLs). NetShow also provides the capability to synchronize different data types on a common timeline. By synchronizing many different types of content, a content provider can generate a more interesting and compelling end product.

The NetShow software architecture is designed to be completely codec independent. This means that the content provider can choose the compression scheme needed for a specific application and is not tied to a proprietary compression scheme. The current release of NetShow On-Demand works with a variety of codecs to enable the immediate authoring of content. The number of codecs supported will continue to increase as the product develops; this means that content providers can leverage improvements in codec technology to deliver better performance and quality of content.

The ActiveX streaming format (ASF) is an important part of the Microsoft streaming architecture. Its streaming format allows multiple types of data — for example, audio objects, video objects, still images, URLs — to be combined into a single synchronized multimedia stream that can be stored on a variety of servers and transmitted over a range of networks. The format does not replace existing formats, such as AVI, WAV, and QuickTime, but rather repackages them for more generalized storage and transport. ASF provides the following key benefits:

•**Scalability.** The format provides support for streams at virtually any bit rate; it can be optimized for low bandwidth networks with no quality of service (QoS) guarantees and for mid- and high-bandwidth networks where QoS guarantees are critical. In addition, ActiveX streaming format is scalable in the formats it supports — from device independent bitmap (.dib files) and WAV to MPEG.

• **Server Independence.** You can store ASF files locally, on a generic HTTP server, or on a Windows NT Server running Microsoft NetShow On-Demand.

• **Media Independence.** ActiveX streaming format complements existing standard media types and formats — for example, ACM, VCM, JPEG, AVI, and QuickTime-rather than replacing them. It repackages the underlying data so that they can be stored and transmitted efficiently. The architecture's format independence will allow it to support other formats, such as MPEG, in the future.

• **Flexibility.** ActiveX streaming format uses a timing model that allows the content author to flexibly synchronize media, such as audio, images, and URLs, to a common timeline. ASF files can include a variety of media, subject to the limitations of the underlying network. In addition, the format permits progressive rendering and stacking of images for rapid replay.

The content author uses ASF Editor to create, test, and compile an ASF file to store illustrated audio content. The tool is designed to handle most of the issues of encoding and timing so that the author doesn't have to. It determines where to place objects — sounds, images, and uniform resource locators (URLs) — so that they appear at the correct time during playback.

The key features of this tool are the following:

• An easy-to-use graphical display of the file timeline and pipe
• Drag-and-drop editing
• Automatic image and audio conversion
• Support for multiple bit rates — 14.4 kbps, 28.8 kbps, and 100 kbps

ASF Editor displays an illustrated audio file so that the author can see when objects will appear and how they are stored. It also has the ability to convert objects from one format or one level of quality to another. On networks with low bit rates, this ability becomes very useful in determining the tradeoffs between sound and image quality.

One example where ASF Editor finds its perfect usage is the creation of advertising content. Many corporations are investing a great deal of money and time in advertising on the Web and in using their Web sites to drive the sales of their products. Illustrated audio provides a great help in this process; content providers can use it to illustrate the benefits of their products to their customers. ASF Editor provides a great authoring paradigm for these Web sites by enabling a very precise synchronization between many images and an audio track.

NetShow On-Demand also provides a set of command-line utilities that allow a content author to quickly convert an AVI or QuickTime video or a WAV audio file to a file so that it can be stored on a NetShow On-Demand Server and streamed to clients.

As an example, the video conversion tool (VidToAsf) facilitates the creation of streaming media content from video tapes. To do this, the content author uses a video capture card to transform the video tape content to AVI (or to another supported video format). The content author uses the card to reduce the number of frames in the AVI file and thereby reduce the amount of data that needs to be sent over the network. After this step, the author uses the conversion tool to convert the AVI file into ASF file; the file is then ready to be stored on the server and streamed to clients.

Using NetShow

Like anything good on the 'Net, in order to "see" a page enhanced with NetShow you need to download a (840K) viewer, as shown in figure 4-1. Then you have to "tell" your browser which application to use to display the content association with the NetShow file extension (ASF and ASX) as shown in figure 4-2.

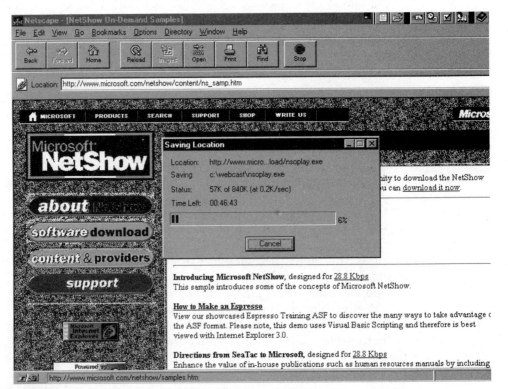

Figure 4-1. Downloading the NetShow player.

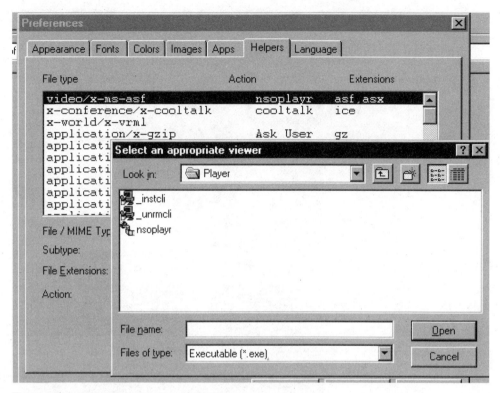

Figure 4-2. Setting up the NetShow MIME type.

As you can see from figures 4-3 and 4-4, NetShow has quite a robust streaming audio and imagery capability. In this six minute video we are given quite extensive instructions on how to get from SeaTac to the Microsoft campus — with a travelogue along the way. The audio was smooth and took little time to download from the NT server where it resides.

The audio used in an ASF file created for delivery through limited bandwidths (such as 14.4 kbps or 28.8 kbps) must be compressed. Compression tends to drop some frequencies, especially those in the high end, resulting in lower quality. Generally, the higher the compression rate, the lower the quality. The following codecs are recommended by Microsoft: audio only at 14.4 kbps — DSP TrueSpeech; audio only at 28.8 kbps — MSN Audio at 17,089; audio only at 100 kbps — MSN Audio at 35,382; audio with images or URL flips at 14.4 kbps — not recommended; audio with images or URL flips at 28.8 kbps — DSP TrueSpeech; audio with images or URL flips at 100 kbps — DSP TrueSpeech or MSN Audio.

Perhaps the most interesting use of NetShow is in its ability to provide a guided tour of either a particular Web site or a set of Web sites as shown in figure 4-5.

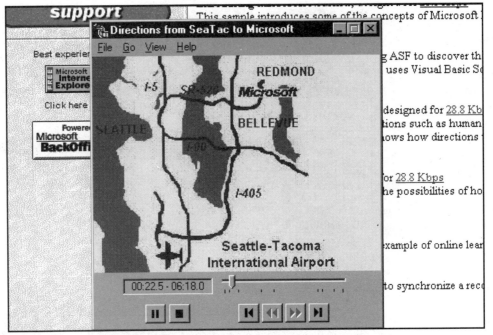

Figure 4-3. Illustrated audio used to provide travel directions.

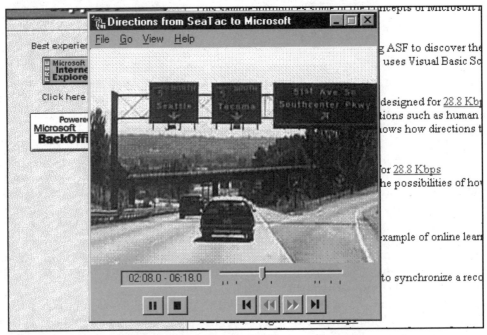

Figure 4-4. Photographs and drawings can be used to illustrate the audio segment.

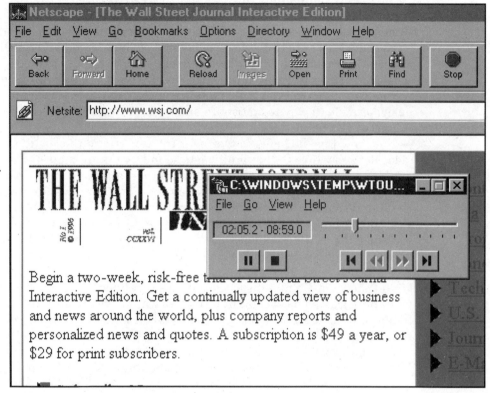

Figure 4-5. Providing a slide show with voice-over.

In this example, we are taken on a tour of interesting places on the Web. It doesn't take a rocket scientist to make the leap to understanding how this capability can be used to provide a slide show with a voice-over for, say, a financial analysts' meeting.

Using NetShow client has certain requirements. Microsoft recommends a 486/50 processor (minimum) Pentium with at least 8 MB RAM for Windows 95 (minimum), but 16 MB is suggested. Those running NT have the following requirements: 16 MB minimum with 32 MB suggested. Of course, a sound card and speakers are required.

Though Microsoft has tested only with its own browser, Internet Explorer, I had no trouble getting it to work under Netscape's Navigator.

The Fun Is In Developing the Content

This book, of course, is not about viewing the content but about making it. Making content requires one to deliver that content. This requires a server and, in the case of NetShow, Windows NT is the server of the moment.

Hardware/software requirements for the server are as follows: 486/66 MHz processor (minimum); PCI or EISA bus (PCI is recommended);

24 MB RAM (minimum) with 48 MB suggested; Ethernet network interface card (NIC); Microsoft Windows NT Server version 4.0; Microsoft NetShow On-Demand also requires Microsoft Internet Information Server 2.0 or greater.

NetShow is actually two products: NetShow Live and NetShow On-Demand. Microsoft NetShow Live delivers audio streams to clients on IP-based networks. The software multicasts data over the network. Multicasting, a technology that sends a single instance of the data to many clients simultaneously, provides a way to distribute audio without using an excessive amount of the network's bandwidth.

NetShow Live includes software for the server and the client. On the server side, NetShow Live Server multicasts sound by taking input through the server's sound card. The NetShow Live Server allows you to start and stop NetShow Live multicasts and to configure NetShow Live features, including the sound source, the sound format, and the IP address and port used for multicasting. Almost any audio source can serve as the audio signal. This can include CD's, AM/FM radios, televisions, VCRs, telephones, electronic instruments, microphones, mobile radios, scanners, baby monitors, alarm systems, and whatever else you can think of.

NetShow On-Demand is essentially the "canned" version of NetShow Live. Once broadcasted most content providers want a way to have users view and/or listen to broadcasts that have already taken place. This is called on-demand publishing — hence the name NetShow On-Demand.

The current version of NetShow enables users to view content from a NetShow server only if that user is not behind a firewall or proxy server, for example, if you "dial up" to browse the Web. Beta 2 of NetShow, which just became available as this chapter was written in November of 1996, includes firewall support for the Microsoft Proxy Server.

The NetShow Server uses UDP as its transport, and most firewalls and proxy servers are not configured to pass UDP traffic. Microsoft is working with firewall and proxy server manufacturers to ensure that their solutions will allow NetShow streams to pass through their systems.

By installing the Microsoft Proxy Server, you have nearly completed the installation requirements for allowing NetShow On-Demand traffic to stream past the Microsoft Proxy Server to a client machine. By default, the Microsoft Proxy Server allows all installed protocols (NetShow On-Demand, VDOLive, etc.) to pass through the proxy. To enable a client to receive Microsoft NetShow On-Demand traffic, an administrator must accomplish two tasks:

1. Create permissions for users on the network to receive "MS NetShow."
2. Install client side Proxy Server code.

The Microsoft Proxy Server documentation details how to perform both of these tasks. For more information, see http://www.microsoft.com/proxy.

In the meantime, it is possible to host ASF (Microsoft's Active Movie Streaming Format) content on standard HTTP servers. This would allow playback through firewalls over TCP/IP, but TCP/IP is generally not well-suited to multimedia and you would lose the error correction and scheduling that make NetShow a good server for streaming content.

Bear in mind that Microsoft has pre-set the sound quality to the IMA ADPCM, mono, 8 KHz, 4 bits/sample so as not to create too much IP traffic on your network. To change this, follow the instructions for setting up the codec in the NetShow Server dialog box. Realize that the higher quality codec you choose, the more traffic you will have on your network.

In order to stream audio and images over very small bandwidth connections, the content author must make some tradeoffs. To play an average AVI file takes about 1.5 Mbps in available network bandwidth. A 28.8 kbps dial-up connection is about 1/50 the size required. Therefore, the content author must take steps to decrease the bandwidth required to play back the content. Means of achieving this include decreasing the number of frames per second, decreasing the frame size, decreasing the number of colors used, and/or compressing the audio and the images.

The NetShow On-Demand authoring tools can help in this process. For example, to play back an AVI over the Internet, the content author would have to use an AVI editing tool (e.g., Adobe Premiere, Avid systems), to decrease the file's bitrate, then use the VIDTOASF tool to convert the AVI to the ASF format.

For very low bandwidths (e.g., 28.8 kbps) it's very difficult to create AVI files that are small enough (in frames per second and frame size) while maintaining high quality levels. In this case, the best recommendation is to select specific images from the AVI, extract them, and the audio, and then synchronize the images with the audio using the NetShow On-Demand ASF Editor. If you do decide to use VIDTOASF to convert very low bit-rate AVIs to the ASF format, Microsoft recommends using the "-leadtime" option with a minimum of 3 seconds. This would be expressed as "-leadtime 3000."

There are two types of Microsoft NetShow files. We've already discussed the ASF format. Another NetShow format is the ASX format. To make support from any browser possible, Microsoft introduced the ASX metafile. The ASX file is created in Notepad or any text editor, contains one line of code, and basically tells the browser to launch the NetShow On-Demand Player, establish a connection with the server, and start streaming the content.

To create content you first have to decide what type of ASF you would like to create and get together the raw materials. ASFs come in the following types:

1. Audio only: you'll need a WAV file or files. You can use the WAVTOASF converter to make the conversion easy, or the NetShow On-Demand ASF Editor to match up multiple WAV files or WAV files with URL flips and create ASFs.

2. Illustrated Audio: you'll need a WAV file or files, and can synchronize them to pictures from scanned images or a digital camera, illustrations in BMP, JPG, or DIB format. The NetShow On-Demand ASF Editor is by far the easiest way to create illustrated audio.

3. Video: you can use VIDTOASF to quickly and easily convert an AVI or MOV (QuickTime) video clip to ASF. Keep in mind that if bandwidth is limited you will need to use an AVI editing tool like Adobe Premiere to edit down the frame size, frames per second, colors, and add compression before converting to ASF. Note that the current version of NetShow does not permit the streaming of MPEG files. To stream MPEGs, first convert the file to AVI then use the VIDTOASF tool to convert it to ASF.

4. URLs: The NetShow On-Demand ASF Editor allows you to synchronize automatic changes to specified URLs at specific times in the audio track. URL-flipping content can be used for guided tours of HTML pages on a site or multiple sites. There are two ways to specify which frame you would like the URL to be launched if the NetShow On-Demand Player is embedded within a Web page. Within the ASF Editor, you can simply name the frame you would like the URL to be launched into when you create the URL using "Add URL." With VIDTOASF and WAVTOASF, append "&&FRAMENAME" to the URL within the ScriptCommand table. The following example shows how to use this syntax within a script file for these two utilities.

```
start_script_table
;URL is a reserved type indicating that the parameter
;should be treated as a URL and launched
;This is an example of how to write a regular URL flip
;in a ScriptCommand table
5.0 URL http://www.microsoft.com
;This is an example of how to specify a frame for the URL flip
35.0 URL http://www.microsoft.com/NetShow/&&DisplayFrame
end
```

If the Player is not embedded, it is not possible for the Player to specify which frame a URL should be launched into. Any frame information will be ignored by the Player when in non-embedded mode.

If you want to convert an AVI to an ASF, the tool to use is the VIDTOASF converter. It allows you to quickly and easily make the conversion. The ASF Editor supports WAV audio files and images and other scripting commands, but not AVIs.

For WAVs, download the tool WAVTOASF and create a batch file (text file with the .bat extension) with the command line for each WAV to ASF conversion. Here's an example:

```
c:\NETSHOW\Tools\wavtoasf.exe -in sample.wav -out sample.asf
c:\NETSHOW\Tools\wavtoasf.exe -in sample2.wav -out sample2.asf
```

You can do the same thing to batch convert AVI or MOV files — use the VIDTOASF command line tool in this case. However, you will want to edit the

AVIs or MOVs to reduce their bit-rate before converting them.

Keep in mind that you need to author content for a specific bandwidth (e.g., 14.4 kbps, 28.8 kbps, 100 kbps, etc.). This is partly because at lower bandwidths if you automatically start to decrease quality or drop frames, it's impossible for it to automatically pick the right frames to drop or degrade. For example, there is a lot of content that contains a person giving a presentation. If some automated process automatically dropped frames to accommodate lower connection speeds, you could end up with a presentation full of blinks, transition slides, and other sub-standard images. Instead, when you use the ASF Editor to tailor ASF files for specific bandwidths, your results are crisper and clearer images.

Microsoft recommends tailoring your presentation for the lowest bit-rate you plan to support, and then using the Template feature within the ASF Editor to migrate your work to the higher bit-rates where you can then further enhance the presentation. Since all components of the project (including ScriptCommands and Markers) are migrated when you use a Template, this can greatly reduce the work needed to produce multiple bit-rate versions of a project.

You can test a newly created ASF file within the ASF Editor by selecting /Stream, /Test. Or just double-click on the file from the Explorer or from File Manager. It won't be streaming, but you can still verify that it plays the way you want it to. The Test Playback functionality is provided for basic content testing purposes. If you have the NetShow On-Demand Player installed, you can select /Stream, /Play. This will start the Player with the ASF you created.

When streaming files over the Internet, packets (collections of data that carry information about your file) can sometimes be lost. When streaming sound over the Internet, lost data results in lower sound quality. But when playing images, most image compression/decompression software (also called codecs) need all of the data to render an image. When data is lost in transit, these codecs then become unable to render the images. The two notable exceptions currently supported by the ASF Editor are uncompressed bitmaps (which don't use a codec) and the NetShow Loss-Tolerant JPEG filter.

The Loss-Tolerant JPEG filter allows data to be lost and an image still to be rendered. If data is lost during transit, the picture quality is lowered, but all of the images in your ASF will still be rendered.

Audio used in an ASF file created for delivery through limited bandwidths (such as 14.4 kbps or 28.8 kbps) must be compressed. Different codecs compress more than others. The higher the compression ratio, the lower the resulting quality of the audio. You can either compress the audio from within the ASF Editor (when you try to add a WAV file to the project timeline and the Editor will notify you if the bandwidth of your audio file exceeds that allowed in the rate you specify), or you can compress the audio in a standard audio authoring tool like the Windows Sound Recorder. In the process of compressing the audio, some frequencies will be lost, especially those in the high end. Also, some codecs are better suited to the human voice, and some are better suited to music. To see a list of codecs installed on your computer, go into the Control Panel, select Multimedia, then Advanced, then Audio and Video Compression Codecs. Many codecs come pre-installed on Windows systems.

Finally, when writing an HTML link to an ASF that is not embedded into Internet Explorer 3.0, you simply use the standard tag as follows:

```
<A HREF="mms://server/path/filename.ASX"<Description></A>
```

If the ASF is to play embedded within Internet Explorer 3.0, you can simply link directly to the ASF from within the NetShow On-Demand object. A sample object tag follows:

```
<OBJECT CLASSID="clsid:2179C5D3-EBFF-11cf-B6FD-00AA00B4E220"
   HEIGHT=134
   WIDTH=312
   NAME=NSOPlay>
   <param name=TransparentAtStart value=False>
   <param name=FileName value="mms://server/filename.asf">
   <param name=AutoStart value="True">
</OBJECT><BR>
```

To make an ASF file (on the external player) play automatically when a user enters a page, simply insert the following tag into your HTML in the header section:

```
<META HTTP-EQUIV="Refresh" Content="2; URL=Filename.ASX">
```

In the Content tag, the first number (2 in this case) indicates the number of seconds until the file should be downloaded. The URL is the name of the ASX Redirector file that points to the ASF file you want the user to view. Please note that if you specify an ASF file, the browser will completely download the ASF file before it is viewed. The end-user will be unable to stream the ASF if you do not specify an ASX file in the META tag.

The NetShow On-Demand Player also supports the TransparentAtStart property, which allows the Player to be invisible until image rendering, thus allowing any background images (such as a table background image) to show through. The following sample shows how to embed the Player in a table with a background image. The background image will show through until the first image is rendered by the player. One convincing way to integrate this feature is to set the AutoStart property to FALSE and use an image with a "Start" button for the table background. Using the ClickToPlay functionality, the user can then click on that image and the ASF will start playback.

```
<table background="myimage.jpg" width="320" height="240">
<OBJECT CLASSID="clsid:2179C5D3-EBFF-11cf-B6FD-00AA00B4E220"
  WIDTH=320
  HEIGHT=240
  ID=NSOPlay>
  <param name="TransparentAtStart" value="TRUE">
  <param name="ControlType" value="0">
  <param name="AllowChangeControlType" value="FALSE">
  <param name="FileName" value="myasf.asf">
</OBJECT>
</table>
```

Downloading the ASF content creation tools (about 1.57 MB) took little time. The ActiveX Streaming Format (ASF) Editor enables you to combine images, audio, and script commands into a single multimedia file that can be streamed in real-time over a network (Internet or intranet).

The ASF Editor provides tools that help you create ASF files as shown in figure 4-6, including an interface for obtaining the audio and image files that you will use to create ASF files. After obtaining the various files, drag them into a

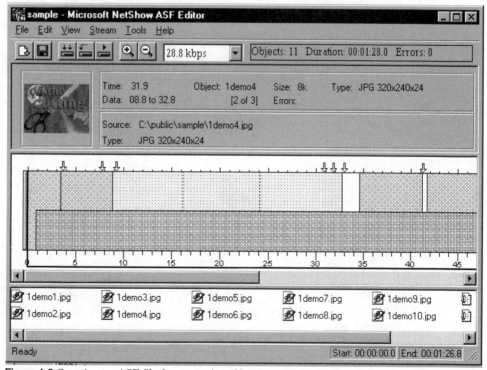

Figure 4-6. Creating an ASF file from a series of images.

window that simulates how files will stream across a particular network bandwidth. If you like how the files will stream, build your ASF file. If you do not like something, ASF Editor includes conversion tools to allow you to edit the files. Using the ASF Editor is fairly simple. An ASF file is created from a series of images (usually JPEG) and some audio and audio files (WAV files). Each of these images and sound files is called an object.

The content developer selects a delivery speed (14.4 kbps, 28.8 kbps, etc.) and then "builds" the ASF file. The ASF file is built from the specified images, URLs and WAV files which are ordered similarly to a presentation. You can add, delete or edit files and rebuild at will. Sound can be easily converted by selecting the sound file and then Edit|Convert to convert the selected audio files to any of the preferred formats which include: Truespeech; MSN Audio 8200; MSN Audio 17089; and MSN Audio 35832.

Selecting New from the file menu, pointing to the appropriate directory and then selecting one or more image files or URL is all it takes to create the image side of the ASF file as shown in figure 4-7.

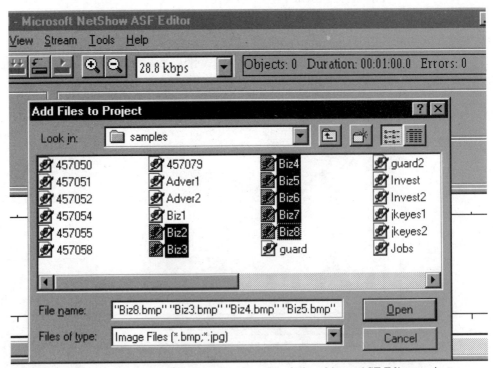

Figure 4-7. Image files and sound files can be selected and placed in an ASF Editor project.

The Presentation Assistant can then be used to synchronize the appearance of images with the audio. The images you use can be selected images from the content window or the images within the time range in the edit window. If you select images from the content window, the order of the images in the content window determines their order in the queue. If you don't select images from the content window, Presentation Assistant uses the images in the time range. When you open the Presentation Assistant dialog box, it places the images into a queue and prepares to play the audio files that are within the time range. You can then play the audio and indicate when you want the images to render. When you are done, the images in the edit window move to the points you indicated.

In the Presentation Assistant dialog box, click Start to begin playing the audio (see figure 4-8). When the audio reaches a point where you'd like to have an image appear, click Drop. Repeat this step until you have either placed all the images (in which case the Drop button will turn gray), or the audio for the time range finishes playing.

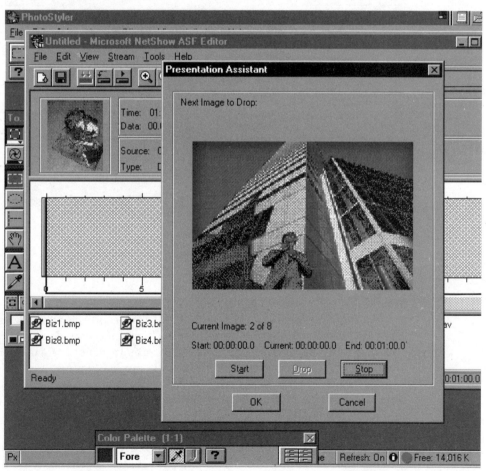

Figure 4-8. The Presentation Assistant is used to synchronize the appearance of the images with the audio. Images are "dropped" into the audio timelines.

After testing it and saving it, if there are no errors, the ASF editor lets you build the ASF file to be deployed on the server as shown in figure 4-9.

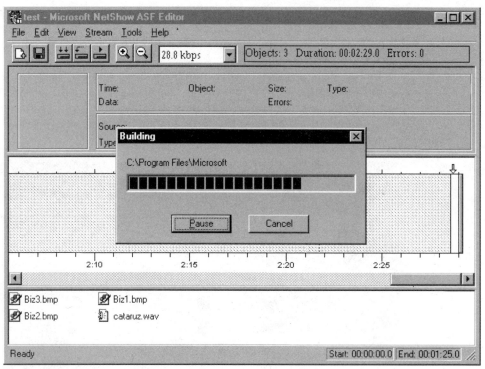

Figure 4-9. Building the ASF file.

The NetShow Live Server

The NetShow Live server is 603 KB and requires the NT server to run. Download it from http://www.microsoft.com/netshow/download/nslservr.exe. It's also an integral component of Microsoft's Internet Information Server version 3.0 and above (http://iisa.microsoft.com/iis3/default.asp). NetShow Live uses IP Multicast to efficiently deliver a stream of live audio information to intranet users. IP Multicast is an open, standards-based way to distribute identical information to many users simultaneously. This contrasts with regular TCP/IP (IP unicast) where the same information may be sent to many clients, but the sender must transmit an individual copy to each user.

NetShow Live multicast file transfer provides another way for network managers to save bandwidth when large quantities of data need to be distributed to many users at the same time (beta 2 version). NetShow Live uses Real Time Protocol (RTP) as its transport protocol. RTP is an industry standard developed under the direction of the Internet Engineering Task Force (RFC 1889/1890).

To hear a NetShow Live multicast requires the following: Windows 95, WindowsNT 4.0 Workstation or Server running Internet Explorer version 3.0 (full version); the NetShow Live Client dlls installed (nlaclnt.exe) and the nlaudio.ocx in the \windows\occache directory;.a Sound Blaster 16 sound card or compatible (with the volume up); an installed and functioning NetShowLive Server on your network. Simply being on the Internet is not sufficient to enjoy NetShow Live sessions. You must have a NetShow Live Client.

There are two pieces to the NetShow Live Client. The first piece is the ActiveX control called nlaudio.ocx, and it should be in your \windows\occache directory. The second piece is the client dll's, installed by running the file, "nlaclnt.exe." You must have both pieces installed at the client to hear audio.

NetMeeting

NetMeeting (http://www.microsoft.com/netmeeting/download/) is at the core of Microsoft's real-time Internet communication strategy and is part of the intrinsic functionality of Windows 95. The NetMeeting platform provides real-time voice and data communications, application sharing, file transfer, whiteboard, and text-based chat.

The NetMeeting platform is based on open ITU (International Telecommunications Union) standards. In its first release, this technology uses T.120 for data conferencing, which is part of the H.323 standard. NetMeeting does not currently include video conferencing capabilities; however, several third-party vendors offer or have announced video conferencing support integrated with NetMeeting. These vendors include Creative Labs Inc., Intel, PictureTel, VDONet Corp. and White Pine Software Inc. Microsoft is planning to add H.323-based video conferencing capabilities to NetMeeting in a future release planned for the first half of 1997.

Data conferencing works over several different transports, including IP, PSTN, and IPX. In addition, vendors can install their own transports for data conferencing. Conference members can be connected over different types of connections at the same time (for example, one over an intranet, one over the Internet, and one dialed in over a modem).

Microsoft has targeted the Windows 95 and Windows NT platforms first, soon to be followed by the Macintosh. Because the NetMeeting platform is based on ITU standards, almost any product adhering to the standards will enjoy the benefits of interoperability.

Microsoft offers these examples of how NetMeeting can be used:

> *A customer is using your product but is having trouble. The customer clicks the Support button or menu item you've added to your application, and gets connected to a member of your support staff. Your support engineer can control the customer's application remotely, and can talk them through the problem.*

All the user needs is a sound card, microphone, speakers, and a network connection. No additional hardware or software is required.

You create a Web page to bring together a community of users with similar interests in a conference. A user surfs to your Web page, sees a roster of participants currently in the conference, and clicks a "Join" button to participate in the conference.

A customer is browsing your Web page over the Internet. When they see something they really like, they click a button on your page to learn more. They get connected to a company representative who can carry on a live conversation with the customer, give presentations shared from their own machine, or lead the customer through the Web site or through applications on the customer's desktop remotely. Control of the mouse and keyboard goes back and forth during the exchange between the customer and your representative; for example, the customer asks questions about a graph your representative shows, your representative explains, and so on.

You and a few of your associates, from your separate offices, collaborate on a report for the meeting you have in an hour. One person can be working from home, connected over a phone dial-in line. You can talk and take turns editing the document in real-time. Note that Microsoft NetMeeting platform is not remote control—someone at each machine must specifically select each application to be shared (that is, a machine cannot see an application running on a remote desktop unless that application is shared by the person at that other end).

The NetMeeting client is now a bundled component with Microsoft Internet Explorer (which is one of the reasons why the download consumes over eight megabytes of hard disk space). It is a real-time Internet voice communications client that provides multi-user application-sharing and data conferencing capabilities with whiteboard and chat functionality.

A user accesses NetMeeting through the Start/Programs menu under Windows 95. Figure 4-10 shows the entry point dialog. First time users are asked to enter some basic (see figure 4-11) information about themselves, such as e-mail address and name. There is also room for comments, which unfortunately has a tendency to be used for more x-rated things than I'd care to admit.

A "User Location Server" is used to maintain a directory of all people connected to a particular system. A private internet/intranet would have its own server name, which could be made easily accessible (the directory, that is) from a Web page. In figure 4-12 we see that we are using Microsoft's public User

Microsoft's View of Webcasting 87

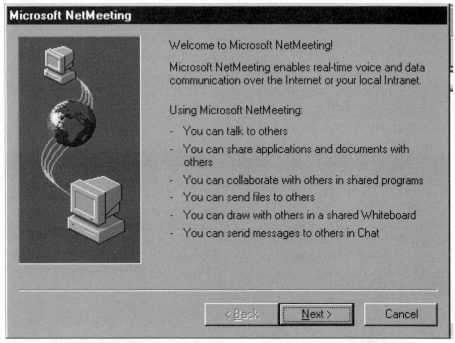

Figure 4-10. Accessing NetMeeting.

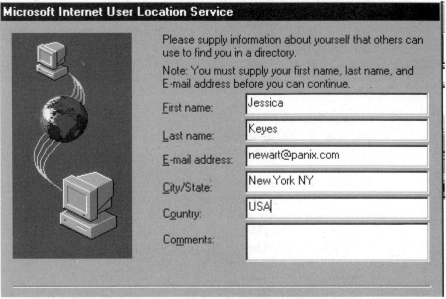

Figure 4-11. NetMeeting tracks some basic information about each user.

Location Server "uls.microsoft.com," Those of you reading this section are advised to immediately download the latest version of Internet Explorer (at the time of this writing it was version 3.0). After installation, click on NetMeeting and register. Once done, you'll be amazed at how quickly people have a tendency to find you. While writing these pages I booted up NetMeeting on my laptop for reference purposes and Greta from Finland said "Hello." That's right, she said hello.

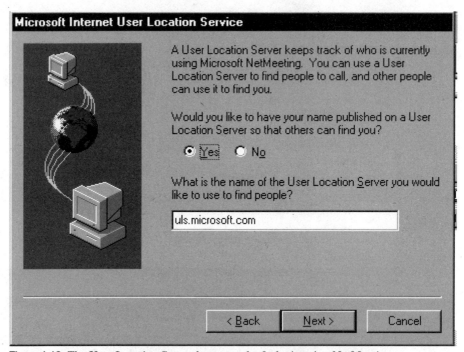

Figure 4-12. The User Location Server keeps track of who is using NetMeeting.

To use the audio capabilities of NetMeeting you have to first connect your audio components to NetMeeting. This is easily done using the product's Audio Tuning Wizard as shown in figures 4-13. After "training" NetMeeting you are now ready to use it.

Figure 4-14 shows what the NetMeeting interface looks like. Clicking on the Call menu item results in a list of NetMeeting users who are online at the moment. After selecting a user just click on Call to initiate a telephone call to the person. Since NetMeeting makes use of your speaker and microphone, its quality is only as good as the equipment you have. My laptop has a rather tinny speaker so it was rather different to hear Greta on the phone.

NetMeeting has a host of other features that make this a great webcasting "plug-in" as shown in figure 4-15. You can send a file in real time; share resources with other people in an online conference either by working alone to

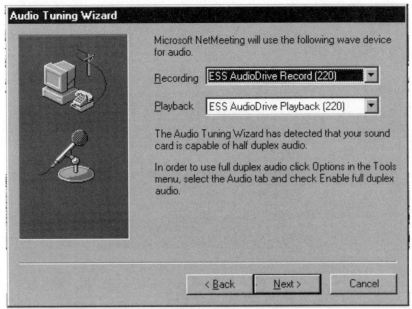

Figure 4-13. Connecting your audio components to NetMeeting.

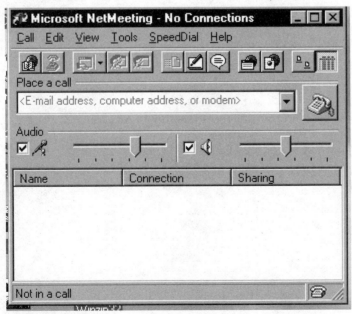

Figure 4-14. The NetMeeting interface.

90   Chapter Four

Figure 4-15. NetMeeting has many features including shared applications, whiteboard and chat.

Figure 4-16. A NetMeeting collaboration.

show the others in the conference or working jointly where each conferencee takes a turn in working on the application; chat and use a whiteboard to share ideas and data.

Figure 4-16 shows how NetMeeting lets folks collaborate using one application. Here Jose and I were using Microsoft Windows Paint to work on an image. Note the Paint menu bar — it's in Spanish. Multipoint Application Sharing enables you to share a program running on your computer with other people in a conference, allowing them to see the same data or information that you have on your PC. NetMeeting works with existing Windows-based programs, allowing applications to be shared transparently without requiring any special knowledge of conferencing capabilities.

When an application has been shared, the other people in the conference see the actions that are performed as the person sharing the application works on the program (e.g., editing content, scrolling through information, etc.). In addition, the person sharing the application can choose to collaborate, allowing other people in the conference to take turns editing or controlling the application. Each member of the conference does not need to have the given application on their system — only the person that is sharing the application.

Figure 4-17 shows the NetMeeting whiteboard. I'm not sure if you can see that I used the pencil tool to scrawl the word "hi" which was seen by those I was collaborating with. The whiteboard program is a multi-page, multi-user drawing application that enables you to sketch diagrams, organization charts, flow charts, or display other graphic information with other people in a conference. Whiteboard is object-oriented (versus pixel-oriented), allowing users to move

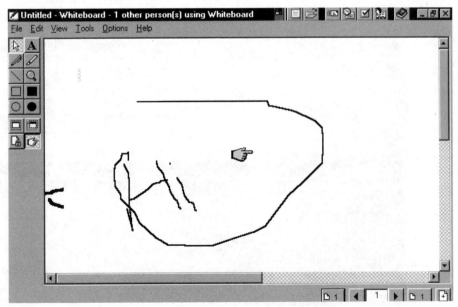

Figure 4-17. The NetMeeting whiteboard. Can you see the word Hi?

and manipulate the contents by clicking and dragging with the mouse. In addition, you can use a remote pointer or highlighting tool to point out specific contents or sections of shared pages. This capability extends the application sharing feature of NetMeeting by supporting ad hoc collaboration on a common drawing surface.

To create your own NetMeeting environment requires you to have your own User Location Server. Organizations using Microsoft Internet Information Server (IIS) can set up their own User Location Service and provide a way for visitors to their site to find each other. Microsoft has submitted a specification on the ULS to the Internet Engineering Task Force as a proposed enhancement to existing standards. Beta 4 release of the User Location Server is now available for downloading http://www.microsoft.com/intdev/msconf/uls.htm). You need to install the final release of Microsoft NetMeeting 1.0 or later to use the User Location Service. Software requirements for NetMeeting ULS are: Windows NT version 3.51 with Service Pack 4, or Windows NT version 4.0 Microsoft Internet Information Server (IIS).

The Microsoft NetMeeting Software Developer's Kit (SDK) can be downloaded from http://microsoft.com/intdev/msconf/.

Surround Video

The simplest of Microsoft's webcasting products to use is Surround Video. From the end-user's perspective, it is the easiest of plug-ins to download. Figure 4-18 shows the dialog the user encounters when he or she attempts to run a Surround Video. Clicking OK not only downloads the plug-in, it installs it as well — a welcome departure from the nuisance of downloading, searching

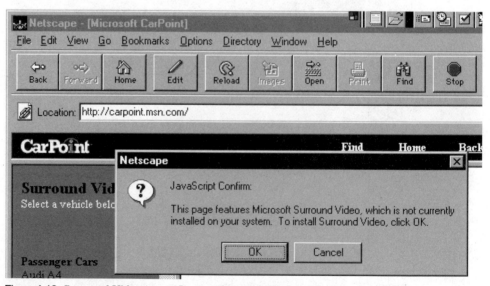

Figure 4-18. Surround Video uses a Java applet to install the player on a user's PC.

for the executable you downloaded (but forgot where you stored it) and then executing it.

Carpoint, the Microsoft site shown in figure 4-19, is an Internet-based marketing brochure that almost lets the end-user sit in the car and get a bird's eye view of the interior. Those that have been to Disneyland have probably seen those 360 degree movies that make you feel you're really there.

Figure 4-19. The Carpoint marketing brochure.

Surround Video does just this. As shown in figure 4-20, you can use your mouse to move your view left, right, up and down. In this way, you can see the side of the car, the roof of the car as well as the back window.

Carpoint (http://carpoint.msn.com/) is the next best thing to shopping for a car in person — take that you unscrupulous salesperson! Actually, Carpoint is actually an online car buying service, although I'm not sure that anyone other than billionaire Bill Gates would really plunk down multi-thousands for a car sight unseen. Still, it's a great example of what four-sense interactivity can do for you.

Carpoint contains information on all types of cars from passenger cars to luxury cars with sports cars, vans and pickup trucks thrown in for good measure. Essentially, it's a visit to the car dealer and a read of Consumer's Reports, or at least Car & Driver, all rolled up into an interactive session. It contains special reports such as "What's in store for the New Model Year" and provides expert opinions. The very best Carpoint feature is that it's free.

Figure 4-20. Rotating the image in any direction using Surround Video.

The feature that makes the Carpoint site webcasting is it's four sense dimensionality. Carpoint provides a sort of virtual simulation (without the new car smell, of course) of test-driving a new car. Using the proprietary Surround Video, Microsoft's 56 kb plug-in, the netsurfer gets a 360-degree view of what its like to drive his or her prospective new wheels.

The Surround Video plug-in, I have to begrudgingly admit, is on the leading edge of webcasting plug-ins. It's no secret that webcasting requires one or more plug-in components to be downloaded to the net. I personally have always thought this was a pain in the colloquial butt. Some of these plug-ins, after all, are 2 megabytes and on a 14.4 modem, one can cook one's dinner before the plug-in is fully loaded. Then there's the challenge of installing the plug-in. More than one net surfer's PC is littered with partially installed plug-in software.

The Surround Video plug-in is mercifully small so kudos to Microsoft for finally understanding what us ancient programmers already knew — there really is a time-space continuum. Next, Carpoint automatically senses whether you have the plug-in and if you don't asks permission to install it — no error messages here when you surf to a page unarmed with the appropriate plug-in. Except for having to close your browser, the install does everything else — even opening your browser to the Carpoint page.

According to Carpoint, "We are pleased to bring this added service to online car shoppers. Getting a chance to see the interiors of best-selling cars and trucks has been a persistent request of armchair tire kickers. And while traditional photography and video go part of the way to satisfying this request, neither television nor print publications are capable of delivering the level of inspection and interactivity found in Carpoint Surround Videos."

Personally I rather liked the BMW 5 series although I got pretty frustrated when I couldn't get the car to take off down the road. Idea for you Microsoft, I want to fly down the road like a bat out of hell, not just get a 360 degree interior view. Still, it's a webcasting-oriented technology that's worth investigating.

The New Microsoft Network (www.msn.com)

When Windows 95 was launched there was a big controversy over whether or not Microsoft was practicing unfair trade tactics by bundling the Microsoft Network (MSN) along with its Windows 95 operating system.

Those of us buying new PCs, which came automatically with Windows 95, naturally gravitated toward MSN, perhaps not so much as a substitute for America Online or CompuServe, but (at least in my case) as a ready, willing, and able access provider for the Internet itself.

MSN never really took off showing that even Bill Gates and Company is capable of failure. But out of the ashes is arising a new breed of MSN. As I put pen to paper MSN is getting ready to go off-line as a proprietary information service and online as an ISP with an intriguing Web site (www.msn.com).

Much of the content that exists on the proprietary system is being re-rendered and out into place on the new and improved site. Although anyone will be able to access MSN, there will be places for members only just like on the older proprietary service. Microsoft describes the different categories of MSN as follows:

> **OnStage** *is the interactive news and entertainment area on MSN where you'll find original and creative programming on six distinct channels. These entertaining and informative "Web shows" offer exciting, interactive content appealing to a variety of interests and attitudes. There's Mungo Park, an online travel magazine for the adventure-minded; Rifff a show for rock and roll fans; and UnderWire, online entertainment and information for women, just to name a few. OnStage has something for everyone!*
>
> **Essentials** *gives you key services for finding time-saving information and making smart purchases.*

This area of the new MSN brings together the advantages and value of online reference, interaction, and shopping. Expedia travel services, Microsoft Investor, Encarta encyclopedia, and Wine Guide are just some of the excellent online services Essentials puts at your fingertips.

Communicate *is your connection to e-mail, chats, discussion forums, and Internet newsgroups. Through Communicate you can exchange information and ideas, as well as participate in both the MSN community and the Internet community at large.*

When you access the www.msn.com site you're told right away that you need the FutureSpash plug-in. The new MSN is very webcasting oriented and FutureSplash (a product by FutureWave) lets you experience vector-based animation on the Web. Because FutureSplash files are remarkably small, animated graphics and drawings play on your Web pages in real time, even over a 14.4 kbps connection. FutureSplash also provides interactive buttons, anti-aliased graphics, outline fonts, and zooming control.

The MSN site is quite smashing as shown in figures 4-21 and 4-22.

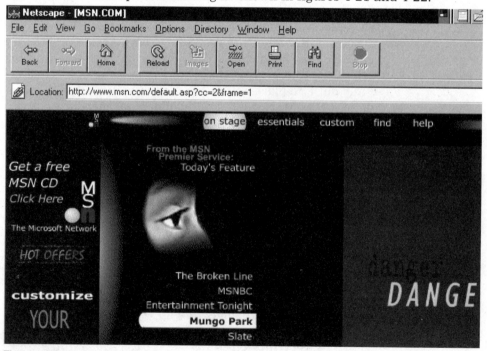

Figure 4-21. The new Microsoft Network.

Microsoft's View of Webcasting 97

Figure 4-22. FutureSplash plug-in provides interactive buttons, zooming and font control.

Resources:

NetShow Content Providers:

The Center for Multimedia
3240 - 118th Avenue S.E., Suite 100, Bellevue, WA 98005
(206) 643-9039, fax (206) 643-9032
email: cfm@msn.com
Web site: http://www.cfmm.com/

Digital Evolution, Inc.
11911 San Vicente Boulevard Suite #225, Brentwood, CA 90049
(310) 440-3377, fax (310) 440-3388
email: epulier@digev.com
Web site: http://www.digev.com

Emerald City Productions
1605 - 12th Ave., Suite 38, Seattle, WA 98122
(206) 328-0595, fax (206) 328-2176
email: emerald@emeraldweb.com
Web site: http://www.emeraldweb.com/

fine.com
1109 First Avenue, Suite 212, Seattle, WA 98101
(206) 292-2888, fax (206) 292-2889
Web site: http://www.fine.com

Free Range Media
117 South Main, Suite 400, Seattle, WA 98104
(206) 340-9305, fax (206) 340-0509, sales (800) 570-3873
email: info@freerange.com
http://www.freerange.com

Saltmine Creative, Inc.
3800 Aurora Avenue North, Suite 360, Seattle, WA 98103
(206) 633-4743, fax (206) 633-0176
email: Webmaster@saltmine.com
http://www.saltmine.com

Tri-Digital Software, Inc.
1818 Westlake Ave. N, Suite 228
Seattle, WA 98109
(206) 232-1885, fax (206) 286-9442
email: mmonrean@tri-digital.com
http://www.tri-digital.com

Chapter

5

Using RealAudio

Progressive Networks RealAudio (http://www.realaudio.com) was probably the first "true" webcasting product on the market. While sound files have always be available to be downloaded from the Web, size and time constraints made this medium virtually useless.

RealAudio is a streaming audio product. *Streaming* is the operative word here. What this means is that it is no longer necessary to fully download a sound byte (or bunch of bytes) down to a client before it begins playing. So, instead of waiting long, agonizing minutes for a sound clip to play, it all "loads and goes" in a matter of seconds.

Like Microsoft's NetShow, RealAudio is available in two modes: live and on-demand. This chapter will focus on the use of RealAudio to build a webcasting system. Before we get started you might want to surf over to AudioNet (http://www.audionet.com) which touts themselves as being the broadcast network on the Internet. It uses RealAudio so you'll get a good sense of what's possible using this medium.

To start yourself out on the road to learning how to develop content with RealAudio, you should download the RealAudio player and experiment with how it works. RealAudio 3.0 RealAudio Player Plus ($29.99), the newest plug-in available as this chapter was written, allows you to play near CD-quality audio over standard modems using its PerfectPlay feature and is available for download at http://www.realaudio.com/cplus/index.html. RealAudio Player Plus also has a scan feature that lets you scan the Web for live music, radio, sports and news. It has preset buttons, like a car radio, that takes you straight to your favorite sites. The free version (i.e. non-CD quality and no scanning) is available from http://www.realaudio.com/products/player/download.html.

The RealAudio Encoder puts sound files through advanced filesize compression while preparing them for use with the RealAudio Server. The advantage of this is that the resulting RA files are extremely small. For example, a WAV file sampled at 22 kHz, 16 bit consumes about 2.6 Megabytes, but encoded into RealAudio at 28.8 consumes only 113 Kilobytes.

The only way to achieve the kind of compression that RealAudio encoding accomplishes is by leaving out some of the soundfile information. The RealAudio encoder does this by identifying which parts of the soundfile are most important. No matter how carefully a file is pre-processed, the 60 k .RA file will never have as great a frequency response or dynamic range as the 2.6 M WAV file.

Current Internet data transmission rates necessitate signal compression prior to transmission of real-time audio. The RealAudio Encoder performs this function within the RealAudio System; the RealAudio Player can only play files that have been encoded using the RealAudio Encoder, and the RealAudio Server can only serve files that have been encoded using the RealAudio Encoder. Thus, the RealAudio Encoder is the bridge between the RealAudio Server and the RealAudio Player. RealAudio content may be created either from previously recorded digital audio files, or from an external audio source.

Pre-recorded files may be in AU, WAV and raw PCM audio formats. External audio may be fed from a recorded source, such as DAT (Digital Audio Tape), CD (Compact Disc), or directly from a mixing console or microphone. Prior to encoding, pre-recorded audio should be preprocessed using one of the various sound editing utilities available to maximize the audio quality of the encoded content. One of these is Cool Edit for Windows, available at http://www.netzone.com/syntrillium. Similarly, when encoding live source audio, the input levels should be prepared and tested as before any professional recording session.

The RealAudio Encoder can encode using two different algorithms. The 14.4 algorithm provides optimal sound quality to end-users with a 14.4 kbps modem connection to the Internet. This algorithm has a high compression ratio optimized for speech transmission. RealAudio 2.0 includes a 28.8 algorithm, which provides RealAudio to end-users with a 28.8 kbps or faster connection to the Internet. This format, although still highly compressed, takes advantage of the added bandwidth and delivers monophonic FM quality audio. The latest version at the time I wrote this chapter, RealAudio 3.0, enhances playback quality.

Providing Web site access to your RealAudio content is similar to creating links between Web pages. When accessing RealAudio content, however, your links are to RealAudio metafiles rather than to other Web pages. Although RealAudio files can also be first downloaded and then played, providing RealAudio content in real-time requires a RealAudio Server. Metafiles tell a visitor's Web browser to launch either the RealAudio Player or the RealAudio Plug-in and to play the desired file.

The RealAudio System can broadcast "live" to the Internet. It can also be used as part of a multimedia presentation. "Live" broadcasting means that visitors to your Web site can listen to your audio from the current point in the broadcast, just like listening to a radio broadcast. A multimedia event is a combination of your RealAudio content and your Web page content. Both of these capabilities are provided with the Windows Live Encoder, which is distributed with the RealAudio Server (http://www.realaudio.com/products/server.html).

Recording Audio Files

The RealAudio Encoder compresses the audio data stream and prepares it for use with the RealAudio Server. This compression is "lossy", which means that some of the information contained in the original audio data stream is removed. To ensure that you will get optimal audio quality after encoding, you must start with a high fidelity recording which utilizes the full dynamic range and has a high signal-to-noise ratio. Using Digital Audio Tapes (DATs) or Compact Discs (CDs) as your source, for example, will result in high quality RealAudio files. In addition, you will have better results if you use simpler audio signals rather than very complex signals.

While it is possible to record directly from a source, pre-processing the sound file before encoding contributes to higher quality sound. For example, a closely miked interview in a studio will encode better than an interview conducted on a busy or windy street.

The audio file used for input to the RealAudio Encoder should use the full range of available amplitude, without exceeding the maximum input level. "Clipping" results if this level is exceeded, and it is heard as a pop or click in the resulting file. When encoded, a RealAudio file with clipping will have high-frequency background noise or static.

If the full amplitude range is not used, the RealAudio files will sound rough. Use your audio editor's "Increase Amplitude" or "Increase Volume" command to adjust the range before encoding the file. Some sound editors have a "Normalize" function that will maximize levels automatically.

Keep in mind that audio files take up a lot of disk space before they are encoded. Once the files are encoded into the RealAudio format, they will use 60 kb/minute (3.6 MB/hour) of disk space.

The RealAudio Encoder allows you to encode files or live streams into RealAudio files or directly to the RealAudio Server for live broadcasts. The Encoder encodes files in real-time. You can browse folders and select files for encoding, or drag and drop files directly onto the Encoder icon. The Encoder window displays information about the audio file's sampling rate before and after compression. You can also enter author, title, and copyright information. This information will then appear in the RealAudio Player window when the user plays the file.

To open the Encoder, double-click on encoder.exe. The Encoder window is comprised of the menu and toolbar, an encoding status display, and four information panels: Source, Destination, Description and Options. Figure 5-1 shows a window with information already partially entered.

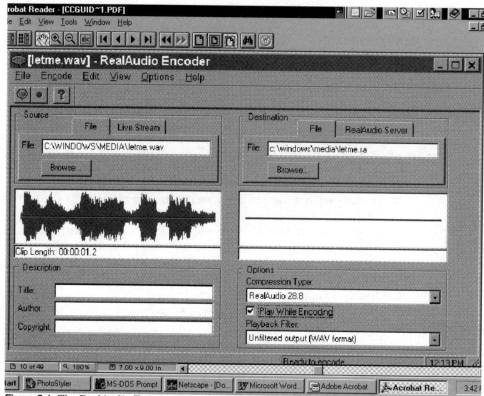

Figure 5-1. The RealAudio Encoder.

The Source panel allows you to choose the type of input source you will be using, either File or Live Stream.

• **File**. A previously digitized audio file; indicates where the input source is located.
• **Live Stream**. A live feed from an event or a studio, or audio from a CD, DAT tape, satellite feed or other high quality source; indicates the sampling rate and resolution of the live stream.

The Encoder automatically detects the audio type of the source file. If for some reason the Encoder cannot recognize the file type, you will be presented with a dialog box that allows you to select the sampling rate, format and resolution of the source file.

The Destination panel has two tabs, File and RealAudio Server. If you do not have the Live Encoder, only the File tab will be enabled. The File tab allows you to specify the location of the RA output file. If you are encoding from a file, the Encoder suggests a default output file with the same name (with an RA file name extension) in the same location as the source file. If this is not the desired location, or you are encoding from a live source, enter the appropriate destination path and the desired filename. If you are using the Live Encoder for a live broadcast, select the RealAudio Server Destination tab.

The central area of the Encoder window displays the progress of the encoder. The information is displayed in both graphical and numerical form. You may choose to view the progress in two different ways, as a waveform or as a straight bar, by toggling Show Audio Signal under the Options Menu. If you select Show Audio Signal, the left graph shows the original audio signal while the right graph displays the decompressed waveform of the RA file being created.

The lower left side of the Encoder window has a Description panel for the RealAudio file. You have the option of providing the title, author and copyright information about the audio file into the corresponding areas. This information will then be displayed in the RealAudio Player and the RealAudio Plug-in. For example, if you type the following information into the Encoder window:

```
Title: ABC News 3 PM 19 July 1995 Pacific Time
Author: ABC News and Information Network
Copyright: 1995
```

When playing the clip, the Player will display the information as shown in figure 5-2. You can change the description field on a file you have already encoded by re-encoding the file with the new description information. To do this select the RA file to change from the Source Panel File tab, type in your new description and select the Start Encoding command from the Encode menu or click on the Start Encoding button on the left of the toolbar.

The lower right portion of the Encoder window allows you to set certain options for encoding your files. This is where you select the Compression Type

Figure 5-2. The RealAudio player.

desired for compressing your audio file. There are two options available: 14.4 and 28.8. The 14.4 compression is best optimized for speech. It yields a file that plays with AM quality, and which can be played over a 14.4 kbps modem. The 28.8 compression supports a greater dynamic range and more complex audio sources than 14.4 compression. 28.8 format files require at least a 28 kbps modem connection to the Internet. If you choose 14.4 compression, you will need to make sure that you have 1.0 kb of disk space available per second of audio. The 28.8 compression requires 1.6 kb of disk space per second of audio. If you would like to listen to the audio file as it is being encoded, you may do so by checking the "Play While Encoding" option in the Options panel. Using this feature, however, may slow down the encoding process. You can choose to listen to either the input file or the decompressed RA output file.

Starting the Encoding Process

After you have selected your input file and output destination, set your compression type and entered the desired description information, you are ready to begin the encoding process. To encode, select Start Encoding from the Encode Menu or click on the Start Encoding button on the left of the toolbar. Once you are familiar with the standard method of encoding you may find that drag and drop encoding or command-line encoding will work for your purposes.

RealAudio supports two types of drag and drop encoding. Clicking on a file and dragging it on to an open Encoder will place the path and filename information into the File field in the Source tab. Enter the description information and other desired settings and click the Start Encoding button to start the encoding process.

To initiate the encoding process, you can also click on the file that is to be encoded, and drag and drop it onto the encoder.exe file. The Encoder window will be open only during the encoding process, so you will not be able to set or change the encoding options. The file is encoded using the source file name and with the last saved default settings. This means that if you have selected Save Default Settings on the Options Menu, the saved settings will determine the compression type, the description information and playback filter used during encoding. If you have not selected Save Default Settings your file will be encoded in RealAudio 28.8 format.

To automate the encoding of multiple audio files, you can specify command-line arguments that direct the Encoder to process an input file and then shut down. The syntax is:

```
ENCODER <file to encode> [<settings file>]
```

where <file to encode> is the digital audio file to encode and <settings file> is the name of an optional settings file. For example,

```
ENCODER complete.wav intro.txt
```

would encode the file complete.wav with the Encoder settings specified in the file named intro.txt.

The <settings file> allows you to specify the compression type and the title, author and copyright strings for the RA file. If not specified, the settings are those most recently stored by selecting Save Default Settings from the Options menu. The settings file is a text file with the following format:

```
[Default Settings]
title = Title String Here
author = Author String Here
copyright = Copyright String Here
Compression = <1 for 14.4 compression or 2 for 28.8 compression>
```

The settings file must start with the [Default Settings] line. For example, if the settings file intro.txt contains the following:

```
[Default Settings]
title = Thank you for installing the RealAudio Player.
author = The RealAudio Team
copyright = 1996 Progressive Networks
Compression = 1
```

the RealAudio Player will display the information contained in intro.txt.

If you place the files you wish to encode and their corresponding settings files in the same directory as the RealAudio Encoder, you will not have to specify the file path. However, if you would like to encode files in other directories, you will need to specify the complete paths to all input files. You will also need to have the RealAudio encoder in your path. For example:

```
c:\raencod\ENCODER c:\files\welcome.wav c:\settings\intro.txt
```

The Encoder is distributed with two command-line utilities, racut.exe and rapaste.exe, which enable you to edit RealAudio files. racut.exe creates a copy of a specified portion of your original file. Cutting files encoded in the 28.8 format can only be done in blocks of 1.44 seconds; if your selected time is not a multiple of 1.44 the utility will round down to the nearest acceptable time frame. You can use the status bar on the Player to determine the time frame of the portion of the file you want to copy. The command uses the following format:

```
racut output.ra input.ra startTime endTime
```

where output.ra is the name of the file to which you want to save the cut portion, input.ra is the file from which to cut and startTime and endTime are the times between which you want to cut out. The time format is: [[[days:]hours:]minutes:]seconds[.tenths] where bracketed arguments are optional. Seconds are the only required value. The time will be interpreted from right to left, so it is not necessary to put a zero into every blank field, unless you are missing an increment between two other increments. For example, if you want to cut from the sixth hour of the first day (set of 24 hour periods) to the third day at four hours and one tenth of a second, your command would look as follows:

```
racut output.ra input.ra 06:00:00 02:4:00:00.1
```

Rapaste.exe is a utility that creates a new RA file from two or more RA files. The command uses the following format:

```
rapaste output.ra input1.ra input2.ra [... input1.ra]
```

where output.ra is the name of the file you are creating, input1.ra is the first file you want in the new file, and input2.ra is the file to be appended to the end of output.ra. The number of input files is limited to the system command-line limits. Splicing a file into the middle of an existing file is a multi-step process. First use racut.exe to create a file that contains the audio up to the point at which you want to insert a new file. Then use racut.exe to create a file with the audio to follow the inserted audio. Finally, use rapaste.exe to combine all three files together. For example, the syntax to put insert.ra into original.ra at 25 minutes would look as follows:

```
racut part1.ra original.ra 00.0 25:00
racut part2.ra original.ra 25:01 50:00
rapaste newfile.ra part1.ra insert.ra part2.ra
```

newfile.ra would then consist of original.ra with insert.ra inserted 25 minutes into original.ra. To protect your original files, you should always work with a copy of your original.

Bandwidth negotiation is a Server feature that allows visitors to your Web site to automatically receive the highest quality format available to their computer, while only requiring one generic link to a particular content file on your Web site. For example, without bandwidth negotiation, to provide content in both 14.4 and 28.8 formats, your Web site would require two hypertext links and two metafiles, one to a 14.4 file and one to a 28.8 file. Using bandwidth negotiation, however, you would only need one hypertext link and one metafile.

Web Site Configuration

Directly referencing a RealAudio file in a Web page would initiate a download of the file prior to playback. To play real-time audio, RealAudio files must be served by a RealAudio Server and played through a RealAudio Player. Metafiles are text files which contain the URL of a RealAudio file. They act as the link between the Web Server and the RealAudio Server.

Imagine your Web page as a sheet of paper containing directions to someone's house. In most situations, you would follow the directions and arrive at that house. For RealAudio files, a Web page is like a sheet of paper that contains directions to a house, and once you arrive at the house, there is another piece of paper attached to that door with a set of directions to another house, which is your actual destination.

When accessing RealAudio from a Web page, the first set of directions is represented by a link to a RealAudio metafile, recognized by a RAM or RPM file name extension. The second set of directions represents a link from the metafile to the RealAudio file, recognized by a RA file name extension. Instead of pointing to the audio file, your Web page will point to a metafile. Unlike the usual HTML link, the metafile does not display information through the browser, but rather, it provides the audio file's URL to the RealAudio Player. The Player uses this information to locate the RA file on the RealAudio Server as shown in figure 5-3.

-**Figure 5-3**. HTML link to a meta file results in the player being displayed and loaded.

The metafile that you create will contain the address of the RealAudio (RA) file or files being accessed by that link. The RealAudio System uses two metafile types: RAM and RPM. Both types of metafiles are created in the same manner. The different file extensions, however, tell the Web browser which application to use to play the accessed file. The RAM file launches the RealAudio Player and the RPM file loads a RealAudio Plug-in instance.

Most URLs begin with a locator type that identifies the protocol being used to exchange information between the client and the server. Common locator types include HTTP and FTP. The locator type used by RealAudio software is PNM. You must include PNM as part of the URL referenced in the metafile.

To create a metafile, open a text editor such as Notepad or Microsoft Word, and type in the URL of the RealAudio file using the PNM locator type and the following syntax:

`pnm://hostname/path`

For example, if you create a metafile to reference a RealAudio file called hello1.ra, the text of the metafile might read:

`pnm://www.server.com/hello1.ra`

If you want more than one file to play when the user clicks on a link, you can create a metafile that contains several URLs on separate lines (with no blank lines). For example:

`pnm://www.server.com/hello1.ra`
`pnm://www.server.com/welcome1.ra`
`pnm://www.server.com/stayhere.ra`

The Player will play these URLs in sequence. Listeners can use the Clip Menu on their Player to move forward and backward between clips in a multi-clip RAM file. Save your file as a "Text Only with Line Breaks" type file using a RAM file name extension. For example, you may wish to save the metafile that references the above RealAudio files as 3track.ram.

To insert a reference to this RAM file in your HTML, reference the metafile within a hyperlink. For example:

`<A HREF="http://www.realaudio.com/3track.ram">Hello!</A>`

Make sure that your Web server is properly configured to understand that the extension RAM refers to the MIME type x-pn-realaudio. Optional arguments are available to give you optimal control over what will be heard and seen on the RealAudio Player when someone clicks on your link. You may choose to start a RealAudio file at a point other than the beginning or to stop playing it before the actual end of the file. You may also change the Title, Author and Copyright information seen during playback.

These options follow the URL and are preceded by a ? and separated from each other by &. The syntax is as follows:

`pnm://www.realaudio.com/test.ra?[option1]&[option2]`

To create a link that starts playing the file from a point other than the beginning of the file append the desired start time to the URL. Use the following format:

```
start="dd:hh:mm:ss.ss"
```

Tenths of seconds are separated from seconds by a decimal point; and the other units of time are always separated by colons. The time will be interpreted from right to left, so it is not necessary to put a zero into every blank field, unless you are missing a step between two other unit. For example:

```
pnm://www.realaudio.com/test.ra?start="30"
```

would start playing test.ra from thirty seconds into the file. To create a link that will play a file up to a specified end point other than the actual end of the file, append the desired end time to the URL, using the following format:

```
end="dd:hh:mm:ss.ss"
```

The specified amount of time is from the absolute beginning of the file. For example:

```
pnm://www.realaudio.com/test.ra?end="5:30"
```

would stop playing test.ra five minutes and thirty seconds from the beginning of the file. To play only a designated section of a file append both the start time and the end time to the URL. For example:

```
pnm://www.realaudio.com/test.ra?start="30"&end="5:30"
```

would start playing test.ra from the thirty second point and stop playing after reaching the point five minutes and thirty seconds from the beginning of the file. You can change the description information that the Player and Plug-in will display by appending the desired change to the end of the URL. The formats are as follows:

```
title="title changes"
author="author changes"
copyright="copyright changes"
```

The Title, Author, and Copyright strings can be changed together or independently. Changing the description information in this manner does not change the description information permanently. It is especially useful, for example, if you have one large RA file that contains your band's entire CD but you want to play each song individually and credit the writer of each song. You could create a multi-clip RAM file as follows:

```
pnm://www.server/band.ra?end="5:30"&title="Song1"
pnm://www.server/band.ra?start="5:31"&end="7:45"
```

```
&title="song2"&author="Joe Smith"
pnm://www.server/band.ra?start="7:46"&end="15:01"
&title="song3"&author="Jane Smith"&copyright="My Music, 1996"
```

Using the RealAudio Plug-ins

The RealAudio Plug-in enables seamless integration of RealAudio into your Web page layout. You can place individual interactive components such as play buttons and volume controls anywhere on the page with the same level of control the HTML IMG tag offers for graphics. For an online demonstration of Plug-ins and associated HTML commands see the Progressive Networks Web page at: http://www.realaudio.com/products/ra2.0/plug_ins/index.html.

Viewing pages that use Plug-ins requires a Web browser that supports Netscape's Plug-in architecture. If you choose RealAudio Player 2.0 Express Setup the Plug-in will install automatically if there is a Plug-in compatible Web browser detected. During RealAudio Player 2.0 Custom Setup, you have the option of installing the Plug-in. Upon successful installation the file npra16.dll or npra32.dll will be located in your Web browser's plug-in directory.

Programming the Plug-in

The EMBED tag specifies Plug-in attributes in HTML pages in much the same way that the IMG tag specifies image attributes. The basic EMBED tag for RealAudio contains only the attributes SRC, WIDTH and HEIGHT, as shown below:

```
<EMBED SRC=metafile.rpm WIDTH=width_value HEIGHT=height_value>
```

For example:

```
<EMBED SRC="sample1.rpm" WIDTH=300 HEIGHT=134>
```

Do not place the EMBED tag within a table.

The SRC attribute specifies the RealAudio metafile to be accessed. As mentioned earlier, the RealAudio Plug-in has the RPM file name extension. This file name extension tells the user's Web browser to load the RealAudio Plug-in rather than the standalone RealAudio Player as shown in figure 5-4. For the end user's Web browser to correctly identify the RPM files, your system administrator must first configure the RPM MIME type in your Web server. End-users do not need to configure their Web browsers to recognize the RPM MIME type. The plug-in architecture will automatically send RPM files to the RealAudio Plug-in. Files with an RPM extension are identical to RAM files except for the extension.

The WIDTH and HEIGHT attributes specify the size of the embedded RealAudio component. Unlike images, Plug-ins do not size automatically. The

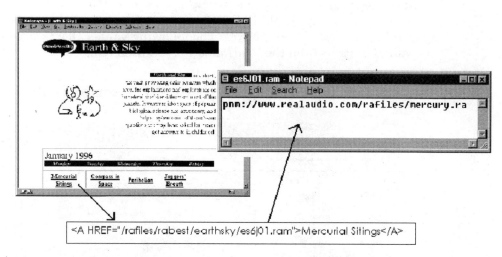

Figure 5-4. The RealAudio file extension dictates whether the plug-in or player will be used.

WIDTH and HEIGHT can be specified in pixels (the default) or as a percentage of the Web browser window (e.g. WIDTH=100%). If the WIDTH and HEIGHT attributes are not included, the Plug-in may appear in an icon-sized square space.

If you want your Plug-in component to maintain an absolute size, specify the size in pixels. If you want the Plug-in to scale with the Web browser window, specify the size as a percentage. For example, if you want to stretch the Position Slider and Status Bar to fit the entire width of the Web browser window, use a WIDTH=100% tag.

Some Web browsers do not support Plug-ins. You can create HTML pages that are enhanced for Plug-ins and also work for other browsers by using the <NOEMBED> tag to include HTML statements that will appear in Web browsers that do not support Plug-ins.

The <NOEMBED> command should appear after an <EMBED> command and should have the following syntax:

```
<NOEMBED> HTML to be ignored </NOEMBED>
```

For example:

```
<EMBED SRC="sample1.rpm" WIDTH=300 HEIGHT=134>
<NOEMBED>
   <A SRC="sample1.ram">
   Play the audio using the standalone Player! </A>
</NOEMBED>
```

would use the Plug-in if the your page is accessed by a browser supporting Plug-ins and display the message "Play the audio using the standalone Player!" if the browser does not support Plug-ins.

You can use multiple EMBED statements to construct a custom interface made up of individual controls. The following values allow you to embed individual controls from the RealAudio Player directly into your HTML layout.

CONTROLS = All (Default view if no control is specified)

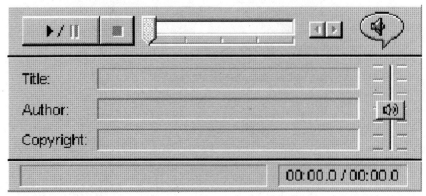

Figure 5-5. Embedding a full Player view.

CONTROLS = ControlPanel

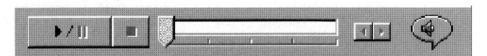

Figure 5-6. Embedding just the buttons and the slider.

Figure 5-5 demonstrates how to embed a full Player view including the Control Panel, Information and Volume Panel and Status Bar. This is also the default view if no CONTROLS attribute is specified. Figure 5-6 shows how to embed the Play/Pause button, the Stop button and the Position slider. This is similar to the panel the Player application displays when none of the options on the View menu are checked.

Figure 5-7 shows how to embed the area Title, Author and Copyright information and a Volume Slider on the right-hand side. This is the same panel that the Player application displays when the Info & Volume option on the View menu is checked.

```
CONTROLS = InfoVolumePanel
```

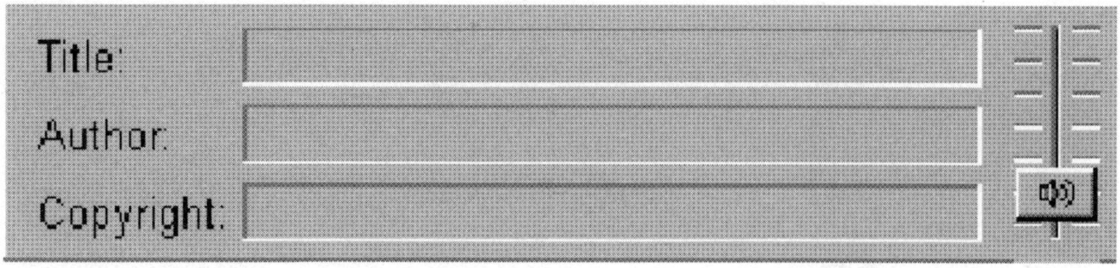

Figure 5-7. Embedding title, author and copyright.

Other values include:

```
CONTROLS = InfoPanel
```
Embeds the area showing Title, Author and Copyright information only.

```
CONTROLS = StatusBar
```
Embeds the Status Bar showing informational messages, current time position and clip length. This is the same panel that the Player application displays when the Status Bar option on the View menu is checked. If you do not embed a Status Bar in your page, error messages will be displayed in the Web browser's status bar.

```
CONTROLS = PlayButton
```
Embeds the Play/Pause button only.

```
CONTROLS = StopButton
```
Embeds the Stop button only.

```
CONTROLS = VolumeSlider
```
Embeds the Volume Slider only.

```
CONTROLS = PositionSlider
```
Embeds the Position Slider (scroll bar) only.

```
CONTROLS = PositionField
```
Embeds the field of the Status Bar showing Position and Length.

```
CONTROLS = StatusField
```
Embeds the field of the Status Bar that displays message text.

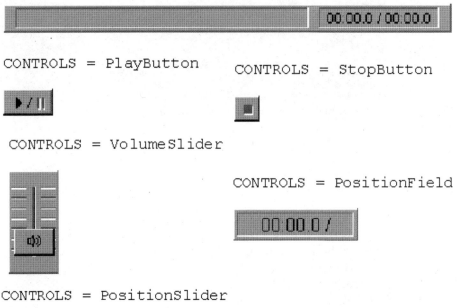

Figure 5-8. Various embed controls.

If your Web page is localized for a language other than English, or you wish to use the description fields to display information other than title, author, and copyright, you may want to remove the Title, Author, and Copyright labels from the information area. Controls that display the Title, Author and Copyright information for a clip, support a NOLABELS=TRUE attribute. For example, using the default is shown in figure 5-9.:

```
<EMBED  SRC="use_lbl.rpm"  WIDTH=350  HEIGHT=80  CONTROLS=InfoPanel
CONSOLE="Tester">
```

or

NOLABELS=FALSE

```
<EMBED SRC="use_lbl.rpm" WIDTH=350 HEIGHT=80 CONTROLS=InfoPanel
NOLABELS=false CONSOLE="Tester">
```

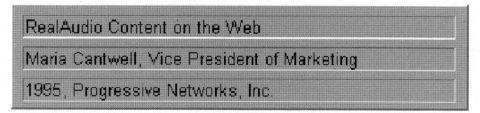

Figure 5-9. The NOLABELS option.

Starting a RealAudio Clip from HTML

Adding an AUTOSTART=TRUE attribute to an EMBED tag tells the RealAudio Plug-in to automatically begin playing when the page is visited. You can use this feature to begin a narration or to play background music. Since only one clip can play at a time, if you specify AUTOSTART for more than one Plug-in instance, only the last Plug-in to load will continue playing. The order in which the source files arrive is dependent on the Web Server and on your browser's cache. This is not necessarily the order in which they are listed. You should use this attribute for only one Plug-in instance per page.

The RealAudio Plug-in allows you to embed any number of RealAudio clips within a Web page. Normally each Plug-in behaves independently of all the others. Sometimes, however, you may want to link two or more Plug-ins together. For example, you might have a Play Button and a Position Slider that work as a pair. To include multiple components that work together, specify a CONSOLE attribute and assign the same value to each instance. For example:

```
<EMBED SRC="sample1.rpm" WIDTH=30 HEIGHT=33 CONTROLS="PlayButton"
    CONSOLE="Clip1">
<EMBED SRC="empty1.rpm" WIDTH=300 HEIGHT=33
    CONTROLS="PositionSlider" CONSOLE="Clip1">
```

Specifying a CONSOLE value of "_master" links the Plug-in to all other RealAudio Plug-ins on the page. Use this value when you want a control such as a Status Bar to display information for all audio clips. For example:

```
<EMBED SRC="sample1.rpm" WIDTH=300 HEIGHT=33 CONTROLS="StatusBar"
    CONSOLE="_master">
```

Because many platforms, including Windows, only support one volume setting for all digital audio, all volume sliders act on all clips and are automatically kept in synch regardless of the CONSOLE name. For this reason, you may wish to include only one Volume Slider on your page, with no reference to an RA file in the RPM file. You can create a dummy RPM file (called something like empty1.rpm) to represent the SRC for the Volume Slider. Since a completely empty RPM file may cause a browser to crash, the dummy RPM file must contain a hard return (ASCII 13).

Each Plug-in instance (each EMBED tag) must have a unique SRC tag. If two EMBED tags have the same source, only the first will appear, and the other will be ignored in the HTML.

You can also use an RPM file as the HREF for a normal hypertext anchor. The Web browser will display the complete Player view at the full size of the browser window. The format is:

```
<A HREF="sample1.rpm">Play sample clip full-screen!</A>
```

In general, it is better to use an embedded control or a RAM file that launches the RealAudio helper application.

Producing RealAudio Events

The Standard RealAudio encoder can create RA files from live sources. The Live Encoder provided with the RealAudio Server has an additional capacity. In conjunction with the use of the Live Transfer Agent (LTA), it enables you to broadcast a live event directly to the Internet. There is also a utility, Simulated

Live Transfer Agent (SLTA), that can take prerecorded material and broadcast it as if it were live.

Live events can be sent over the Internet in real-time using the RealAudio Live Encoder and the Live Transfer Agent (LTA) Application included with the RealAudio Server. To set up the RealAudio System for live events, the machine that has the RealAudio Encoder needs to be located where the sound is to be transmitted from, and the machine that runs the LTA needs to be located where there is enough bandwidth available for transmission to the Internet. There needs to be a TCP/IP network connection between these two machines.

When live events are to be sent directly from the Encoder to the RealAudio Server for delivery over the Internet, they need to be processed through the LTA before being sent to the RealAudio Server. The Live Transfer Agent must be located on the same machine as the RealAudio Server. Live audio is fed into the Encoder's computer through a line that runs from a microphone to the microphone input jack or through a line that runs from a mixing console, CD player or other line level output device to the line input jack on the computer's audio card (see figure 5-10). To ensure high quality RA files, verify that you are using the proper input for the source you are using and that your input volumes are adjusted properly.

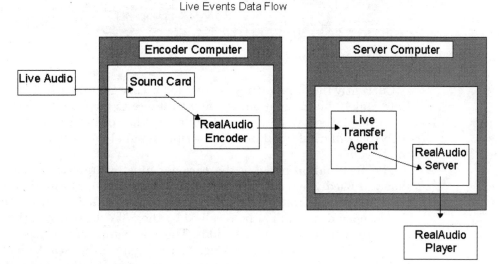

Figure 5-10. RealAudio Live.

As soon as the audio is encoded, it is sent directly to the Server computer, where it is processed by the LTA and delivered to the RealAudio Server. The Server sends RealAudio packets to users who are listening to the live event through a link on a Web page.

The LTA is a command-line application with the following usage:

```
lta -b <path/to/rafiles> -p <port#> -w <password>
```

where <path/to/rafiles> is the path to the directory where the LTA will place the encoded files received from the Encoder, <port#> is the TCP port on which the RealAudio Server receives files from the Encoder, and <password> is the password shared by the LTA and Encoder. The password protects the live event from being accessed by outsiders during broadcasting. If the -p command is left out of the command-line, the default port 7069 will be used. To see options available for the LTA command-line, type: lta -v.

Once the LTA is started, the RealAudio Encoder can be opened and set up to start the encoding process. The encoding process occurs in real-time. As soon as audio is fed into the Encoder, it is encoded and sent to the Server computer. In the Encoder, select the Live Stream tab from the Source panel, and the RealAudio Server from the Destination panel (see figure 5-11).

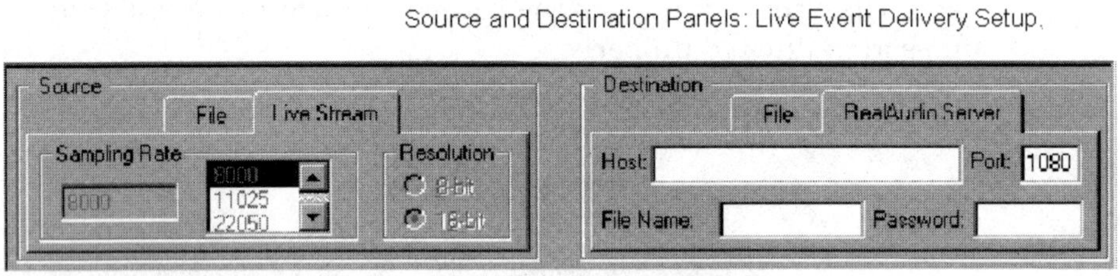

Source and Destination Panels: Live Event Delivery Setup.

Figure 5-11. Source and destination panels.

Currently the only settings available for Live Stream are 8000 Hz Sampling Rate and 16-bit Resolution. If you would like to have a description of the live event displayed by the RealAudio Players that connect to it on the Web site, then you will need to fill in the Description panel in the lower left-hand side of the Encoder.

The Destination panel of the Encoder must contain the same information that you used when starting the LTA. If any of the information in this panel does not correspond with the information you specified when starting the LTA, the encoded data will not be received by the LTA. The Host is the name of the computer where the Server resides. The File Name will be used in a RAM file to access the live event. It will also be the name of the RealAudio file once the live event finishes. Port is the port number that the Encoder will use to send the encoded RA data. The password must be the same password used to start the LTA.

Options for encoding a file are found on the lower right side of the Encoder. You must choose the Compression Type that is needed for the live event. 14.4 compression will allow people with 14.4 kbps or faster modems to listen to the event, while 28.8 compression limits the audience to those who have 28.8 kbps or faster modems. Note that the 14.4 algorithm was optimized for speech transmission and is not recommended for music applications. Since the 28.8 algorithm can deliver more data it will provide higher quality audio. You will need 1.0 kb of disk space per second of audio when encoding using 14.4, and 1.6 kb per second of audio when encoding using 28.8.

To start the live broadcast, select the Start Encoding command from the Encode menu or click on the Start Encoding button on the toolbar. To end the live broadcast, select the Stop Encoding command from the Encode menu or click the Stop Encoding button on the toolbar. When the LTA stops receiving data, it sends important header information to the RealAudio file which enables the file to be accessed later. If a break in the transmission occurs and this header is not written, the file will not be a usable RealAudio file.

If you restart the LTA with the same path and file name as a previous event, the LTA will overwrite the existing RA file. This is an important consideration. Reusing the same output file name can simplify Web page maintenance since the RAM file for a recurring event would not need to be changed. For example, if you broadcast news at 6:00 every night, you could have the LTA write to a generically named file 6pmnews.ra. You could reference 6pmnews.ra in your RAM file, and your Web page could always be linked to the same, unchanged RAM file. If, however, you wanted to maintain an archive of your broadcasts you would need to rename the RA on a daily basis since the LTA will overwrite the existing RA file.

In order to reach the largest audience you will probably want to encode both a 14.4 and a 28.8 version of the event you are broadcasting. To accomplish this you will need to run two simultaneous Encoders and LTAs as well as provide two links on your Web page. The Encoders should be set up with different port numbers and output file names.

The RealAudio 2.00 Server allows for the "live" delivery of non-live events through the SLTA (Simulated Live Transfer Agent). It takes a previously encoded RA file and provides a live-like stream to the Server for distribution to RealAudio Players.

A RealAudio Player will see clips broadcast using the SLTA as a "live" clip and will always connect at the current point of the clip, which is offset from the time when the SLTA was started. The SLTA is run from the command-line using the following arguments:

```
bin/slta -b <basepath> -i <nameofinputfile> -o <nameofoutputfile>
```

The <basepath> should be the same basepath the Server is using. <nameofinputfile> is the previously encoded RA file you want to broadcast. If -o <name of output file> is omitted, the name will default to live.ra. The RealAudio Server waits 30 seconds after the end of the file to give the Players time to disconnect and then it deletes the output file.

Synchronized Multimedia

With the RealAudio System, you can provide real-time audio on-demand. In addition to basic audio content, RealAudio allows you to create real-time on-demand multimedia presentations using the *cevents* utility (provided with the RealAudio Server). These presentations can be as simple as a narrated slide show of your home page or as intricate as a multiframe training program that the viewer controls.

One of RealAudio's features is the ability to synchronize Web pages with audio. Thus the audio can be used as a "time-line" to display new pages or frames in the Web browser or to update its content, enabling the creation of Internet slide shows, presentations, guided tours and site walk-throughs. The end-user can have full random access (fast forward and rewind), and the Web browser content will automatically be synchronized with the audio.

The RealAudio system stores the information for the synchronized events in a file with an RAE file name extension. This file is automatically located by the RealAudio Server when the listener opens the RA file. The RealAudio Server streams audio and event information to the Player. As the event information is streamed to the RealAudio Player, the RealAudio Player then sends information to the Web browser telling it when to update the page's content.

The RealAudio Plug-in will work with synchronized multimedia events. However, since sending the Web browser to a new URL will unload the RealAudio Plug-in when the HTML page is unloaded, it is best to create separate frames for the RealAudio controls and for the changing images.

Creating a synchronized multimedia event is a three-step process:

1. Use a text editor to create an input file specifying the display time for each URL.
2. Use the cevents command-line tool to generate a binary file from the text input file.
3. Place the resulting RAE file in the same directory as the RA audio file.

Begin by creating a list of the URLs that you want to be shown during your presentation and the times within the RealAudio clip when they should be displayed. The syntax for each entry should follow the format:

```
u<space>starttime<space>endtime<space>URL for event
```

Where u stands for URL event (each line starts with the letter u), starttime is the time into the audio clip when the new event is shown, endtime is the time into the audio clip when that event ends, and URL (generally beginning with "http:" or "file:") is the URL for that event (usually an HTML document). The time format is: [[[days:]hours:]minutes:]seconds[.tenths].

The lines of the input file must be in ascending order of start time. The end time should be at least one-tenth of a second before the start time of the next event. The following example shows how an input file might look:

```
u 00:00:10.0 00:00:59.9 http://www.RealAudio.com/
u 00:01:00.0 00:02:00.0 http://www.mysite.com/ page2/
```

This input file tells the Player to send the Web browser to the RealAudio home page at ten seconds into the audio clip. At one minute into the audio clip, the Web browser will display a page from "www.my_site.com."

The input file may also contain comment lines beginning with the # symbol. These comment lines are ignored by the event creation tool and are a good way to document the date that the file was created.

You will need to create a RealAudio binary event file from the text file you just created. The command-line utility cevents is provided for this purpose. It uses the following syntax:

```
cevents <input text file> <output event file>
```

where <output event file> is the same name as the audio file with which it will be associated. For example, to a create synchronized multimedia presentation to accompany paradise.ra, you would generate paradise.rae using the following command:

```
cevents paradise.txt paradise.rae
```

Copy the RAE file to the same directory as your RA file. The RA and RAE files must have the same name except for the file name extension. The RealAudio Server will automatically detect the file and send the event information to the Player, which then sends it to the Web browser.

The RealAudio Player can also read local RAE files just as the Server does. To test the RAE file locally, place it in the same directory in which the corresponding RA file is found. The URLs within your input file for CEVENTS can refer to local files. When passed to the Web Browser, partial path names will be interpreted as relative to the current working directory. For maximum reliability, specify complete paths as shown below:

```
u 10.0 45.0 file:c|/media/test2.html
```

Using Frames

Some Web browsers support a feature which allows the browser window to be divided into multiple regions. Each region is called a frame and can display a separate URL such as a graphic or document. For an introduction to frames visit Netscape's Web site.

A frame document describes the sub-HTML documents or frames that will make up a window. The basic structure of a frame document is similar to that of a normal HTML document except that the FRAMESET tag replaces the BODY tag. Each frame is defined by the FRAME tag. In order to effectively use

RealAudio each FRAME tag needs the SRC and NAME attributes. The SRC points to the URL to be displayed in the frame. The NAME attribute assigns a name to the frame so that it can be targeted by links in other documents. The example below shows a simple frame document that would create two frames:

```
<HTML>
<FRAMESET ROWS="105,*">
  <FRAME SRC="banner.html" NAME="banner">
  <FRAME SRC="lyrics.html" NAME="Lyric">
</FRAMESET>
</HTML>
```

Frames and RealAudio content are synchronized in the same way that a regular Web page and RealAudio content are synchronized: a RAE file. The difference lies in the addition of the targeted frame name to the text file that is used to create the RAE file. The syntax for each entry should follow the format:

```
u<space>starttime<space>endtime<space>&&framename&&<space>
URL for event
```

Where u stands for URL event (each line starts with the letter u), starttime is the time into the audio clip when the new event is shown, endtime is the time into the audio clip when that event ends, && is a delimiter, framename is the frame name as specified in your frame document, and URL (generally beginning with "http:" or "file:") is the URL for that event (usually an HTML document). The time format is:[[[days:]hours:]minutes:]seconds[.tenths].

The lines of the input file must be in ascending order of start time. The end time should be at least one-tenth of a second before the start time for the next event.

The example below shows an RAE input file for a Web site that displays lyrics as a song plays. Each verse is displayed within a frame called LyricFrame.

```
u 00:00:10.0 00:00:35.0 &&Lyric&&http://www.songs.com/ver1.html
u 00:00:35.0 00:00:50.0 &&Lyric&&http://www.songs.com/ver2.html
```

Making Quality RealAudio Recordings

As with most projects, the quality of what you get out of the RealAudio system depends heavily on what you put in. Good quality equipment is a must. You wouldn't consider opening a radio station with only a portable cassette player, would you? Make sure you have a good environment in which to record. A quiet, carpeted room should be adequate.

Equipment to do this need not be outlandishly expensive. Think about what it is you hope to achieve, decide on a budget, and consult with your local recording studio equipment dealer. They should be able to come up with a working solution, be it hardware, software, or a combination of both. Most importantly, make sure that they are going to send someone out to help you install your system. What would take a knowledgeable engineer half a day to set up could frustrate a novice for weeks.

Also note that some people's voices are more suited to recording than others. Professional announcers are paid not only for their reading abilities, but also for their pacing, dynamics, inflection, and most importantly vocal tone. Bear this in mind when choosing the person behind the microphone.

There are a number of steps you can take to get the best possible sound from your RA files:

1. Use a Good Original Source

A high-quality audio source is probably the single most important variable in determining your final audio quality. Progressive Networks uses satellite signals, audio Compact Discs, or Digital Audio Tapes. When creating sounds from scratch, they use professional-quality microphones. You can make sound files from low-quality analog cassettes, tiny condenser microphones, or anything else — but the hiss and distortion in the resulting sound file will have a substantial adverse effect on clarity after the file is encoded into RA format.

You should always encode from 16-bit (not 8-bit or mu-law) sound files. It is also recommend to digitize at a 22050 Hz sample rate. Although the encoder will also accept 8000 Hz and 11000Hz sample rates, 22050 Hz yields the best results.

2. Set Your Input Levels Correctly.

Setting correct levels is absolutely crucial. When creating your original sound file, the input level should be set to use the full range of available amplitude, while avoiding clipping. Clipping is audible as a high-frequency crackling noise and is what happens if you try to send too much input to your soundcard (or any other piece of audio equipment).

When digitizing with your sound card, first do several test runs and adjust your input level so the input approaches but does not exceed the maximum level. You can adjust this on the mixer page of your sound card utilities. Look for the Input Levels or Recording Levels option. Most mixer pages have some sort of visual display where you can see how much sound is coming in. Make sure there are no peaks above maximum. These are generally indicated by a red light somewhere. Be conservative with your levels; you never know when someone will get excited and speak much louder, or when a great play at a sports event will make a crowd roar. Differences in volume levels can be evened out later.

Sound files that do not use the full amplitude range will produce poor-quality RealAudio files. If the amplitude range of an existing file is too low, you can use your audio editor's Increase Amplitude or Increase Volume command to adjust the range before encoding the file. Most sound editors have a Normalize function that will maximize your levels automatically.

Note, however, that better quality will be achieved if the levels are set correctly at the time of recording. The good news is that once you set your input levels correctly, they generally will not need to be reset. If you are reasonably consistent with your recording practices, you'll save yourself a lot of trouble in the long run.

3. Use High-Quality Equipment

High-quality equipment will produce better results and save you a lot of headaches in the long run. Every piece of equipment in the audio chain, from the microphone to the soundcard to the software, will have an effect on your RealAudio files. If you intend to be a commercial RealAudio content provider, you should invest in professional quality audio equipment. This need not be a crippling investment, but it does mean you will have to purchase from a professional recording equipment dealer, not your local computer/hi-fi/gadget store.

4. Select Appropriate Material

RealAudio 14.4 was optimized for speech delivery. If you want to encode music for transmission over 14.4 phone lines, remember that the simpler the source, the better chance that the encoded version will be faithful to the original. There isn't enough bandwidth in a 14.4 line to do a harmonically complex signal (like a full orchestra) justice. Many folks have used music successfully in their 14.4 clips as background, where fidelity isn't as important an issue.

With RealAudio 28.8, a whole new world of music possibilities arise. The increased bandwidth allows an improved dynamic range and better frequency response, with less artifacts. Virtually any kind of music can now be delivered in real-time across the Web.

Those who are attempting to encode audio more professionally should keep these RealAudio hints in mind:

1. Correcting DC Offset

Sometimes when files are digitized, something known as DC offset creeps in. This is when the digitized waveform is not correctly centered around the 0 volts axis. Most of this is due to improper grounding of soundcards. Some soundcards are worse than others; to see how bad your soundcard is try recording silence. You should in theory see nothing in you waveform window, but you'll probably see a flat line just slightly above or below the 0 volts axis. This is DC offset.

This can wreak havoc when you attempt to process your waveform, and can add a low rumbling sound to the encoded file. Luckily most editors have a built in facility to take care of this. Some call it *Centering the Wave* and are automatic; others allow you to adjust DC offset manually (+/-). In this case you'll have to find out precisely what your DC offset is by running a statistics command or something similar. Then you'll have to correct it. For instance, if your average DC offset is 45 you'll want to offset the wave by -45.

Obviously if you are doing a live broadcast, you'll have to live with whatever DC offset you have. Proper balanced wiring between all your audio components will help minimize this as well as any ground loops.

2. Noise Gating (or Expansion)

Noise Gating, or downward expansion, eliminates unwanted background noise which becomes audible during pauses in the audio (e.g. when an announcer pauses, or there is a gap between programs). Signals above a certain volume level are left alone, but below this level the signal is turned down or even off, depending on how heavy the gating or expansion is. Setting up a noise gate or expander is straightforward. Most budget compressors have a noise gate built in.

To use noise gating, set the threshold control so that the gating or expansion occurs when there is no desired audio, but not so high that the beginnings of words or music that you want to hear are chopped off. It takes a bit of time, but remember to err on the side of caution just in case the next person in the program has a softer voice.

If your gate or expander has a range control, set this to around 5 — 10 dB. This means it will turn down the "noise" sections a little, but not turn them off altogether. That way you'll hear if the gate is cutting something off that you want to hear, and you can then readjust the threshold setting accordingly.

3. Compression

One of the side effects of RealAudio encoding is artifacts — sounds that weren't there before encoding. These can be heard sometimes as rumbling or distortion in the signal. These artifacts appear at a relatively constant low level, whether the original soundfile was loud or quiet. Louder files tend to mask these quiet artifacts. RealAudio recommends feeding the encoder a loud signal. However, we are limited by the loudest section of the file being encoded. If we could turn down the loudest section, we could turn the overall volume of the soundfile up. A compressor helps us accomplish this.

Compression reduces the difference between the loudest and quietest sections of the incoming signal. Sections that exceed a user-defined threshold are turned down. Now that these loud sections have been turned down, we can turn the overall volume of the soundfile up. This will substantially help your programs take advantage of RealAudio's available dynamic range. How much the sections are turned up or down depends on how much compression you use.

How much compression should you use? The exact settings will be determined by experience and by referring to the manual that comes with your equipment or software. Here are some rough guidelines which should be helpful in most situations:

For speech, use moderate to extreme compression (4:1 to 10:1). This guarantees the resulting signal will be loud enough to mask artifacts which are more apparent in RealAudio 14.4.

With RealAudio 28.8, the dynamic range is greatly increased, and the artifacts are greatly reduced so the need for compression is not as great. A compression ratio of between 2:1 and 4:1 is generally more than enough. With music, compression effects are more readily apparent. These effects may or may not be pleasing — the person doing the encoding will have to use his or her judgment.

4. Equalization

Equalization (or EQ) changes the tone of the incoming signal just as you can on your home stereo or car radio. This is done by boosting (turning up) or cutting (turning down) certain frequencies. Using EQ, we can boost frequencies that we like (where the important content is) and cut frequencies where noise or unwanted sound is. By doing this, we can give the encoder a big hint about which sound information to keep. The RealAudio encoder discards a lot of the high end, or treble information. This can make files sound dull. To compensate for this, it helps to boost the middle frequencies or midrange. This will also make speech sound more intelligible.

Most good mixing boards will have a midrange EQ knob. Sometimes you can choose which frequency to boost, other times this is preset at the factory. If not, or if you are using a graphic equalizer or audio processing software, you'll want to boost at around 2.5 KHz.

If your equipment does not have a mid-frequencies EQ knob, you can obtain a similar result by turning the low and high EQ knobs down and then turning the overall volume back up (note, though, that this is not as effective as boosting the *mids*, which attacks the problem at its source).

The amount that you should turn up the midrange depends on your EQ equipment and source file. A little experimentation is necessary. Try adding some *mids* to a short section of a piece to be encoded and check it with the RealAudio Player. If it is a bit muddy or hard to understand, try adding a little more. You can keep going until the knob won't turn anymore, or until the result starts to sound too harsh.

For RealAudio 14.4, it is important to try and make the voice as full as possible in the middle frequencies. This is where the majority of speech information is contained. What we are trying to do is lift the voice away from any background noise. Remember to listen to the resulting RA file; what may sound harsh before encoding might help a weak voice.

Some signals can be improved by rolling off (turning down) the bass frequencies as well.

Side effects of the RealAudio 14.4 encoder are sometimes audible as a lower voice shadowing the original. This is particularly noticeable with women speakers. When this effect is too prominent, try rolling off the bass and encoding the result. The artifacts will not disappear, but sometimes they will be quieter. Be careful not to make the voice sound too thin or brittle.

For RealAudio 28.8, much more of the fidelity of the original recording is retained so you won't need to worry about EQ as much. It still helps to boost at around 2.5 KHz to compensate for the high frequency loss, but boosting too much will make music sound thin and tinny.

5. Normalization

Normalization is a process included in most audio recording software whereby the computer calculates exactly how much it can turn up the volume of a file without distortion. Because we always want to feed the encoder the loudest files possible, this is a very handy function. This is why you can afford to be fairly conservative with your recording input levels, and then let your program's normalization function take care of the rest.

Normalization should be the last thing you do. If you normalize your file, and then ADD some EQ, you'll end up with distortion. (If you add after you've maximized you will exceed.)

The RealAudio encoder sometimes chokes on peaks when they are too close to the maximum. Normalizing to 95% of maximum usually avoids this. If your Normalization option will not let you specify a percentage, simply turn down the overall volume after you normalize using the volume or amplify option in your audio software.

The RealAudio Server

At the tail end of 1996, Progressive networks had a "sale" where you could purchase a five stream RealAudio server for just $495. By the time you read this page, this deal will more than likely be over. But, then again, Progressive Networks may have another super deal. Try http://www.realaudio.com/products/server/easystart/index.html and see what happens.

RealAudio Servers are priced by the stream. The five stream deal above meant that five people could listen to a RealAudio broadcast simultaneously. If you believe your site is going to be far more popular than that then you have to purchase a Server with greater capabilities — obviously at a higher price.

Figure 5-12 shows pricing for RealAudio Servers as of November 1996.
You may evaluate the RealAudio Server free for thirty days. The evaluation package includes a fully functional five stream RealAudio Server 2.0. and an Evaluator Guide for evaluating RealAudio Server 2.0.

Simultaneous Streams*	License Price**	Upgrades & Support***	Total
5	$495	$100	$595
20	$1,895	$995	$2,890
50	$4,495	$1,995	$6,490
100	$8,495	$2,995	$11,490
> 100	Contact Server Sales Center for details.		

Figure 5-12. RealAudio price list. Call (206) 674-2228 for streams > 100.

Evaluators must fill out an on-line form which is then e-mailed to Progressive Networks. Your return mail will contain a URL, username, password and license key for downloading and installing your developer copy of the RealAudio server, SDKs and other tools.

Once you get access to the server software you must upload it to your server. My service provider has a UNIX-based Sun so I downloaded the executable for the Solaris. Figure 5-13 shows how to use FTP (file transfer protocol) to first create a subdirectory named realaudio and then copy the file to that subdirectory.

```
ftp> mkdir realaudio
257 MKD command successful.
ftp> cd realaudio
250 CWD command successful.
ftp> put solaris_tar.z
200 PORT command successful.
150 ASCII data connection for solaris_tar.z (206.15.6
226 Transfer complete.
local: solaris_tar.z remote: solaris_tar.z
6538646 bytes sent in 13 seconds (5e+02 Kbytes/s)
ftp>
```

Figure 5-13. FTPing the executables for the Solaris.

My next step is to decompress the file. Since this is a gzipped tar file, I have to unzip it first by typing:

```
gzip -d solaris_tar.z
```

This expands the 6-meg file to well over a 10-meg file. My next step is to untar the file by typing:

```
tar xvf solaris_tar
```

These commands are executed under a TELNET session. Your service provider or system administrator probably already has the tar and GZIP utilities on the system, so try typing the commands first. If the utilities are not on your system you can probably download them from http://www.shareware.com (do a search for tar under the UNIX operating system). Figure 5-14 shows what this looks like along with a partial output.

```
> tar xvf solaris_tar
x pnserver/, 0 bytes, 0 tape blocks
x pnserver/bin/, 0 bytes, 0 tape blocks
x pnserver/bin/win_mon/, 0 bytes, 0 tape blocks
x pnserver/bin/win_mon/_inst32i.ex_, 297325 bytes, 581 tape
x pnserver/bin/win_mon/_isdel.exe, 8192 bytes, 16 tape bloc
x pnserver/bin/win_mon/_setup.dll, 10240 bytes, 20 tape blo
x pnserver/bin/win_mon/_setup.lib, 24443 bytes, 48 tape blo
x pnserver/bin/win_mon/data.z, 1698963 bytes, 3319 tape blo
x pnserver/bin/win_mon/setup.exe, 47616 bytes, 93 tape bloc
x pnserver/bin/win_mon/setup.ins, 3809 bytes, 8 tape blocks
x pnserver/bin/win_mon/setup.pkg, 327 bytes, 1 tape blocks
x pnserver/bin/win_mon/uninst.exe, 269312 bytes, 526 tape b
x pnserver/bin/win_enc/, 0 bytes, 0 tape blocks
x pnserver/bin/win_enc/lencinst.exe, 596334 bytes, 1165 tap
x pnserver/bin/monitor, 483004 bytes, 944 tape blocks
```

Figure 5-14. The contents of the RealAudio tar file.

The RealAudio server installation process creates a directory called pnserver. Its files are shown in figure 5-15. Before anyone can use these files permissions must be altered as follows:

```
> ls -l
total 14
drwxr-xr-x   5 online   wen       512 Nov  7 07:15 bin
drwxr-xr-x   2 online   wen       512 Nov  7 07:15 doc
drwxr-xr-x   2 online   wen       512 Nov  7 07:15 logs
drwxr-xr-x   4 online   wen       512 Nov  7 07:15 rafiles
-rw-r--r--   1 online   wen      1247 Apr 26  1996 readme.txt
-rw-r--r--   1 online   wen       826 Apr  1  1996 server.cfg
```

Figure 5-15. The contents of the pnserver directory.

```
chmod -R 644 *
chmod 750 bin logs rafiles
chmod 755 bin/*
```

The download comes with an Adobe Acrobat file (raserver.pdf), located in the doc directory, which is a 100-page manual that is searchable as well as printable. Rehashing what's in this particular manual is really beyond the scope of this book. I would like, however, to touch on a few points that you should be aware of.

RealAudio Player users typically gain access to audio content via the World Wide Web. References to RealAudio files are embedded in HTML documents provided by a Web server. The method of interaction between the RealAudio Server and the Web browser is shown in figure 5-16

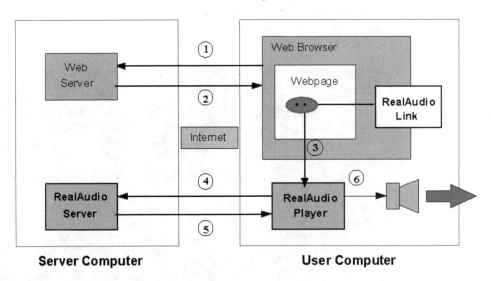

Figure 5-16. Web browser and RealAudio interaction pathways.

When the user clicks on a RealAudio link (1), the HTML document on the Web page accesses a metafile. The metafile is a document that contains the Universal Resource Locator (URL) of the audio file on your RealAudio Server. The URL is sent by the Web server to the user's browser (2), and then to the RealAudio Player (3). The RealAudio Player is configured as a helper application for your Web browser. The RealAudio Player requests the audio file from the RealAudio Server (4), which delivers the audio stream to the Player (5), where it is played (6).

Currently, the server runs on the following platforms: 6 DEC Alpha: Digital UNIX v3.2 and Windows NT 3.51; Hewlett-Packard PA/RISC: HP/UX 10.01; Intel 486, Pentium: Microsoft Windows NT 3.51, BSDI 2.0, LINUX 1.x, including ELF, and FreeBSD 2.x; IBM Power PC: AIX 4.0; Sun SPARC: SunOS 4.1x and Solaris 2.x; Silicon Graphics: IRIX version 5.2. Make sure you download the executable for your particular operating system.

The software requires approximately 2 MB of disk space. Compressed audio documents require approximately 1.1 kB per second of audio for 14.4 format and 2.4 kB per second for 28.8 format; 1 hour of 14.4 format audio requires 3.6 MB of memory and one hour of 28.8 format audio requires 8 MB of memory.

The RealAudio Server requires at least 10 kbps for 14.4 format and 22 kbps for 28.8 format for each client connected to the Internet backbone. Therefore, a 56 kbps leased line can only accommodate approximately five simultaneous 14.4 kbps connections. A T1 line, by contrast, can accommodate over 100 simultaneous 14.4 connections, and is recommended for commercial RealAudio Server applications. Figure 5-17 outlines the number of streams an Internet connection can support. The bandwidth consumed by other applications (e.g., the Web server) should be taken into account when estimating the number of simultaneous users that can be accommodated.

Internet Connection	RA 144 Streams	RA 288 Streams
Frame Relay (56Kbit)	5	3
ISDN (64Kbit)	6	4
ISDN (128Kbit)	12	8
T1 (1.5Mbit)	150	90
Ethernet LAN (10Mbit)[3]	560	350
T3 (45Mbit)	4,500	2,700
100BaseT/FDDI LAN (100Mbit)	10,000	6,000

Figure 5-17. Numer of RealAudio streams versus Internet connection type.

The file server.cfg, located in the pnserver directory of your server, needs to be modified before RealAudio will work. If you downloaded an evaluation copy, then an e-mail will be sent to you with this information. Those using the CD will find the information included in the shipment.

You can edit server.cfg using your preferred text editor. The two configuration settings required to start your RealAudio Server are CustomerName and LicenseKey. These should be placed after the line #Licensing Details. Also examine your existing RealAudio the PnaPort number entry and the BasePath entry. If the PnaPort entry is set to 7070 or is not present in your existing configuration file, this means it is using the default port 7070. You will have to change the port number for the RealAudio 2.0 Server before starting and testing it. This will allow your existing server to continue running, while testing the RealAudio 2.0 Server.

If you have any problems starting the RealAudio 2.0 Server on this port because another application is using it, you will need to select a different port number and use this port number instead of 7070. For example, to connect to the server using the 7071 port, you must add :7071 to the PNM URL. This makes the URL become pnm://<my.server>:7071/sound1.ra.

Starting the server is platform dependent. For UNIX, change directories to the pnserver directory of the RealAudio Server. Start the RealAudio Server by typing:

```
bin/pnserver server.cfg
```

Note that the RealAudio Server "detaches" from the shell and runs in the background as a daemon process; the prompt will return immediately. You will have to press CTRL+C to end the process.

Once the RealAudio Server is started, you can test it by attempting to play the clips provided in the directory rafiles. Open a RealAudio Player on any Macintosh, Windows or UNIX computer that supports RealAudio Players and can access the RealAudio Server via a network.

Figure 5-18. Using the RealAudio Open Location dialog.

Use the Open Location dialog, on the File menu to enter the URL of the test file sound1.ra as shown in figure 5-18. <my.pnserver> is the DNS name or the IP address of the computer with the RealAudio Server installed. If you've assigned it to something other than port 7070, you will need to specify that port as follows:

```
pnm://myserver.com:7071/sound1.ra
```

There can be any number of reasons why the sound won't play. Check your error log file which is located in the logs directory under the filename pnerror.log. The most common error is forgetting to change permissions and the second most common error is "port in use..

The RealAudio Server is distributed with a basic default configuration file that you used and just tested. The RealAudio Server also supports three operational configurations. By adding to the default configuration parameters, you can customize the RealAudio Server to your needs.

The RealAudio Server can run as multiple processes within a single machine on all of the supported UNIX platforms. The RealAudio Server starts the required number of processes and shares the total number of streams among those processes. Incoming streams are automatically balanced across the

Server's individual processes. This allows more efficient use of system resources. This option can be configured either in the configuration file or on the command line. The RealAudio Server can take advantage of symmetric multi-processing, if available.

The command-line option on starting the RealAudio Server is -t n, where n is the total number of processes required. For example, starting the RealAudio Server with bin/pnserver -t 5 server.cfg will start 5 processes. Since this configuration parameter will affect your computer's CPU usage, you should experiment to find the optimal number of processes for your system.

The RealAudio Server supports clustering of individual RealAudio Servers. This allows single RealAudio Servers to be grouped together to provide support for large stream requirements. The cluster is established with a control Server and a number of sub Servers. The control RealAudio Server allocates incoming connection requests from RealAudio 2.0 Players to the least busy sub Server. RealAudio 1.0 Players can only connect to the control Server. Once the maximum number of connections to the control Server is reached additional RealAudio 1.0 Players will not be able to connect until there are streams available; RealAudio 2.0 Players will continue to be passed on to the sub Servers as long as there are streams available. Individual RealAudio licenses are required for each RealAudio Server in the cluster.

The RealAudio Server also supports the ability to subdivide the stream capacity of your Server between multiple accounts. This feature, called RealAudio Hosting Service, is controlled by your license. This feature allows the RealAudio Server's capacity to be allocated to guarantee certain content or individuals stream access. A configuration entry is created for each individual or organization that requires RealAudio Server stream.

During the initial stages of installation you will probably be making many changes to the server.cfg file. It is possible to force the server to re-load this file by delivering a HUP signal to the Server to force it to re-examine its configuration:

```
kill -HUP <processId>
```

where <processId> is the process id of the RealAudio Server. If you do not know the process id, check the pid file or run ps to obtain it. The exact parameters for ps depend upon the version of UNIX you are using.

Before the Web server will handle RealAudio metafiles properly, you must configure it to recognize them as the following MIME:

```
audio/x-pn-realaudio (files with a RA or RAM file extension)
audio/x-pn-realaudio-plugin (files with a RPM file extension)
```

The MIME type is communicated in the HTML header sent to the user's Web browser. It tells the Web browser to activate the RealAudio Player on its computer. If you do not configure the MIME type correctly, the user's Web browser will try to download the content of the RealAudio file rather than activate the RealAudio Player. If this happens the user will need to empty the cache on their Web browser.

After I installed the server I manually started it by first changing directories into the top level directory of the RealAudio Server and then typing:

```
bin/pnserver server.cfg
```

Once tested you will want to start it automatically. The instructions for doing this are quite different depending upon the operating system. Interestingly, it is far more cumbersome to start it from the NT side than from the UNIX side where you merely add the command to the boot-time scripts of your UNIX system. Since the boot-time scripts generally reside in files or directories beneath the /etc subdirectory you'll need the system administrator to perform this function. RealAudio server, in other words, is not something you can sneak into your operating environment.

Stopping RealAudio is easy as well. On the NT side you merely click on the Stop button in the Services Control Panel. Under UNIX if you know the process id, use the following procedure, while logged on with the same user id as the Server (or as super-user):

```
kill <processid>
```

If you don't know the process id you can enter the command: kill cat logs/pnserver.pid from the pnserver directory.

To verify that the RealAudio Server is stopped, use the appropriate ps command for your system.

Performance Issues

The Internet is not an error-free medium: there are a number of factors that can interfere with the quality of the audio being delivered to your users. Audio packets can be lost during delivery through the Internet if they hit slow routers, or if the network is especially busy. Recurrent problems may indicate that you need to modify your connection to your Internet service provider.

To monitor audio quality, you should occasionally use the RealAudio Player to make an Internet connection to the links on your Web page. When the connection is made, open the Statistics window for the RealAudio Player to monitor the percentage of packet loss that is occurring. If the audio quality is poor, it is likely that your users are experiencing the same.

Since RealAudio files use 10 to 19 kbps while playing, you should first check the configuration file for the number of connections to ensure that your Internet connection can handle the peak throughput; refer to Maximum Audio Connections for more details.

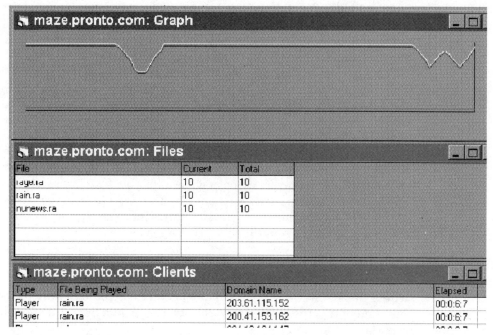

Figure 5-19. The graphical System Manager.

If you determine that there is a high packet loss level, your first step will be to consult your Internet provider. You may need a faster Internet connection or there may be other problems with your Internet service.

The RealAudio System manager provides continuously updated information about current connections to the RealAudio Server. There is a Windows-based System Manager and a UNIX command line System Manager. The System Manager can be opened from any computer that has a network connection to the RealAudio Server.

The graphical interface System Manager is run from Windows 95 or NT and can monitor a Server running on any platform. The System Manager contains three windows where you can view clients currently connected, files being played, and a graphical interpretation of all connections for the past two minutes as shown in figure 5-19. This highly versatile interface allows you to choose how you would like connection information interpreted and displayed.

For example, you may wish leave the System Manager open on a corner of your screen with just the Player connections shown as a graph, allowing you to get a visual sense of the connection patterns on your Web site. Your System Manager will be located in the c:\pnserver\bin\win_mon directory if you are running your Server on a Windows NT machine and in the pnserver/bin/win_mon directory if you are running your Server on a UNIX platform. Copy all the files from your System Manager directory to a temporary folder on the Windows machine which you want to act as the System Manager.

The RealAudio Command Line System Manager is used from a UNIX machine. It can monitor a Server running on a Windows or UNIX platform. Information provided by the System Manager includes number and status of Player connections, System Manager connections, Unknown connections, which are connections that are currently being negotiated with the Server, and Total connections, which includes all of these. This information can then be used to monitor activity on the RealAudio Server on a regular basis.

The System Manager runs in two modes: interactive and non-interactive. When the System Manager is in the non-interactive mode, information is automatically appended to STDOUT every 5 minutes, unless that time span is modified by the -l command. The System Manager will accept commands from the command line; however, it does not prompt you. The interactive mode is started with the -i command, which enables the System Manager to print prompts and accept commands from the command line. The System Manager resides in the bin directory. From the bin directory type

```
monitor [options] <host>[:port]
```

where <host> is the DNS hostname of the RealAudio Server you wish to monitor, and port is the TCP port which the RealAudio Server uses to accept clients and the options can be:

```
h/? to prints a list of commands.
c to do a quick Server check and then exit.
i to start the  interactive System Manager mode.
l <update frequency>  to quote a time, in seconds, between each log update.
k to d reverse DNS lookups.
p <password> to specify a password to use.
v  to print version information and exit.
```

Encoding Audio

You may download the RealAudio encoder for free from http://www.realaudio.com/products/encoder.html. The RealAudio Encoder compresses audio into the RealAudio format and enables users to create RealAudio content by compressing digital audio files in common formats and converting them to RealAudio format.

RealAudio files created with the Encoder are delivered over the Internet with the RealAudio Server. The RealAudio Player can play RealAudio files delivered by the Server over connections of 14.4 kbps or better and RealAudio files that have been pseudo-streamed from Web servers.

As this chapter was written the RealAudio converter (for Windows 95 the size was about 800 K) was available for: RealAudio Encoder 3.0 for Windows 95, NT; RealAudio Encoder 2.0+ for Windows 95/NT, PowerPC, Linux, Solaris

RealAudio Encoder 2.0 for Mac 68K, and other UNIX platforms.

Figure 5-20 shows how the RealAudio Encoder works. On the left side you enter the information about the source file. The encoder's browse function lets you look for WAV files. WAV files already compressed using another codec will not work, however, so be sure that you keep your WAV files in a decompressed mode if you're going to use them in a RealAudio encoding process.

Since every file on my hard disk was already compressed I went searching and found some decompressed Windows files. The one I choose was a Jungle noise. Note the description information which I entered for the sound clip. The RealAudio Encoder automatically detects the sampling rate, format and resolution of a source file and displays them in the Format box. If the Encoder cannot recognize these attributes, a dialog box appears where you can specify the information. When you have selected the file to encode, a graphical representation of the file appears below the Source pane and the length of the clip is displayed. You can choose not to display the Audio Signal by clearing Display Audio Signal from the Options menu.

When I first started experimenting with RealAudio I was driven crazy by the fact that RealAudio files are not usually saved to the end-user's disk. I wanted to demonstrate the use of this product to a client on my own PC and had a devil of a time trying to locate a RealAudio sound clip that I could save to my own

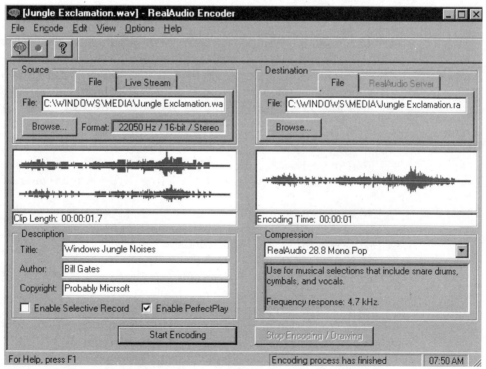

Figure 5-20. The RealAudio Encoder.

disk. This is because the Encoder allows the content developer to decide whether or not to allow the RealAudio Player Plus users to save the RealAudio signal to disk. To do so requires the content developer to select Enable Selective Record before the Encoding process.

Once I selected a file I merely clicked on the Encode button and let the encoder do its stuff. The Options menu permits you to select whether or not you will hear a playback while encoding as well as lets you decide whether you want to see an audio signal.

The RealAudio Encoder converts WAV, AU, and PCM files into the RealAudio format. The original source files may be recorded at a variety of sampling rates. To generate RealAudio files, start with a file in one of the following formats:

WAV: 8 kHz, 11 kHz, 22 kHz, 44 kHz in 8- or 16-bit format, monophonic
AU: 8 kHz, 22 kHz, 44 kHz, monophonic
PCM: 8 kHz, 11 kHz, 22 kHz, 44 kHz in 8- or 16-bit format, monophonic

If your audio is in a format not supported by the RealAudio Encoder, you can convert it using a variety of sound editing tools available for the Windows platform to convert the file to a supported format.

There are actually two versions of the Encoder for Windows: a free Encoder available for download from Progressive Networks Web site and a Live Encoder that is included when you purchase RealAudio Server. You can encode a static file using either Encoder. Only the RealAudio Encoder included with RealAudio Server can deliver live content for broadcasting live events.

If you want to allow RealAudio Player Plus users with 14.4 kbps modems to experience RealAudio files encoded for a higher bandwidth by partially downloading audio data before beginning playback, select Enable PerfectPlay.

RealAudio Live

The RealAudio Encoder included with RealAudio Server can deliver live content for broadcasting live events. To deliver live content, you need:

- A live audio source
- A computer running a RealAudio Encoder
- A server running a RealAudio Server

To encode and broadcast live content:

1. Click the Live Stream tab in the Source frame.
2. In the Description pane, enter the Title, Author, and Copyright information for your RealAudio output. These fields are optional.
3. If you want to allow RealAudio Player Plus users to save your RealAudio signal to disk, select Enable Selective Record.
4. In the Destination pane, click the RealAudio Server tab.

5. In the Host box, type the domain name or the IP address of the RealAudio Server computer.
6. In the Port box, type the port number from the PnaPort configuration setting in the RealAudio Server configuration file.
7. In the File Name box, type a name for the live clip being encoded. This is the filename part of the URL that goes in the metafile (RAM) used to access the live broadcast.
8. In the Password box, type the password from the Encoder Password configuration setting in the RealAudio Server configuration file.
9. In the Compression pane, select the appropriate compression type.
10. Click on the Start Encoding button to begin encoding the input and sending the data to the specified RealAudio Server.

Bandwidth Negotiation

File organization is the key to bandwidth negotiation. A single link on a Web page, which references a directory with three RealAudio files encoded, may use different algorithms. The following steps explain how the RealAudio Player and RealAudio Server determine which file to play based on bandwidth.

1. The user clicks a link to a RealAudio metafile on a Web page.
2. The Web server returns the metafile to the Web browser and based on the RAM file extension, sets the MIME type of the metafile to audio/x-pn-realaudio.
3. The Web browser looks up the MIME type of the metafile, starts RealAudio Player as a helper application, and passes it to the metafile.
4. RealAudio Player reads the first URL from the metafile and requests it from RealAudio Server. Based on its preference settings, RealAudio Player also sends a list of RealAudio compression types it supports.
5. RealAudio Server checks the directory specified by the URL and begins streaming the highest bandwidth file supported by RealAudio Player.
6. The name of the RealAudio file specified in the URL in the metafile is actually a directory on the RealAudio Server computer with the RA filename extension. Within that directory are the individual files for each format.

The raconv utility helps you arrange your files into the organization required for bandwidth negotiation by generating the directory with the RA extension and placing the appropriately renamed files in that directory. The utility uses information in the RealAudio file to determine how to rename the file. Because the utility renames files, keep a back-up of your original files until you are sure that the process was successful.

RealAudio Service Providers

If you don't want to set up your own server or your service provider doesn't want to install RealAudio for you then the following list of RealAudio enabled service providers will be of help to you:

Internet Direct	602-222-2888	sales@direct.net
XS Media	602-994-2202	sales@xsmedia.com
ConXioN	408-291-0300	inquiry@conxion.com
CTS Network	619-637-3600	info@cts.com
Dev-Com	800-241-7066	sales@dev-com.com
Earthlink Network	800-876-3151	sales@earthlink.net
Rocky Mountain	800-900-7644 x2235	sales@rmi.net
Global Datalink	407-841-3690	admin@gdi.net
Access America	770-667-7200	sales@america.net
Synet, Inc.	708-271-1500	mikew@synet.net
Digital Marketing	301-249-6501	og@digimark.net
Continuum Internet	718-788-8013	info@cipsinc.com
Digital Telemedia	212-255-0827	jgardner@dti.net
Interactive 8	212-807-1762	info@interactive8.com
CDS Internet	541-773-9600	info@cdsnet.net
Teleport Internet	503-223-0076	support@teleport.com
Intelecom Data	401-885-4243	info@ids.net
digitalNation	703-642-2800	sales@dn.netWolfe
CompuTech	509-624-6798	info@iea.net
Internet Canada	416-363-8518	vpa@ican.net

Chapter 6

Using VDOLive

The use of video on the Internet represents a broad, new market category which is called desktop video broadcasting. VDOnet's product strategy reflects the view that this market is made up of two types of users: current users of video that want to find new ways to deliver existing video and to create new video for the Internet; and individuals or small organizations that want to use this new and powerful medium to communicate with customers, friends, family, and associates. Examples of how video can enhance Internet communications include: Internet marketing can be enhanced with promotional videos such as movie previews or travelogs; individuals or small companies can produce personal video classified ads or business cards for the Internet; or corporations can add executive presentations, interactive product and service demonstrations, and training videos to their Web sites.

Where Chapter 5 gave you an introduction into audio webcasting using RealAudio as a guide, this chapter will delve into the vagaries of audio-video webcasting using, as an example, a product called VDOLive.

First, An Example

Before we start, I'd like to spend a few moments demonstrating just how a typical webcast looks from an end-user's perspective. This mini-tour uses both RealAudio, which we learned about in the last chapter, and VDOLive, which we are going to learn about in this chapter. As we run through this example notice the way in which Microsoft, the host of the webcast event, structured their pages so that you can follow their well thought out template.

Back in October of 1996, Microsoft held their Site Developer's Conference in San Jose, California. Because I couldn't attend I decided to attend the "simul-

142   Chapter Six

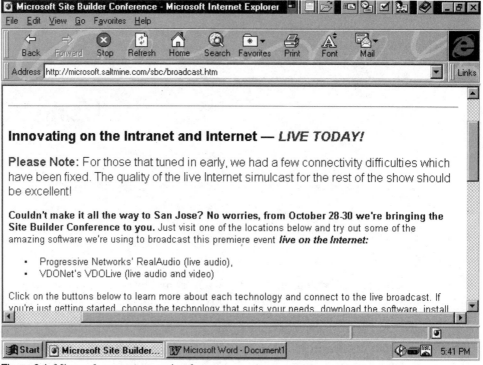

Figure 6-1. Microsoft announces a simulcast.

cast" instead. A simulcast, in case you couldn't figure it out, is the simultaneous transmission of a "live" event on the computer.

In figures 6-1 and 6-2 Microsoft announces the simulcast — well in advance of the event. Notice that it gave viewers several choices: they could either hear it using RealAudio or see and hear it using VDOLive. They also advised on-line attendees that they should download the plug-ins necessary to attend the event.

Microsoft provides a table that makes it quite plain what is required to attend the event. Do you want audio only? Then download RealAudio. Have a PowerMac? Then download VDOLive.

For this event, Microsoft maintains the plug-in for RealAudio ActiveX on its own server as shown in figure 6-3. If you've read chapter 5, you'll recognize the

Technology	Broadcast Type	Operating Systems	Minimum Connectivity Requirements
VDOLive	Video/Audio	Win95,WinNT,Win3.1,PowerMac	14.4 kbps
Real Audio	Audio	Win95,WinNT,Win3.1,Mac,Unix	14.4 kbps

Figure 6-2. Giving the end-user webcasting choices.

Using VDOLive 143

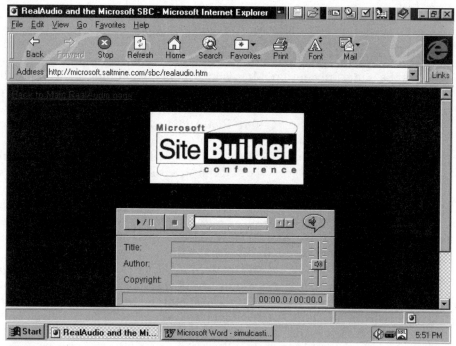

Figure 6-3. The RealAudio Player.

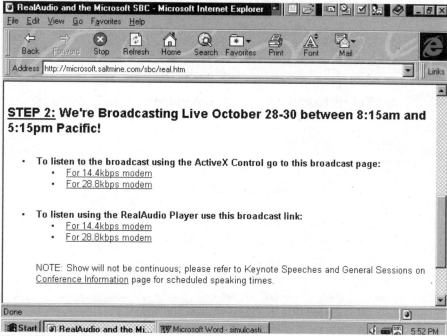

Figure 6-4. Choosing between ActiveX or not ActiveX.

RealAudio player.

In figure 6-4 Microsoft continues to cover all bases. The site gives you a choice between 14.4 and 28.8 kbps. Microsoft is well aware that there are lots of folks with less than optimal communications equipment. By providing a 14.4 kbps audio only option, Microsoft widened its audience dramatically. The company is also well aware that many people have already downloaded the RealAudio plug-in that doesn't use ActiveX, so rather than exclude them from the conference, the regular RealAudio plug-in was provided along with the ActiveX version.

Microsoft provides the same options with VDOLive, as shown in figure 6-5. If you decided that you wanted the VDOLive option, the Microsoft screen takes you directly to the VDO site, as shown in figure 6-6.

It's at this point that the prospective attendee might actually get lost. The VDO site has lots of goodies — an Internet phone, the VDOLive server along with the VDOLive viewer. My advice to you is to point your end-users directly to the plug-in download.

When we finally get to the download, we're given a choice of platforms as shown in figure 6-7. Note that the PowerMac is less than half the size of the Windows 95 plug-in, a true testament to the multimedia capability of the Macintosh platform.

Our first taste of VDOLive is impressive as shown in figure 6-8. We click the old-fashioned TV set and, voila, we're in business as shown in figure 6-9. The

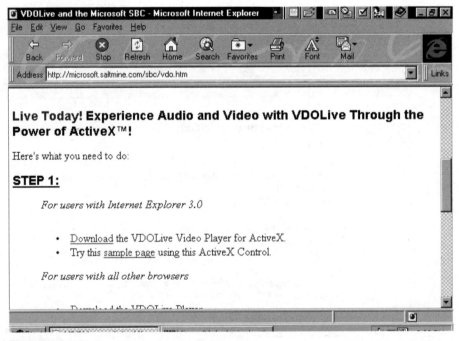

Figure 6-5. VDOLive options.

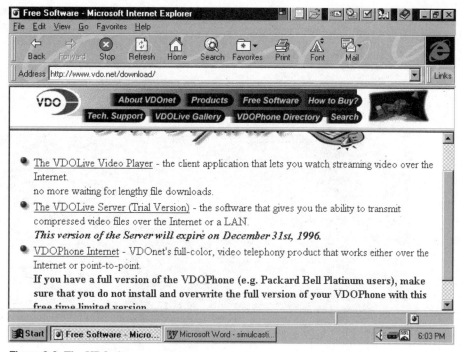

Figure 6-6. The VDO site.

Select a platform to download		
Platform	File Name	File Size
Windows 95	vdol3220.exe	727K
Windows NT	vdol3220.exe	727K
Windows 3.1x	vdol1620.exe	478K
Power Macintosh	vdolmac.hqx	294K

Figure 6-7. VDOLive choice of platforms.

sound was as good as RealAudio but, note, that the image is dependent on a couple of things:

• how fast your connection is
• the size of your monitor
• the resolution of your monitor

I watched the simulcast on my laptop, which is obviously small. While I had no trouble seeing and hearing the speakers, I did have some trouble viewing

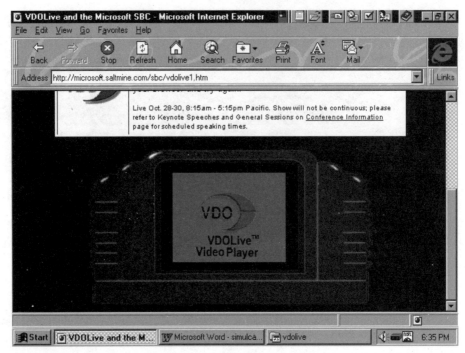

Figure 6-8. Our first view of VDOLive.

the slide presentations even though I zoomed in as much as I could, as shown in figure 6-10. Because I was attending the conference using my laptop's 14.4 modem, although I saw the speaker very well, his movements were rather jerky. I did have much better results on my 17 inch, high-res monitor using a 28.8 modem. I'm sure that an ISDN connection would have been superb.

Aside from Microsoft, VDOLive is already in use by nearly 150 Web sites, including major news and information companies, technology companies and

Figure 6-9. The VDOLive view of the speaker.

Internet service providers.

The Public Broadcasting Service (PBS) is using the technology to bring PBS

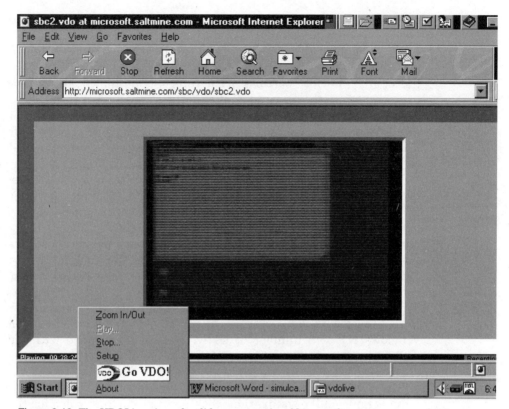

Figure 6-10. The VDOLive view of a slide presentation. Not exactly easy to see on a laptop.

video programming to the Internet, while CBS News Up-to-the-Minute has been broadcasting VDOLive-enabled reports from its Web site since December, 1995. The technology is also being used by Grolier Interactive, Preview Vacations, and many others to enhance their Web sites.

The VDOnet technology has also been used in live Internet broadcasts of key presentations at the October, 1995, Internet World conference sponsored by Mecklermedia Corp. The technology was also used to broadcast highlights of the NAB (National Association of Broadcasters) '96 show and of major speeches being delivered in conjunction with the American Israel Public Affairs Committee's Annual Policy Conference to a worldwide Internet audience.

The VDOnet Technology

VDOnet represents a whole new breed of webcasting over the Internet. While Mbone might be fine for some folks, the majority of those who want to webcast over the Internet have no desire to build their environment from the ground up. VDOnet's products do it all for you.

VDOnet's technology is specifically optimized for the Internet since it adjusts to the available bandwidth on-the-fly. This is called "bandwidth scalability" which is important because video being transmitted over the Internet needs to be able to accommodate any connection, at any time.

To accomplish this, VDOnet uses two core technologies. The first is a scalable compression algorithm that can compress video small enough to run over the small bandwidth portions of the Internet but allows the quality of the video to increase with the size and quality of the connection at the other end. The second core technology is a set of communications protocol which maintains the integrity of the video as it makes its way through what some refer to as the "bumpy roads" of the Internet. When combined, you get motion video that can be used by virtually anyone on the Internet, regardless of their connection.

There are several VDOLive products. The VDOLive Video Server enables professionals to publish video over any TCP/IP-compliant network (such as the Internet or a corporate network). It allows the capture, compression, and storage of video and audio to provide real-time playback. It needs to store only one copy of each video, which it can then play back at variable speeds, ranging from dial-up modem through T-1 connection speeds, maximizing the quality of the video for each connection. The VDOLive Video Server works with any HTTP server to easily add video or audio to any Web site. The VDOLive Video Server comes with built-in editing and compression tools which run on a Windows 95 PC equipped with video capture capability. The VDOLive Video Server runs on Windows NT or a number of UNIX platforms equipped with video capture capability. It can be configured for delivery of over 100 simultaneous video streams.

The VDOLive Personal Server brings video and audio broadcasting to individuals and small organizations looking at publishing video for their personal communication needs. The personal server can be configured for delivery of two simultaneous video streams, handles two-minute video clips, and serve up to 28.8 kbps modem connections. It can run on a Window NT personal computer platform and is easily upgraded to the VDOLive Video Server. VDOLive Video Servers are now available at prices of less than $100 per video stream (for more than 100 streams). The VDOLive Personal Server is available at no charge by downloading it from http://www.vdo.net.

Future versions of its product line will include multicast server capabilities which will enable simultaneous broadcast of scheduled events and two-way Internet video communications — which will allow video telephony over the Internet.

VDOnet Corporation has also launched the VDOCast Center for Multicasting. The purpose of the VDOCast Center is to bring together different parties such as content providers, Internet service providers, advertisers, and technology companies united by the common goal of making multicasting a standard part of doing business on the Internet. NBC Desktop Video, Cisco Systems Inc., and PBS (Public Broadcasting Service) are already working with VDOnet to make video programming widely and easily available on the Internet.

The VDOCast Center for Multicasting will be based in Palo Alto, California with a second targeted for New York. The Center will be responsible for defining a carefully phased roadmap and for building technology, media, and other corporate partnerships for enabling multicasting on the 'Net.

The fundamental philosophy underlying VDOCast technology is that it is not practical to build a whole new Internet infrastructure to enable multicasting. Therefore, the technology at the core of the VDOCast Center is a new technology from VDOnet which, simply put, goes from the video source to the "POP" (point of presence on the Net) — while protecting the quality of the video — and then distributes the video directly to the user.

How Does VDOLive Work?

VDOnet (http://www.vdo.net) really livened up the Web with the introduction of its VDOLive server and toolset. VDOLive technology enables you to incorporate video and audio in Internet Web sites and efficiently delivers video over a variable bandwidth computer network, such as the Internet, using scalable compression algorithms using a TCP/IP-based scalable transmission protocol. VDOLive also offers software only direct delivery of video from the Web site to the user's screen, without downloading. VDOLive works in much the same way as RealAudio:

- Capture and compress your video and audio data using VDOLive Tools.
- Store on the VDOLive Server computer.
- Create an HTML link from your Web page to the video file.
- Viewers use the VDOLive Video Player to request and play your video files.

The VDOLive Server sends compressed data over a TCP/IP connection and the VDOLive Video Player decodes and displays the video. The TCP/IP network is usually the Internet, but could also be a LAN, intranet or any other TCP/IP network.

Each time a VDOLive Video Player, also called a "client," connects to a VDOLive Server to request video, the Server determines the bandwidth available in that particular connection. For as long as the client remains connected the VDOLive Server performs "dynamic scaling."

Compression of video and audio data is necessary in order to minimize the bandwidth required to efficiently transmit this data. The better the compression, the faster the data can travel over narrower lines.

The VDOLive compression algorithms are highly efficient. They enable the transmission of higher quality video than other compression schemes at any given bandwidth: even as low as 14.4 kilobits per second (kbps). VDOLive compression works together with the VDOLive Server's scalability to adjust the rate of transmission to the bandwidth available on the receiving end, while preserving the best possible balance of motion and resolution for the connection.

150   Chapter Six

The VDOLive Player

The VDOLive video player for Windows 95 (vdol32b2.exe) has the following requirements: 80486, 66 MHz or higher; 8 MB of RAM or more; 14.4 kbps modem or faster connection and a sound card.

It is easily downloadable from the vdo.net site and can be automatically activated from a Web page, or the end-user can open the player and have it make a "call" to a video clip as shown in figure 6-11. Notice the "what's playing" button on the player which automatically links you to a page on the VDO.net site.

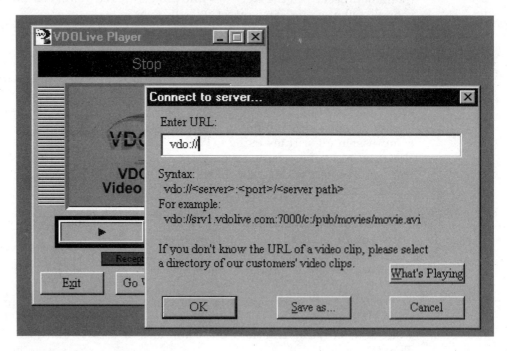

Figure 6-11. The VDOLive player.

The VDOLive Server

The Token File includes all the parameters that define how the Server and Tools work. Once it is installed properly, the Server and Tools read necessary information from the Token File. If the Server or Tools cannot find the Token File, they operate based on default values defined for a Personal Server and Tools.

On the UNIX platform, the Token File is installed in the same directory as the VDOLive Video Server files (the default is /usr/local/vdosrv). On the Windows NT platform the default location is C:\WINNT35\SYSTEM32. I have a UNIX server so the rest of the discussion is UNIX-oriented, although the steps you take are pretty similar to what you would do if your server were NT.

The VDOLive Token File, like the RealAudio server.cfg file, contains several parameters that need to be specified for the video server to be properly configured. These include: the audio codec which defines whether VDOWave I or II is available for use; maximum playback and compression time per clip; expiration date of server and tools; host name or IP address of the computer on which the VDOLive Video Server runs; organization or company name; maximum allowed number of concurrent users; maximum allowed throughput per channel.

If you do not have a Token File or have not installed the Token File properly, your VDOLive Video Server and Tools will run as a Personal Server and Tools. This means the Server and Tools will function according to limited default values.

The Personal Server and Tools are capable of compressing up to one minute of video and/or audio data at a maximum video encoding rate of 128 kbps using any of the four compression modes included with the VDOWave II audio codec. It is capable of serving up to two clients at the same time for clips up to one minute long at a maximum transmission speed of 128 kbps per client (the Personal Server does have an expiration date. The one I downloaded was set to expire on 12/31/96).

The VDOLive Video Server for UNIX is available for the following systems. The required processor is listed in parentheses:

Free BSD : version 2.05 and above (80x86)
SGI Irix : version 5.3 and above (MIPS)
Linux : 1.2.13, both a.out and elf versions (80x86)
SunOS : version 4.13 and above (SPARC)
Solaris : version 2.4 and above (SPARC)
AIX : version 4.1 and above (RS 6000)
BSDI : version 2.1 and above (80x86)
DEC : OSF1 (Alpha)

The VDOLive Video Server is also available for Microsoft Windows NT and runs as a Service of Windows NT. The VDOLive Video Server is compatible with both Server and Workstation versions of Windows NT.

VDOLive Video Server and Tools run on different operating systems but are packaged together. Therefore, you must first run a self-extracting executable under Windows NT or Windows 95, then copy the Server installation file to UNIX. Nothing in the documentation tells you what to do should you not have a Windows PC available. The Windows pre-installation does provide you with the self-extracting installation file appropriate for your system. For example, Free BSD uses the vdosrv.fbsd executable and SGI Irix uses the vdosrv.irix executable.

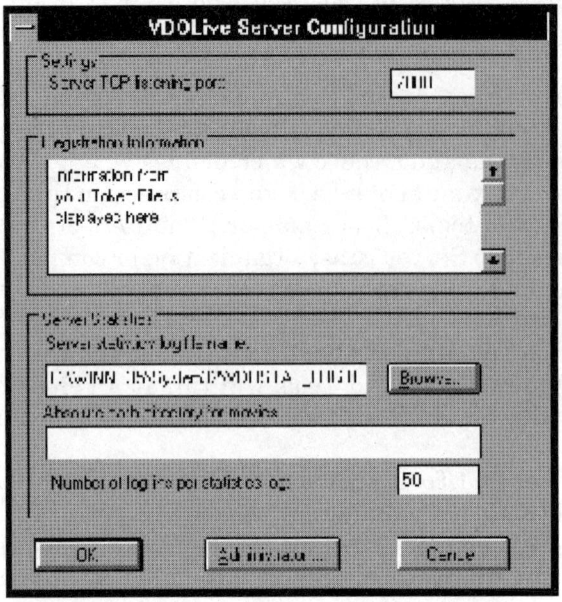

Figure 6-12. Windows server configuration window.

You can only install the VDOLive Video Server if you have super-user privileges on the UNIX computer which means that either you must be the system administrator or have permission from one. Once the executable has been FTP'd and permissions set to executable using the chmod +x filename command, you login as root and type the appropriate file name at a command prompt. On-screen instructions pretty much take you the rest of the way, although the Windows version is far simpler to read as shown in figure 6-12.

After installation, copy the modified Token File to the installation directory and then perform an initial test of the VDOLive Video Server by typing:

```
/usr/local/vdosrv
if you've installed the server in the /usr/local directory
```

This command can be added to the system initialization file so that the VDOLive Video Server starts up automatically each time you boot the computer or it can be started manually each day by typing the command above. Default settings have been defined for all functions and it's probably best to leave them as is for the first go-round. Once you're a bit more experienced you can fine-tune them.

The Video Server Log

Each connection to your VDOLive Video Server is registered and logged to this

Field Name	User	IP Address	Company	email
User Info	John White	201.177.101.64	A.S.E.	jwhite@ase.com
User Info	Tina C.	212.555.121.20	R.V.A.	tinac@rva.com

Time	Bytes	Login time	Login date	kbps
6	7733.2	17:02:36	01/25/1996	13
11	482.25	17:03:11	01/25/1996	20

#users	Video File Name	End Status
1	c:/pub/movies/clip1.avi	Normal
2	h:/pub/vdolive/clip7.avi	User Stop

Figure 6-13. VDOLive server information.

file, unless you set the Server to "do not log." The data recorded here can be analyzed and used for billing, marketing and other business purposes. One way to perform analyses such as these is to load the file into a spreadsheet or database program as shown in figure 6-13.

The log file provides valuable data such as how many users have requested video from your server at different times of day; how many times a particular clip has been played and the bandwidth obtained by each user.

Using VDOLive Tools

The VDOLive Tools include a capture tool, VDO Capture, and a compression tool, VDO Clip. The VDOLive Tools run on Windows 95 and Windows NT. These tools can be used in conjunction with other video capture, editing and compression tools.

VDO Capture software converts analog video, such as VHS or Beta SP magnetic tapes, and from analog audio, to digital format. The conversion process requires use of a video capture card (e.g. Miro, VideoLogic, Creative Labs, Intel) together with VDO Capture, and a sound card if audio is to be captured as well. VDO Capture is not an editing tool.

VDO Clip edits and compresses previously captured, uncompressed video and audio. Finally it will encode this data using VDOLive technology. The compressed files, saved in AVI format, are ready for transmission by the VDOLive Video Server over any TCP/IP network.

The capture card must support the following operations in order to work with VDO: capture color depth of 16 bits per pixel (RGB 555) or 24 bits per pixel (RGB 888); 8-bit color is supported, but not recommended for use; 32-bit color is not supported; to capture motion video, your capture card must be able to support a capture rate of 15 frames per second (fps); to capture video for use in flip mode, a capture rate of two frames per second is sufficient; capture of raw (uncompressed) video or capture and compression to a Microsoft Video for Windows compatible format.

VDO Capture: Capturing video

Set aside disk space before beginning capture to achieve a higher number of successfully captured frames than without pre-allocation of disk space. If your data exceeds the space you allocated, the file will enlarge automatically as necessary, however, the advantage of pre-allocation is lost when this happens. Therefore, you may want to allocate about 20% more space than you expect to need.

Calculate the amount of disk space you should allocate as follows:

```
Total Bytes Required =
Bytes required for video + Bytes required for audio,
```

where:

```
[width of frame (pixels) * height of frame (pixels) * bits per pixel]
divided by 8 = bytes per frame

# of bytes per frame* # of frames per second * length of planned cap-
ture (seconds) = Bytes for video

16 kb per second of audio = Bytes for audio
```

Here's a sample calculation:

Image Size: 160*120
Color: 24 bits per pixel
Rate: 15 frames per second
Total capture: 30 seconds
160 pixels wide * 120 pixels high = 19200 pixels per frame
19200 pixels per frame *24 bits per pixel=460800 bits per frame
460800 bits per frame divided by 8=57600 bytes per frame
57600 bytes per frame * 15 frames per second = 864000 bytes per second
864000 bytes per second * 30 seconds of video = 25920000 bytes required for video (=25312.5 KB or 24.72 MB)
Audio: 16 kb per second * 30 seconds = 480 kb
Total Disk Space Required: 25312.5+480=25792.5 kb (25.19 MB)

   Both space and file name must be set (from the File menu) as shown in figure 6-14. Other parameters are:

• Capture Frame Rate. This is the number of frames per second (fps) at which video is captured. Capture at 10-18 fps for best results.
• Capture Time Limit. Capture is timed in seconds.
• Capture Audio. Check this box to capture audio together with video. Uncheck

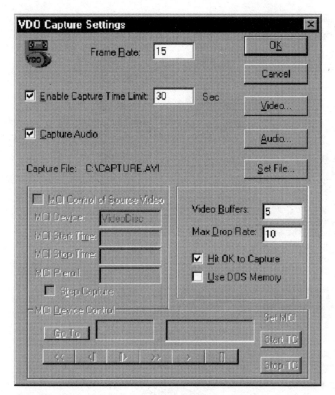

Figure 6-14. VDOLive capture settings dialog box.

to capture video only.
- Video Format.
- Audio Format.
- MCI Control of Source Video.

Supported capture formats are 16-bit and 24-bit color as shown in figure 6-15. Changing the audio format is just as easy as shown in figure 6-16.

In the Options/Video Source menu, make sure the setting corresponds to the type of connection between your capture card and your video deck. If you don't see a picture in the capture program's viewport, your settings are probably wrong.

In the Options/Video menu select the default setting which is 160 x 120 (frame size) and 24-bit color. In the Options/Audio menu the default setting is 8 kHz, 16-bit mono. These settings are required by the VDO compressor program, which is used right after the video is captured.

Finally, select Capture Video from the Capture menu. Once stopped, the captured file will be saved to your hard drive.

Although the majority of VDOLive content developers will not be professional broadcasters, VDOnet still provides a professional level interface. If you

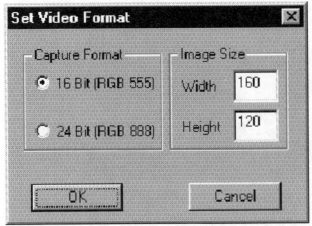

Figure 6-15. Capture settings: set video format.

Figure 6-16. Changing the audio format.

are working with professional level video equipment, you may wish to use this convenient and precise method of controlling source video. You must have a physical connection between your video source hardware and your computer as well as the appropriate MCI device driver installed. MCI related options in VDO Capture is disabled in the menu if you do not have the required configuration.

VDO Clip: The compression tool

You will use the compression tool with the media you just captured or an AVI or WAV file you're using from elsewhere. The clip is now available for editing, compressing and saving. Files that are not multimedia, such as bitmaps, cannot be opened in VDO Clip using the File|Open command. This type of data can be pasted in from other applications and will be displayed in the main window of VDO Clip.

Editing, for the purposes of work using VDO Clip, means manipulating the order of the information in an audio or video stream as shown in figure 6-17. The editing functions are listed under the Edit menu of VDO Clip and include Cut, Copy, Paste and Delete. Use these functions to rearrange the sequence of video frames, to remove portions of the data in a stream or to add data to a stream. Select the data to be edited in order to enable the editing functions; selecting, for the purposes of editing in VDO Clip, means highlighting using a selecting function.

To edit video or audio data:

1. Select (highlight) the video frames or the portion of the audio stream you want to edit.
2. Apply any of the standard editing functions from the Edit menu. These functions (Cut, Copy, Paste and Delete) remain disabled until data has been selected.

Along with editing media, VDO Clip has a host of capabilities including: merging audio and video files and converting audio from an unsupported format. However, its main role is to compress the video.

Compression is the process in which you take video and or audio data and encode it by applying compression algorithms to the data. This allows your encoded data to travel quickly, and with minimal loss, over the relatively narrow data lines that make up much of the Internet. VDOLive Tools compression

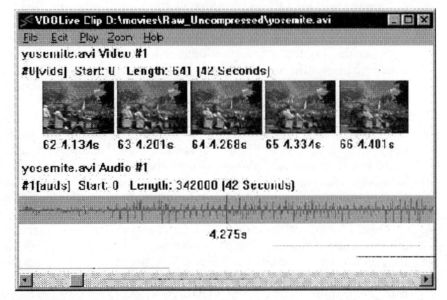

Figure 6-17. Manipulating the order of the information in an audio/video clip.

uses VDOnet's VDOWave algorithms; this algorithm, and other compression algorithms, are also called "codecs" (coder / decoder).

The compression mode defines the speed of the motion in your compressed video. VDOnet provides several modes:

1. **Movie**: fastest motion of all the modes. This is the correct mode for video.
2. **Flip**: slower motion than movie. This is another option for video.
3. **Storybook**: no motion; still images change at pre-defined rate. This is the mode to use for graphics.

Consider the length of time for which you expect to use your files when choosing a compression mode. If your content is going to be used for a long period of time, consider preparing an archive copy. This way, if your audience changes over time, you can prepare new files from the archive copy at different rates and in different modes. If your content changes frequently, use the mode and rate best suited to your current audience since there are unlikely to be great changes in the types of users viewing your content over a short period of time. Save disk space by preparing only the files you can actually use.

The encoding rate defines the maximum amount of information (video data) which is included in the compressed file. This is expressed in kilobits per second (kbps), which refer to the bandwidth necessary to transmit the information. Audio is compressed and transmitted at a relatively constant rate of 6 kbps. If the user's connection has sufficient bandwidth, he will receive all the information included in a file; if not, he will receive as much information as his connection allows.

Viewers will be able to see video at the rate allowed by their bandwidth of their connection; this will sometimes be lower than the maximum encoding rate you set. If this happens, the VDOLive Video Server will scale (in this case, decrease the amount of information it sends to the user) to the user's available bandwidth. Should more bandwidth become available to the user during the connection, the Server scales (now increases the amount of data being sent to the user) accordingly.

At higher encoding rates, more information per frame can be included in the compressed data. Therefore, one way to achieve good results with complex images (such as fast motion) or large (over 160*120 pixels) image sizes is to compress at a relatively high encoding rate. Bear in mind, though, that in order to benefit from these high-quality video clips, your VDOLive Video Server must be able to serve them at a high bandwidth per client allowance, and your users must have sufficient bandwidth to receive the clips at a relatively high speed.

To achieve smooth motion, a high percentage of frames from the captured (or other source) video must be preserved in compression. Higher encoding rates include a greater number of frames. The higher the video encoding rate, the longer it takes to compress the data. Files compressed at a high video encoding rate mean more data for the VDOLive Video Server to read and serve. The higher the video encoding rate, the larger the resulting file.

The VDOLive Video Server gives priority to audio data, then scales video data to the bandwidth available in a particular connection, up to the maximum of the encoding rate at which the file was compressed. Be sure to check with the Administrator of your VDOLive Video Server to see that the Server is configured to transmit at a rate compatible with your encoding rate. Your VDOLive Video Server must also be configured to serve individual client connections at a rate compatible with your encoding rate. If you compress a movie at 256 kbps, for instance, but your VDOLive Video Server is limited to serving clients at a maximum of 64 kbps per connection, your users will not receive the full benefit of your high-compression rate files.

VDOLive Movies provide full motion video to users. These movies are created from high-quality captured video and audio data, compressed at higher video encoding rates than other VDOLive videos and bring high-quality color and motion video to your users.

Movie Mode works best when your viewers are Internet users with connections of 28.8 kbps or faster, or when the movies are going to be played over a LAN or Intranet, when each user generally has a relatively high bandwidth connection.

Figure 6-18 shows VDO Clip compression options while figure 6-19 shows the interface which enables you to configure the encoding rate and mode (i.e. movie, flip, etc.).

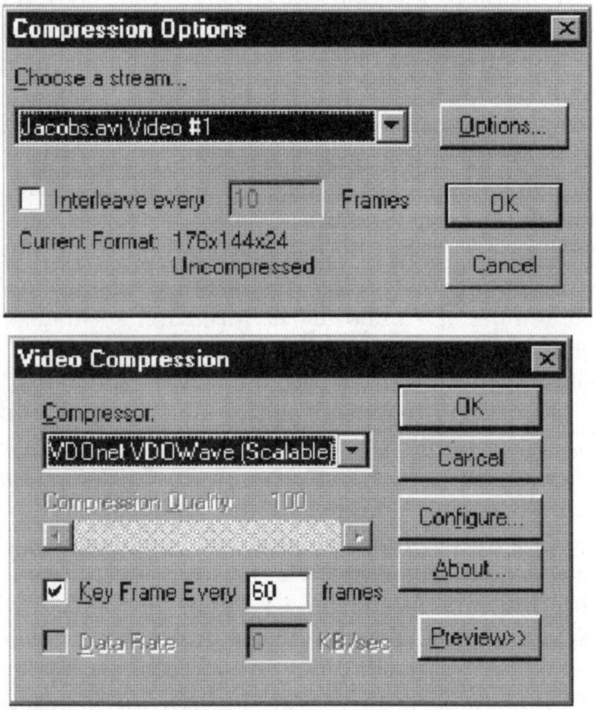

Figure 6-18. VDO compression.

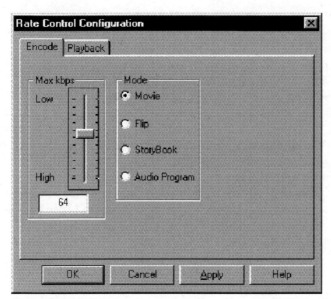

Figure 6-19. VDO clip rate control configuration. Movie Mode selected.

Where movies are a great vehicle for those with fast Internet connections, alas, most of us are using connections no greater than 28.8 kbps. Flip Mode enables you to create high-quality videos with a lower degree of motion than VDOLive Movies. This means that your viewers with only medium speed to slow Internet connections can still receive high-quality images even though their bandwidth cannot support full motion. You can use the same captured video for creating flip mode videos as you would for creating VDOLive movies. Flip mode compression will allow Internet users with modem connections from 14.4 kbps-28.8 kbps to see your webcast.

Frames of the captured video are dropped automatically during encoding (compression) to accommodate the fps maximum transmission rate for this mode. The reduced number of frames also ensures higher image quality in each frame. You cannot choose which frames to drop.

Since most users, even those with high-speed connections, have limited bandwidth, there is a tradeoff between motion and image quality that determines what data gets through to the viewer and what data is lost. If motion is your highest priority for video, then compress in movie mode. If you are willing to reduce motion in order to send higher quality images, use flip mode.

Storybook Mode provides graphic images (not video) synchronized with an audio stream and is intended for use when your viewers are Internet users with low bandwidth connections, such as 14.4 kbps modems, or when your content is graphics only, not video. You define the interval for which each graphic will be displayed and coordinate the changing pictures with your audio.

Although VDO Clip can be used to edit this type of webcast, most professionals will probably use a video editing tool, such as Adobe Premiere or

Ulead's Media Studio instead.

Your viewers will see every frame of the content compressed in this mode; no frames will be dropped during transmission because of Server scaling. Additionally, the VDOLive Video Player displays a message telling viewers they are seeing a storybook. Create storybooks, and compress in Storybook mode when:

• Your content is still graphic images, not video.
• Your users have low-bandwidth Internet connections, such as 14.4 kbps modem connections.

Possible uses of this mode are for any training or marketing presentations, an "art gallery" storybook file, where you show still images of paintings or art pieces, with or without an accompanying musical track or narration, or for an online illustrated book, with the accompanying narration.

Several steps are involved in creating the material for your storybook before you compress:

• Assembling all your images either in VDO Clip, or in a video editing program such as Adobe Premiere or Ulead's Media Studio.
• Synchronizing the images with the audio and determining the length of time for which each image will be shown.
• You will achieve best results when you set a display interval of one frame every 10 or more seconds.

To create and compress a storybook using Adobe Premiere:

Make sure that the audio format is supported by VDOLive compression, that the images are in a size and color format supported by VDOLive compression and that all the images are the same size and in the same color format as each other.

1. Import (File|Import) graphic images and audio stream into your Project Window.
2. Move the audio stream and images from the Project Window into the Construction Window. You can either set the duration for each image as you move it, or adjust the duration by dragging the right border of the images.
3. Open the Make Movie dialog box (Make|Make Movie).
4. In Output Options|Type, select VDOnet VDOWave I for audio compression.
5. In Output Options|Type, set Interleave to every eight frames. Click OK to return to the Make Movie dialog box.
6. In Make Movie|Compression, select the Method: VDOnet VDOWave (Scalable).
7. Click Configure and select Storybook mode. Click OK to return to the Compression Settings dialog box.

8. Make sure the Optimize Stills option is deselected (unchecked). In Compression Settings|Special Processing|Settings, make sure the Better Resize option is deselected (unchecked). Return to the Compression Settings dialog box.
9. In Options, set frames per second to 1.
10. In Options, set the key frames to every 1 frame.
11. Click OK to return to the Make Movie dialog box.
12. Name the file.
13. Save.

Audio Programs are files of compressed audio. They include, and are limited to, only one frame of video at the beginning of the clip. Create audio programs whenever you have only audio content. The video frame at the beginning can be a picture, corporate logo or any other image and is displayed throughout the audio program.

Radio programs are easily adapted to this format, as are audio clips you use to explain your products or services. Additional uses of this format include interviews, training instructions, press releases and news.

The only audio sampling rate compatible with VDO Clip is 8 kHz. However, if you have audio that was captured at another sampling rate there are several options for converting it to 8 kHz before compressing it. Below you will find three different ways to change the audio sampling rate.

GoldWave is a shareware digital audio editing tool that can be downloaded

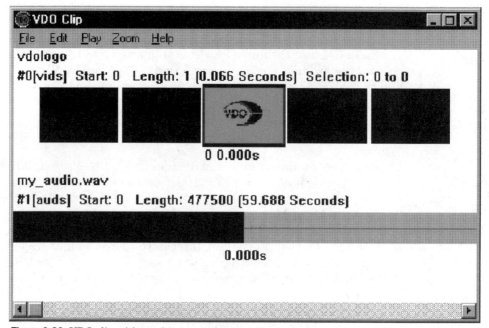

Figure 6-20. VDO clip with one bitmap and one audio stream.

at http://web.cs.mun.ca/~chris3/goldwave. GoldWave is excellent at sampling rate conversion with minimal audio degradation.

1. Open the AVI file in Clip and cut and paste the audio track into GoldWave
or
2. Use File | Open to open the WAV file in GoldWave.
3. Select Resample from the Effects menu.
4. Select 8000.
5. Hit OK.
6. Cut and paste the audio track back into Clip.

Using the Windows Sound Recorder program:

1. Open the AVI file in Clip; select the audio stream and cut and paste it to the Windows Sound Recorder. Or, if your audio and video tracks are separate files, open the audio file in Sound Recorder.
2. Select File | Properties | Convert Now.
3. In the Sound Selection window, let Format remain PCM.
4. Open Attributes and choose 8 kHz, 16 bit, mono.
5. Click OK in the Sound Selection window. Converting Now displays.
6. When conversion has ended, click OK in the Properties window.
7. Choose Copy from the Edit menu, then paste the audio stream back into VDO Clip.

Using the VDOLive Clip program:

1. Open the AVI file in Clip.
2. Select File | Driver options.
3. With the video stream selected, hit Options.
4. For the compressor select Full Frames (Uncompressed).
5. Hit OK.
6. Select the audio stream.
7. Select Options.
8. For the Format, select PCM (no compression).
9. For the attributes, select 8,000 Hz, 16 bit, mono.
10. Hit OK.
11. Hit OK again.
12. Select File | Save As and type in a file name.
13. Hit Save.

This will convert the file to 8 KHz audio without compressing it. Once the conversion to 8 KHz audio is finished, open the new file in Clip and compress it as usual.

The HTML Connection

Although your end-users can launch your carefully crafted video clips right from the VDO Viewer, for the best effect you'll need to write some HTML to make video look like it naturally fits into your site.

Add video to WWW pages by using text or graphic links to lead to the video once a user clicks on the link, or by creating Plug-in or "embedded" video.

Embedded video can play directly from your Web page, in a frame, without using the external VDOLive Video Player. Currently VDOLive Plug-in video is only supported for Netscape's browser versions 2.0 and higher. A "broken image" icon is shown to viewers using any browser other than Netscape to display a Web page with Plug-in video.

Before you begin you must make sure you set up the MIME type for the VDOLive Video Server application on your HTTP server:

MIME type: video
Sub type: vdo
File extension: vdo

Creating links between Web pages and video clips is done in two steps:

1. Creation of a VDO file, which resides on the http Server
2. Link from the Web page to the VDO file

Files with the suffix VDO contain the URL (Uniform Resource Location) for the video file. The VDOLive Video Player decodes files in AVI format. The URL contains the following information:

• Resource type: the resource type for VDOLive video is vdo://
• Server address: identification of the server where the AVI file is located by its host name or IP address (use only one of the two possible addresses)
• Port number: the TCP port used by the server (default is 7000)
• Path: Complete location of AVI file

The URL syntax is:

```
vdo://VDOLiveVideoServerHostName|Server IP
address[:Server TCP port]/FileNameOnServer.avi
```

Where:

"vdo://" = the protocol being used (resource type). The colon and the forward slashes must be included. Backslashes (\ ) do not work.

"VDOLiveVideoServerHostName|Server IP address/" = the host name or the IP address of the VDOLive Video Server. This location must be followed by a forward slash (/) not a backslash (\ ). If the location includes the server port number (see below), the slash should follow the port number.

"Server TCP port" = TCP listening port number on the server (default value is 7000).

"file name on Server" = full path of the video file with either "|" used (a WWW convention) or ":" after a drive letter. In this case, "|" is a vertical line as above, but does not represent "or." The path should include the drive and directory location (Windows 95/NT) or the /path, relative to the root directory (UNIX), as well as the file name. Slashes within a path may be forward (/)or backward (\).

To play the file birds.avi located in c:\movies on server17.vdolive.com at port 6500, the .vdo file would look like this for an NT Server:

```
vdo://server17.vdolive.com:6500/c|\movies.avi
```

To play the file birds.avi located in /movies on server24.vdolive.com using the default TCP port of 7000, the /vdo file would look like this on a UNIX server:

```
vdo://server24.vdolive.com/movies/birds.avi
```

You can create VDO files using any text editor or by using the on-line vdo file generator on the VDOnet Web site. This program can be found at: http://www.vdo.net/tech/howto/vdoed.html.

A video link is the HTML code behind the words or graphic users click on to request video. Each video link should point to one VDO file. The "pointer" is in HTML and is stored on the HTTP (Web) server. A link from a Web page to VDOLive video typically has this format:

```
<a href="http://VDOLive VideoServer IP address/path/filename.vdo">
Some Text </a>
```

To create a link create a separate text file with an extension of VDO (.vdo) on your Web server for each clip. For a VDOLive clip called bird.avi in /pub/movies where the IP address of your video server is 111.222.333.444, create a text file called bird.vdo with one of the following lines, depending on which VDOLive Video Server you have:

```
NT: vdo://111.222.333.444:7000/c:/pub/movies/bird.avi
```

-or-

```
UNIX: vdo://111.222.333.444:7000//pub/movies/bird.avi
```

Create an HTML link to the .vdo file as follows:

```
<a href="http://www.vdolive.com/vdofiles/bird.vdo" >Click here to
view the video</a>
```

How to Create Embedded (Plug-in) Video

The following is the <embed> tag as defined by Netscape:

```
<EMBED>
```

This tag allows different kinds of documents of varying data types to be embedded into an HTML document. It has three default attributes: SRC, WIDTH, and HEIGHT. It may also contain optional parameters that can be sent to the plug-in handling the embedded data type.

```
SRC=<URL>
```
The URL of the source document.

```
WIDTH=<size in pixels>
```
The WIDTH attribute specifies the width of the embedded document, in pixels.

```
HEIGHT=<size in pixels>
```
The HEIGHT attribute specifies the height of the embedded document, in pixels.

```
PARAMETER_NAME=<PARAMETER_VALUE>
```
There can be an infinite number of parameters passed to a plug-in. Examples of parameters are PLAY_LOOP=TRUE, or CONTROLS=FALSE. Parameters are specific to each plug-in.

Examples:

```
<EMBED SRC="MyMovie.mov", WIDTH=150, HEIGHT=250 CONTROLS=TRUE>
<EMBED   SRC="DoomGame.ids",   WIDTH=400,   HEIGHT=300   SPEED=SLOW
LEVEL=12>
</EMBED>
```

To create a Plug-in:

1. For each clip, create a separate text file with an extension of VDO. Store the VDO file on your HTTP (Web) server.
2. For a VDOLive clip called "bird.avi" in the directory /pub/movies and the IP address of your video server is 111.222.333.444, create a text file called bird.vdo with one of the following lines, depending on which VDOLive Video Server you have:

3. `NT: vdo://111.222.333.444:7000/c:/pub/movies/bird.avi`
 -or-
 `UNIX: vdo://111.222.333.444:7000//pub/movies/bird.avi`
4. Create an HTML link to the VDO file:

```
src = "http://webserver/directory name/.vdo file name"
autostart = { true or false }
loop = { true or false }
stretch = { true or false
```

When stretch is true, the size of the video image adjusts to fit the size of the Plug-in window. When stretch is false, the video is centered in the designated area. Although you can size the video to any dimensions you want, when you specify width=1 and height=1, Netscape makes the video fill the page, whatever the page size is.

For example:

```
<embed
src="http://www.vdolive.com/vdofiles/bird.vdo"
autostart=false loop=false stretch=true width=160 height=128>
```

Following is an example of HTML you can use to create a video link for embedded video displayed inside a graphic (such as a television). This example uses four pieces of a graphic (the sides of the frame) cut to resemble one graphic when placed around the embedded video clip.

```
<html>
<head><title>Block image TV</title></head>
<body bgcolor=#000000>
<img border=0 src="tvtop.gif"><br><img border=0 src="tvleft.gif">
<embed src= "/bloopers.vdo" autostart=false width=160 height=120 stretch=true>
<img border=0 src="tvright.gif"><br>
<img border=0 src="tvbottom.gif">
</body>
</html>
```

Embedding a video in an HTML page is done using the Netscape EMBED tag. The tag requires several arguments:

```
SRC="name of .vdo file pointing to the video"
HEIGHT=plug-in height in pixels
WIDTH=plug-in width in pixels
STRETCH=TRUE/FALSE
```

AUTOSTART=TRUE/FALSE

Example:

```
<HTML>
<HEAD><TITLE>Example of HTML page with embedded
video></TITLE></HEAD>
<BODY>
<EMBED SRC="blade_runner.vdo" WIDTH=160
HEIGHT=128 STRETCH=TRUE AUTOSTART=TRUE>
</BODY>
</HTML>
```

A "broken image" icon occurs when an HTML page is viewed by a browser which does not support the VDOLive plug-in. At the moment, embedded videos can only be viewed using Netscape version 2.0 or higher on MS-Windows systems. The problem can be partly solved by generating HTML on the fly using CGI or server-side includes.

CGI defines the environment variable "HTTP_USER_AGENT" that can be used by the server to determine the type of browser and operating system used on each HTTP request. For example Netscape Navigator Gold, version 2.02, running on Windows NT will set the variable to: Mozilla/2.02Gold (WinNT).

You can easily check how each different browser sets the variable by creating a simple CGI script that returns the value of HTTP_USER_AGENT.

Once we know the type of browser used and the operating system, we can generate a page that will contain either embedded video (for Netscape 2.0 or higher running under Windows) or a link to a .vdo file (on any other combination). The following is a sample PERL script that checks for browser type and OS and generates a page accordingly:

```
#!/usr/bin/perl
$agent=$ENV{'HTTP_USER_AGENT'};
# Are we using Netscape 2.0 or higher?
if(index($agent,"Mozilla/2")!=(-1)) { $netscape=1 }
# Are we using Windows?
if(index($agent,"Win")!=(-1)) {$windows=1 }
 # Generate page
print "Content-type: text/html\n\n";
print "<HTML>";
print "<HEAD><TITLE>Sample CGI Script</TITLE></HEAD>";
print "<BODY>";
# Determine whether to use a link or embedded video clip
if($netscape && $windows) {
  print "<EMBED SRC=\"someclip.vdo\">";
} else {
```

Buying VDOLive

Those of you who use an Internet Service Provider to host your domain are in for some bad news. Few ISPs will let you purchase and install VDOLive. These unlucky folks will have to either talk their ISPs into buying the product and then renting its use on a monthly basis or start a search for an existing user of the product that you can rent "time" from. A third option is to purchase

The VDOLive Video Server		
Concurrent streams	Price	Basic annual support
5	$1,199.00	$360.00
10	$1,995.00	$599.00
25	$3,995.00	$1,199.00
50	$7,495.00	$2,249.00
100	$11,995.00	$3,599.00

Figure 6-21. VDOLive price list.

your own server hardware to run all of the webcasting software we've talked about in this book. No doubt, you've probably already run into this problem when you tried to install RealAudio as well.

Now that we're experts in VDOnet products, let's move on to Netscape to find out what they have to offer webcasters.

Chapter

7

Webcasting with Netscape

Netscape is in the unfortunate position where, because it wants to remain a player in the Internet arena, it must be continually innovative. That means that Netscape must enter every Internet market — including webcasting.

Netscape has done so in several products as well as a host of relationships with third-party plug-in developers. CoolTalk, a product by recently acquired InsSoft, Inc. is bundled right along with the latest releases of Netscape Navigator and is targeted as a direct competitor of Microsoft's NetMeeting.

The Netscape Media Server, which lets developers serve up real-time audio, is based on open standards and implemented with open protocols. The Media Server is one of the components of Netscape's Live Media product category. The other components are LiveAudio, LiveVideo and Apple's QuickTime. This chapter will present an overview of Netscape's offerings with lots of information about how to deliver content using these offerings.

CoolTalk

CoolTalk, as shown in figure 7-1, is actually a product developed by InSoft, Inc. but is bundled with the most recent version of Netscape Navigator, much like NetMeeting is bundled with Microsoft's latest browser version (5.7 meg if you selected Netscape 3.01 with components for Windows 95 at http://www.netscape.com/comprod/mirror/client_download.html). You may download CoolTalk by itself from http://home.netscape.com/comprod/products/navigator/cooltalk/download_cooltalk.html.

After downloading, CoolTalk must be configured (Setup Wizard). It didn't seem to like my IBM Aptiva Mwave soundcard, but worked quite well with the ESS soundcard installed in my laptop. Configuration involves listening to

Figure 7-1. CoolTalk is Netscape's competitive offering to Microsoft's NetMeeting.

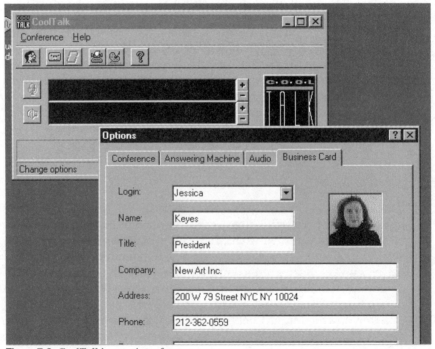

Figure 7-2. CoolTalk's user interface.

sound clips and telling the setup program whether it sounded as if it were in the right pitch and then recording your own voice and playing it back. Finally, if setup was successful, you get to fill out your business card (figure 7-2) which contains information about you as well as your photo.

CoolTalk is a real-time audio and data collaboration tool specifically designed for the Internet to enhance interpersonal communications and avoid long-distance phone charges. CoolTalk provides full-duplex audio conferencing, allowing both users to speak and be heard simultaneously. Again, like Microsoft's NetMeeting, CoolTalk includes: a Chat Tool and a Shared Whiteboard for textual and graphical data conferencing.

CoolTalk's user interface is also shown in figure 7-2. The overlapping window was displayed when I selected Conference|Options. The Options menu also enables you to modify settings for Conferencing, answering machine incoming message storage locations and audio connection. CoolTalk defaults to a 14.4 kbps connections using the Netscape multimedia server (http://live.netscape.com). The icons on the face of the user interface provide a quick way to start a conference, a chat or whiteboard collaboration.

To start a new conference, you will first need to locate the person that you want to conference with. If you have conferenced with the person before, their Internet address will appear in your Address Book. If not, they may be registered with the IS411 Server. Finally, you can enter their name manually in your Address Book.

To invite a user that appears in your Address Book, double click on their name and an invitation will automatically be sent to them. To invite someone registered with the IS411 Server, double click on their name in the listing. If the person you want to invite is not listed in your Address Book or on the IS411 Server, type their Internet Address in the space provided on the Address Book page.

The IS411 Server is a service that enables you to locate other CoolTalk users, and to provide your name and address to other users. If you want to register with the IS411 Server so that other users can locate you, click on the "Make me available through server" box. When this box is selected, your name and Internet address will appear to other users that are connected to the same IS411 Server that you are.

To invite another CoolTalk user that is registered with the IS411 Server that you have selected, select Start from the Conference menu. When the Open Conference dialog opens, select the IS411 Directory tab. A listing of the users who are registered with the IS411 Server will appear. To invite one of them, double click on their name in the list. To add a user found on the IS411 Server to your Speed Dial Bar, highlight their name in the list and click on the Add to Speed Dial button.

When you send out an invitation to another user, CoolTalk will contact their host and check to see if CoolTalk is running. If they are running CoolTalk and are not participating in another conference, they will be invited to join your conference. Once they act on your invitation, you will be notified of the result.

CoolTalk can be set to react to conference invitations that it receives in three different ways. It can accept all invitations, refuse all invitations, or you can set CoolTalk so that it gives you the option to accept or decline each invitation individually. To set this behavior, select Options from the Conference menu. Click on the Conference tab when the Options dialog opens. Select the behavior that you prefer.

After you join or start a conference, you can leave it at any time by selecting Leave from the conference menu. When you leave the conference, you will be asked for confirmation, and if you click on Yes, the connection will be closed.

CoolTalk provides users with real-time audio communications capabilities. When you are in a conference with another user and you have your audio card(s) configured properly, you will be able to conduct a conversation as though you were using a conventional telephone.

In order to facilitate audio communications, CoolTalk's interface includes meters that monitor audio record and playback. The record meter includes two controls, the Silence Sensor and Echo Cancellation. The red marks show the Silence Sensor Setting, the white marks show the Echo Cancellation setting. There are also buttons that allow you to increase and decrease the relative Record and Playback levels next to the audio meters.

The Silence Sensor is designed to prevent CoolTalk from sending audio when the user is not speaking. When the record meter is below the Silence Sensor marks, no audio is sent.

The Echo Cancellation setting is similar to the Silence Sensor. It sets the level at which audio is sent when the other conference member is speaking. Your microphone can pick up audio played by your speakers, and transmit it back to the other conference member, causing them to hear an "echo."

The CoolTalk Answering Machine enables users to send you messages if you are away from your computer and they attempt to conference with you. Its operation is analogous to that of an answering machine used with a normal telephone, with some improvements. Like a real answering machine, the CoolTalk Answering Machine connects after a few rings and plays an outgoing message. It then records a message from the calling party and saves it to a file on disk. When you return to your keyboard you can play back recorded messages.

In order to play back an incoming message, highlight in your Incoming Message list and click on the Play button. The message will begin to play, if you want to stop playing the message click on the Stop button. When a message is selected, the Business Card Photo of the sender will appear in the upper right-hand corner of the Answering Machine window. To sort your incoming messages click on the headings in the Message List. To erase the message that is currently selected, click on the Delete Message button. To return the message sender's call, click on the Call Back button. To save the message as a Wave file on your disk, click on the Save WAVE File button.

CoolTalk Chat

The Chat Tool enables you to send textual information to another person. It consumes few network or CPU resources, and is particularly useful if you are using other network applications in addition to CoolTalk.

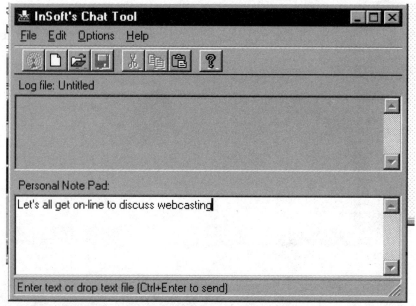

Figure 7-3. CoolTalk Chat's note capability.

By selecting Post Note Pad from the File menu, you can send the contents of your Personal Note Pad to the other member of your conference as shown in figure 7-3. The message you post will be added to your Log window, as well as that of the other conference member. You can also use Include File to import a text file. After you have loaded a file into your Personal Note Pad, you can edit the contents before sending it to another conference member.

CoolTalk Whiteboard

With the Whiteboard (figure 7-4) you can open and share image files, as well as interactively edit the Whiteboard's canvas and mark up any images you import. The Whiteboard supports a number of graphics formats, and is capable of capturing images from the Windows 95 desktop.

In most cases you will not be creating images from scratch or typing your messages (you can use Chat for that). The Whiteboard is most effective to share a pre-existing image as shown in figure 7-5 by using File|New to open an image file. Since everyone is "sharing" the same "Paint"-like tool, the resdesign of the room in figure 7-5 can be worked on in collaboration fairly effectively.

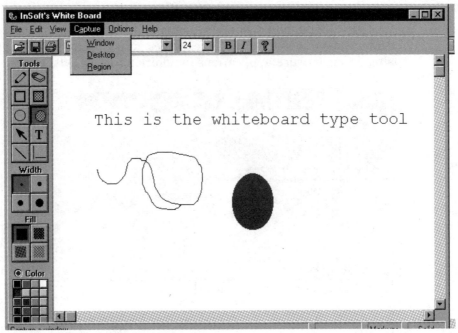

Figure 7-4. CoolTalk whiteboard.

Figure 7-5. An image on the whiteboard.

The following graphic formats are supported: Windows Bitmap; CompuServe GIF; ZSoft Paintbrush PCX; TIFF Revision 5.0; JPEG; Sun Raster; and Truevision TARGA.

There is another way to paste something onto the Whiteboard. CoolTalk permits you to select part or all of your desktop, under the CoolTalk interface. There are three different options for capturing images. In order to capture the contents of a window, select Window from the Capture menu. To capture a window's contents, click on that window. If you want to capture an entire window including its frame, you should click on the title bar. To capture a specific area of the desktop, select Region from the Capture menu. Press the left mouse button to anchor one corner of the area that you want to capture, then drag the cursor until the area you wish to import is surrounded by the bounding box. When you release the mouse button, the area will be captured. To capture the entire desktop, select Desktop from the Capture menu.

Once you have captured an image, it will be imported to the canvas. A bounding box that shows the outline of the area you captured will appear, and you can position the box where you wish to place the image. Click the left mouse button to place the image. To preview the image before placing it, hold down the Shift key as you position the box.

Figure 7-6 shows the secrets of my trade. Since I was writing this chapter when I had the CoolTalk Whiteboard in use, when I selected Capture Desktop it captured my word processing session. Even if you don't intend to use

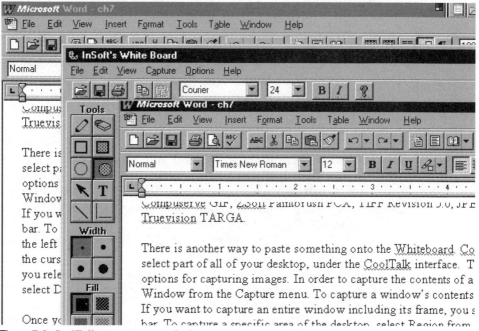

Figure 7-6. CoolTalk captures your desktop.

CoolTalk for collaboration, this is still a great screen capture utility.

The Whiteboard's canvas has two distinct layers, the markup layer and the image layer. The markup layer consists of drawings made using tools from the Toolbox, including Circles, Squares and drawings with the pencil. Items pasted into the Whiteboard from the clipboard are also part of the markup layer.

On the other hand, the Image layer contains images captured from the desktop using the items on the Capture menu, and Images loaded from disk. The Eraser tool and Clear functions from the Edit menu recognize items on each layer, so that you can erase either just markups or both markups and images. To select between the two when you are using the Eraser, click on the Image/Markups button on the lower right-hand corner of the Whiteboard. There are separate items in the Edit menu for Clear Markups and Clear Whiteboard. You can also toggle between the two from the Options menu.

In October of 1996, Netscape announced Netscape Communicator, an integrated client software product that users need every day to communicate, share data and access information on Intranets and the Internet. Netscape Communicator is an integrated product for open e-mail, groupware, editing, calendaring and Web browsing on Intranets and the Internet.

Netscape Communicator integrates in one product five powerful components that work together: Netscape Navigator 4.0 browser software, Netscape Composer HTML authoring software, Netscape Messenger electronic mail, Netscape Collabra group discussion software, and Netscape Conference real-time collaboration software. For corporate users on an Intranet, Netscape also announced Netscape Communicator Professional Edition, which adds Netscape Calendar scheduling software and Netscape AutoAdmin for centralized user management by MIS professionals.

Netscape Communicator comes with the recently unveiled Netscape Inbox Direct service. Inbox Direct is an innovative new content delivery service that harnesses the rich-text messaging capabilities of Netscape Messenger to deliver messages with all the richness of the Web — right to users' e-mail box every morning at no cost. More than 40 companies are now providing content to Netscape Inbox Direct subscribers, driving subscriptions to over 500,000 in less than two weeks of availability. The 40 companies include Axel Springer Verlag, CMP Media, The Daily Telegraph, The Gartner Group, Inc., The HotWired Network, The New York Times, Times Mirror Magazines (Sporting News, Ski Magazine, Skiing Magazine, Golf Magazine, Yachting), US News and World Report and Ziff-Davis' ZD Net AnchorDesk.

Two of the components of this new software bundle are of interest to webcasters:

Netscape Collabra whose information can be accessed from their site at http://home.netscape.com/comprod/announce/faq_c.html#collabra, is an open standards-based group discussion software. New features include easy access to public or private discussion forums; HTML editing tools to create and post Web documents to discussion groups; search tools that locate information on multiple forums; and off-line message reading and posting capabilities for mobile users.

Netscape Conference (information about this product is located at http://home.netscape.com/comprod/announce/faq_c.html#conference) is a real-time collaboration software that lets users simultaneously share information and talk to co-workers on the Internet. Features include audio-conferencing based on powerful compression technology; shared whiteboard, chat and file transfer capabilities; voicemail capability; and the ability to dial Internet phone numbers by e-mail or IP address.

LiveMedia

Figure 7-7. Netscape Navigator now includes support for standard sound formats.

LiveMedia is an open environment for interoperable voice and video communication, audio and video streaming built right into the Navigator environment. It is based on a host of open standards (RTP, RSVP, GSM and other open audio codecs; MPEG, H.261, and other open video codecs).

Since Netscape is treating it as part of their Navigator platform, developers can build an application that uses audio or video or telephony easily by taking advantage of the platform features within the application via APIs.

LiveMedia is actually several components. As shown in figure 7-7 Netscape Navigator now includes native support for standard sound formats such as AIFF, AU, MIDI, and WAV along with providing the ability to play standards-based video formats. The Media Server delivers high-quality streaming audio publishing capabilities, making it easy and cost-effective for companies to create and deliver rich, audio-enabled content and applications. You can synchronize audio with HTML documents, plug-ins, Java applets, and JavaScript for a dynamic multimedia experience. Your company can now go beyond simple text and graphics in its electronic communications, using the power and efficiency of real-time audio delivery over open Internet protocols.

Netscape Media Server

Netscape worked closely with Progressive Networks, the makers of RealAudio, to jointly develop the Real-Time Streaming Protocol (RTSP). Real-Time Streaming Protocol. RTSP is based on the following Internet protocols: TCP, UDP, RTP, and IP Multicast. RTSP has been submitted to the Internet Engineering Task Force (IETF).

Netscape Media Server is open and extensible. It can stream a variety of file formats and has a modular architecture to accept plug-and-play support of future or custom file formats. Currently Netscape Media Server supports three file formats: WAV, AU, and LMA. Hundreds of tools exist to author and edit audio in WAV format, and all of this content can be streamed from a server with no content modifications. The LMA format is a new file format, supported by several tools' vendors, that encapsulates audio compressed using a new class of audio codec, called a variable bit-rate codec. Media Server ships with several codecs, including Voxware's RT-24 and RT-29, offering ultra-low bit-rate encoding of monaural speech.

Any server-class CPU is adequate for Netscape Media Server to stream audio. A machine with audio-recording capabilities is needed for broadcasting real-time live audio broadcasts. No additional software is needed.

Netscape Media Server is scalable and bundles several high-quality audio codecs, so high-quality audio is possible at low bandwidths. You can achieve broadcast-quality stereo at modem speeds of under 28.8 kbps, and with IP Multicast support, thousands of listeners can tune in to the same network stream.

The Media Server, which is now in Beta format, can be downloaded for a trial from http://home.netscape.com/comprod/mirror/server_download.html and is available for both the Windows NT and UNIX platforms.

Netscape Media Server can unicast or multicast both stored audio clips and live feeds. You can choose to loop a stored audio file and serve it as a live feed. Using this method for specific applications can help alleviate network traffic problems on high-demand sites.

For example, a theater site can record a listing of all the movies that are currently playing at its theater, along with show times, special offers, and ticket prices. It can loop the file and multicast it. A customer who tunes in to the multicast in the middle can simply stay tuned until the file starts playing again from the beginning.

You can also use Media Server to synchronize audio with HTML documents, Java applets, and JavaScript applications using LiveConnect. The result is a dynamic user experience that integrates text, graphics, and audio to facilitate more effective communication.

For example, a business site can provide a multimedia presentation of its benefits policies that includes videos with synchronized audio narration. Or, a motion picture site can present synchronized audio and video clips from a new movie.

LMSP is a protocol used for on-demand access of multimedia objects such as stored real-time audio files and live real-time feeds. LMSP is a hybrid protocol that uses Session Control Protocol (SCP) over TCP for control messages and non-real-time data and optionally uses Real-time Transfer Protocol (RTP) over User Datagram Protocol (UDP) for real-time data delivery.

Netscape Media Server automatically detects the bandwidth of a connecting client and delivers compressed audio that is optimized for the bandwidth. This helps ensure high quality for every connection. You can create Media audio files using the Netscape Sound Converter included with Media Server. You can also use the Sound Converter to compress WAV files.

You can record audio files to serve with the Media Server using any recording device appropriate for creating audio files. When you record your files, you can use the Sound Converter to optimize the recording format for a specified codec. To provide the best quality audio for a client, regardless of the bandwidth it uses, you can create multiple files for the same audio content. You can compress each file at a compression level most efficient for a particular bandwidth. Then, each client can play the audio file best suited for the bandwidth it uses. You can also create files compressed most efficiently for specific platforms.

You can group the audio files into sets that are either platform independent or platform specific using an audio metafile (LAM). An audio metafile is a special Media Server file type that provides the location of your Media Server and the locations of your audio files to clients. For a multimedia presentation, it also includes a timeline to synchronize an audio file with another medium, such as a video, that is included in the presentation.

To make your audio content available to clients, you create HTML pages in which you embed the Media Player controls. Clients must also have the Media Player plug-in installed in their browsers. The Media Player controls appear in a rectangular space, which can be in a frame separate from other content you include in a page.

For example, you could include a header frame, a main frame that contains text, images, or a video, and a plug-in frame that contains the Media Player controls. You can also embed multiple sets of controls in a single HTML page to allow clients to play multiple audio files.

Media Server includes a Java class, LiveAudioPlayer, and a Java interface, LiveAudioObserver, that allow you to write your own interface to the Media Player plug-in. When you embed the Media Player plug-in in an HTML page, you can hide the Media Player controls and display your own interface instead. You can choose to write your interface in Java or JavaScript.

The installation of the Media Server is not as straightforward as the RealAudio Server so we won't get into the details of its installation. Instead, I will summarize the installation procedure.

Before you install the server, you should do the following:

1. Make sure DNS is running. If you do not have DNS, you need to use IP

addresses.
2. Create an alias for the server.
3. Create a user account for the server.
4. Choose a unique port number for the server.

Before you install the Media Server, you should be logged in with the user account that the server will use. You should be logged in as the root, unless you plan to install the server on a port greater than 1024 or the location where you plan to install the server (the server root directory) is writable with your current login status.

When you install the Media Server, the installation program checks to see whether you already have a Netscape server installed. Then, it does one of the following:

1. If you have a Netscape server installed, the installation program adds the administration server components for the Media Server to the existing administration server.
2. If you do not have a Netscape server installed, the installation program installs an administration server. Then, it adds the administration server components for the Media Server.

A series of files are installed as shown in figure 7-8. You must also configure your HTTP server to support the audio/x-liveaudio MIME type. Be sure to add audio/x-liveaudio to your MIME type file and associate the file type .lam with it.

The Server Selector and the Server Manager configure and administer the Media Server. The Server Selector lets you: choose a server to configure; install multiple servers; remove a server from the list of servers you can configure; configure your administration server; and start and stop a server (figure 7-9).

Directory/File	Description
/usr/ns-home/bin/lmspd/admin/bin	Administration CGI scripts
/usr/ns-home/bin/lmspd/admin/html	Administration server HTML pages
/usr/ns-home/bin/lmspd/admin/icons	Administration server images
/usr/ns-home/bin/lmspd	Media Server executable
/usr/ns-home/bin/lmspd.conf	Media Server configuration file
/usr/ns-home/bin/lmspd.so	Shared library for administration server

Figure 7-8. Media Server files.

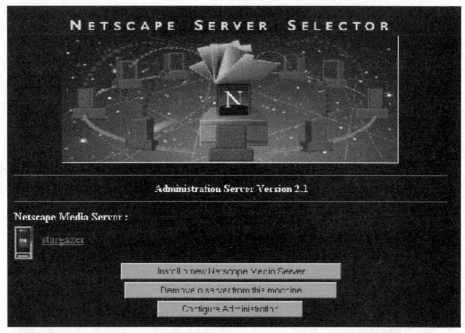

Figure 7-9. The Server Selector lets you configure and administer the Media Server.

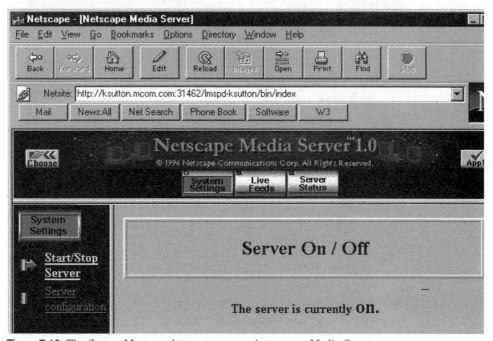

Figure 7-10. The Server Manager lets you start and stop your Media Server.

The Server Manager, shown in figure 7-10, lets you: start and stop your Media Server; configure your Media Server; start and stop a live feed; and check the status of your Media Server.

Running the Media Server is pretty much point and click oriented, at least in the Windows environment. For example, to start a live feed choose Live Feeds|Start Live Feed. The Media Studio window appears. Choose Audio|Start recording to start the live feed. Choose Audio|Properties to change any file options. The Media Studio Properties window appears as shown in figure 7-11.

After you create your audio files, you can use the Media Converter to compress the files at bit rates that are appropriate for specific bandwidths. For example, for a particular audio file, you could create a set of files that are targeted for these typical bandwidth settings:

14400
28800
56000

After creating multiple files for the same audio content, you can create a live audio metafile (LA) that specifies a default file to play and any other choices that are available for specific bandwidths.

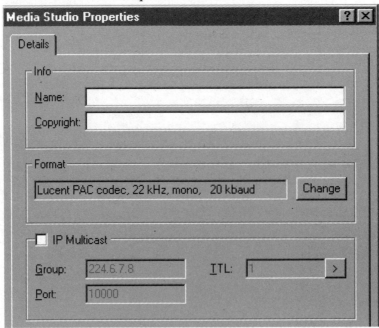

Figure 7-11. The Media Studio properties window.

You can also choose to create sets of files that are compressed most efficiently for specific platforms. In a LAM file, you can define sets of files for these platforms:

Solaris
HPUX
DECUX
MAC68
MACPPC
WIN16
WIN32INTEL
WIN32ALPHA
WIN32PPC
WIN32MIPS

For each platform, you can specify the files to play for specific bandwidths. The Media Converter includes the following codecs that you can use to compress your files:

GSM 6.10: Global System for Mobile Telecommunications codec for speech compression. It compresses data at a rate of 13.5 kbps. This codec is also included in the Windows 95 and Windows NT operating systems, and is included with the UNIX and Macintosh Media Clients.

RT24: Voxware codec for speech only. It compresses data at a rate of 2.4 kbps.

Super Sound Plus Music: Lucent perceptual audio codec, an all-purpose music codec. It compresses data at rates of 8 kbps mono, 12 kbps mono, 18 kbps mono and stereo, and 24 kbps mono and stereo. This codec can be used to create a .la file only.

IMA ADPCM: International Multimedia Association Adoptive Differential Pulse Code Modulation. This codec provides high bit-rate, low complexity compression. It is also included in the Windows 95 and Windows NT operating systems, and is included with the UNIX Media Clients.

You can use the Media Converter to convert and record audio files. To convert a file double click the Sound Converter icon. The Media Converter Window appears as shown in figure 7-12. Detailed information is available by clicking on the icon as shown in figure 7-13.

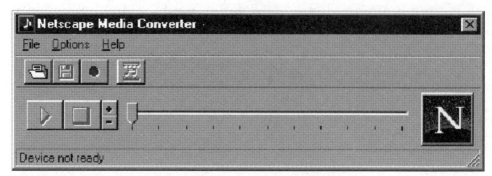

Figure 7-12. The Media Converter converts and records audio files.

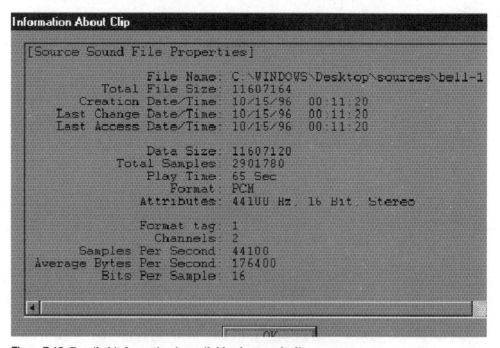

Figure 7-13. Detailed information is available about each clip.

When you select File|Convert the Conversion Wizard appears. The Conversion Wizard guides you through the process of compressing the file. To use the templates provided, select Express Conversion. To use more advanced options, select Custom Conversion.

You can select from various conversion templates as shown in figure 7-14. With the custom conversion option, you can specify more advanced compression options and create your own templates.

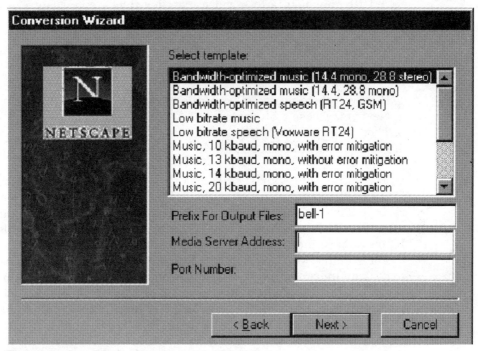

Figure 7-14. A multitude of conversion templates.

Next, you select a target bit rate for the file. You can choose from the following:

All rates
Below 14400 bits per second
14400 - 28800 bits per second
28800 - 64000 bits per second
Above 64000 bits per second
Custom range

If you choose custom range, you can specify the range of bits per second for the target bit rate. Next, you can select a codec to use to compress the file. From a drop-down menu, you can choose from all the codecs included with the Sound Converter and all other codecs that are installed on your system. After selecting a codec, you can choose to create a WAV file or an LMA file. The Conversion Wizard recommends a file type for you.

Finally, you can enter the following for the file:

1. A name for the file
2. Copyright information

188   Chapter Seven

3. A URL that points to a codec installer that a client can use to install an appropriate codec if one is not installed on the client machine.

You can also use a wizard to record audio. The Recording Wizard guides you through the process of recording a file.

1. First you choose the quality of the recording
2. Next you choose a bit rate
3. Then you choose a codec
4. Finally, you can click on Record

You can design your HTML pages in any way you want, with or without frames. When you include the Media Player controls, the controls appear in a rectangular space on the page. Using attributes of the EMBED tag, you determine the width and height of the rectangle and the specific controls it contains. If you want, you can place the controls in a separate frame.

For example, you can include a header frame that contains a header for the page, a main frame that contains text, images, or a video, and a plug-in frame that contains the Media Player controls. Figure 7-15 shows a sample HTML page with the Media Player controls in a separate frame. In addition, you can choose to embed the Media Player in an HTML page, but hide the controls and

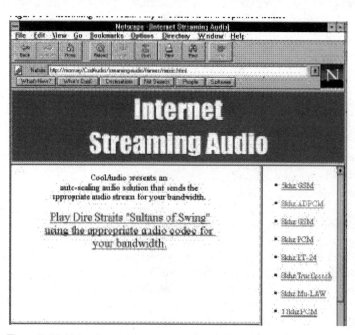

Figure 7-15. Using frames to separate the media controls from the content.

display your own interface.

When you embed the Media Player controls in an HTML page, you can specify one of the following: a live audio metafile (LAM) that provides the location of your Media Server, and the locations of the audio files that are available to play or the live feed to access; and the name and location of a specific audio file to play or live feed to access

When you specify a LAM file, you can define a set of audio files that are available for specific bandwidths or platforms. The server can send the file that is compressed most efficiently for the bandwidth or platform the client is using. When you specify the name and location of a specific audio file to play, you can specify only one file.

LiveAudio

Like RealAudio, LiveAudio enables streaming audio so that you don't have to wait to download a sound player or launch a separate application to play sound files. LiveAudio automatically identifies and plays all major sound formats embedded in or linked to a Web page.

Programming LiveAudio into your Web site is simple using the <EMBED> HTML tag:

```
<EMBED
SRC="/comprod/products/navigator/version_3.0/multimedia/audio/livaud.aif"
   AUTOSTART=false
   VOLUME=100
   WIDTH=144 HEIGHT=60
   CONTROLS=Console>
</EMBED>
```

LiveAudio plays audio files in WAV, AIFF, AU, and MIDI formats. Audio controls appear according to the size specified in the WIDTH and HEIGHT parameters in the EMBED tag. You can create an audio console with any of the following six views.

1. Console: consisting of a Play, Pause, Stop, and volume control lever.
2. SmallConsole: consisting of a Play, Stop, and volume control lever (upon invoking this view of the applet class, a sound will "autostart" by default). This view will have smaller buttons than the standard Console buttons.
3. PlayButton: a button that starts the sound playing.
4. PauseButton: a button that pauses (without unloading) the sound while it is playing.
5. StopButton: a button that ends the playing of sound and unloads it.
6. VolumeLever: a lever that adjusts the volume level for playback of the sound (and adjusts the system's volume level).

These views may be used many times on one Web page, with all the view instances controlling one sound file, or many sound files, depending on how the file is called in the HTML or JavaScript. These controls can be called by other applets to do things like control the systems universal volume. HTML syntax follows:

```
<EMBED
SRC= [URL]
AUTOSTART=[TRUE|FALSE]
LOOP=[TRUE|FALSE|INTEGER]
STARTTIME=[MINUTES:SECONDS]
ENDTIME=[MINUTES|SECONDS]
VOLUME=[0-100]
WIDTH=[# PIXELS]
HEIGHT=[# PIXELS]
ALIGN=[TOP|BOTTOM|CENTER|BASELINE|LEFT|RIGHT
|TEXTTOP|MIDDLE|ABSMIDDLE|ABSBOTTOM]
CONTROLS=[CONSOLE|SMALLCONSOLE|PLAYBUTTON|PAUSEBUTTON|STOPBUTTON|
VOLUMELEVER]
HIDDEN=[TRUE]
MASTERSOUND
NAME=[UNIQUE NAME TO GROUP CONTROLS TOGETHER SO THAT THEY CONTROL
ONE SOUND]..
</EMBED>
```

where:

SRC=[URL] is the URL of the source sound file.

AUTOSTART=[TRUE|FALSE]. Setting the value to TRUE allows the sound, music, or voice to begin playing automatically when the Web page is loaded. The default is FALSE.

LOOP=[TRUE|FALSE|INTEGER]. Setting the value to TRUE allows the sound to play continuously until the stop button is clicked on the console or the user goes to another page. If an INTEGER value is used, the sound repeats the number of times indicated by the integer.

STARTTIME=[MINUTES:SECONDS]. Use STARTTIME to designate where in the sound file you would like playback to begin. If you want to begin the sound at 30 seconds, you would set the value to 00:30 (implemented only on Windows 95, NT, and Macintosh).

ENDTIME=[MINUTES:SECONDS].Use ENDTIME to designate where in the sound file you would like playback to end. If you want to stop the sound at 1.5 minutes, you would set the value to 01:30 (implemented only on Windows 95, NT, and Macintosh).

VOLUME=[0-100]. This value must be a number between 0 and 100 to represent 0 to 100 percent. This attribute sets the volume for the sound that is playing [unless the MASTERVOLUME (see NAME attribute below) is used, then this value sets the sound for the entire system]. The default volume level is the current system volume.

WIDTH=[# PIXELS]. This attribute is used to display the width of the console or console element. For the CONSOLE and SMALLCONSOLE, the default is WIDTH=144. For the VOLUMELEVER, the default is WIDTH=74. For a button, the default is WIDTH=37.

HEIGHT=[# PIXELS]. This attribute is used to display the height of the console. For the CONSOLE, the default is HEIGHT=60. For the SMALLCONSOLE, the default is HEIGHT=15. For the VOLUMELEVER, the default is HEIGHT=20. For a button, the default is HEIGHT=22.

ALIGN=[TOP|BOTTOM|CENTER|BASELINE|LEFT|RIGHT|TEXTTOP|MIDDLE|ABSMIDDLE|ABSBOTTOM]. This attribute tells Netscape Navigator how you want to align text as it flows around the consoles. It acts similarly to the IMG tag.

CONTROLS=[CONSOLE|SMALLCONSOLE|PLAYBUTTON|PAUSEBUTTON|STOPBUTTON|VOLUMELEVER]. This attribute defines which control a content creator wishes to use. The default for this field is CONSOLE.

HIDDEN=[TRUE]. The value for this attribute should be TRUE, or it should not be included in the EMBED tag. If it is specified as TRUE, no controls will load and the sound will act as a background sound.

MASTERSOUND. This value must be used when grouping sounds together in a NAME group. This attribute takes no value (it must merely be present in the EMBED tag), but tells LiveAudio which file is a genuine sound file and allows it to ignore any stub files. Stub files have a minimum length necessary to activate LiveAudio.

NAME=[UNIQUE NAME TO GROUP CONTROLS TOGETHER SO THAT THEY CONTROL ONE SOUND]. This attribute sets a unique ID for a group of CONTROLS elements, so they all act on the same sound as it plays. For example, if a content creator wishes to have one sound controlled by two embedded objects (a PLAYBUTTON and a STOPBUTTON), they must use this attribute to group the CONTROLS together. In this case, the MASTERSOUND tag is necessary to flag LiveAudio and let it know which of the two EMBED tags actually has the sound file you wish to control. LiveAudio ignores any EMBED(s) with no MAS-

TERSOUND tag.

If you want one VOLUMELEVER to control multiple NAMEs (or the system volume), create an EMBED using the VOLUMELEVER CONTROL. Then set NAME to MASTERVOLUME.

LiveAudio includes the ability to defer loading a sound file until the Play button is pushed. This enables a Web page designer to comfortably embed several sounds on one page, without worrying about page load time.

To implement this feature, the Web designer must create a file like the following:

```
<SCRIPT LANGUAGE=SoundScript>
  OnPlay(http://YourURL/YourSound.aif);
</SCRIPT>
```

This file should be saved and named as a sound file (such as script1.aif). When the Play button is pushed, the URL you defined for the OnPlay function is loaded.

Coding Examples

To play a sound as a background sound for a Web page:

```
<EMBED SRC="mysound.aif" HIDDEN=TRUE>
```

To have several CONTROLS controlling one sound file:

```
<EMBED SRC="mysound.aif" HEIGHT=22 WIDTH=37 CONTROLS=PLAYBUTTON NAME="MyConsole" MASTERSOUND>

<EMBED SRC="stub1.aif" HEIGHT=22 WIDTH=37 CONTROLS=PAUSEBUTTON NAME="MyConsole">

<EMBED SRC="stub2.aif" HEIGHT=22 WIDTH=37 CONTROLS=STOPBUTTON NAME="MyConsole">

<EMBED SRC="stub3.aif" HEIGHT=20 WIDTH=74 CONTROLS=VOLUMELEVER NAME="MyConsole">
```

To use a SMALLCONSOLE:

```
<EMBED SRC="mysound.aif" HEIGHT=15 WIDTH=144 MASTERSOUND CONTROLS=SMALLCONSOLE>
```

LiveAudio is LiveConnect enabled. LiveConnect is a family of technologies that enable live, real-time communication on an HTML page among Java, JavaScript, and Navigator plug-ins.

The following functions will work in JavaScript to control a loaded LiveAudio plug-in:

Controlling functions (all Boolean):
```
play('TRUE/FALSE or int','URL of sound')
stop()
pause()
start_time(int seconds)
end_time(int seconds)
setvol(int percent)
fade_to(int to_percent)
fade_from_to(int from_percent,int to_percent)
start_at_beginning() = Override a start_time()
stop_at_end() = Override an end_time()
```

State indicators (all Boolean, except *, which is an int):
```
IsReady() = Returns TRUE if the plug-in has completed loading
IsPlaying() = Returns TRUE if the sound is currently playing
IsPaused() = Returns TRUE if the sound is currently paused
GetVolume() = Returns the current volume as a percentage *
```

As a result, all <EMBED> tags on your screen can now include the NAME parameter, as in:

```
<EMBED NAME="MyMovie" SRC="steve.avi"... >
```

It's now possible to reference the object MyMovie in JavaScript, as in:

```
function StartTheMovie(){
  document.MyMovie.play();
}
```

Some plug-ins can create callbacks, which can be defined as follows:

```
// Called whenever the movie advances
function AviFrameCallback(frame_number) {
    // code here
}
```

Although LiveAudio's flip side is LiveVideo, Netscape also supports Apple's QuickTime as a video standard. OFFWORLD (http://www.headspace.com/offworld/index.html), a sort of Myst Internet equivalent, makes extensive use of the Apple QuickTime plug-in to deliver movies, ambient sound, and QuickTime VR panoramic views. The QuickTime plug-in comes bundled with Navigator 3.0 but does not include the QuickTime VR component which needed to be

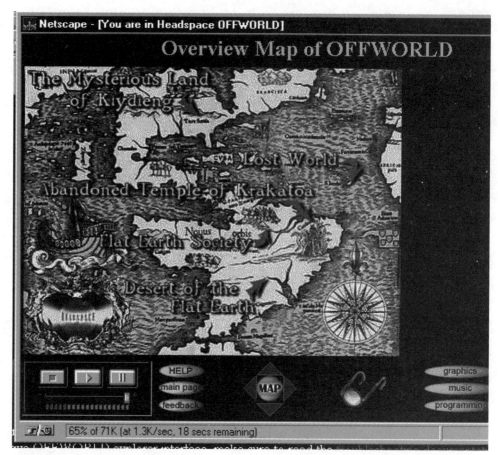

Figure 7-16. The Offworld multimedia experience.

downloaded from Apple's QuickTime virtual reality (VR) Web site http://qtvr.quicktime.apple.com. If you are using Windows, be sure to download QuickTime from http://quicktime.apple.com.

As you can see from figure 7-16, OFFWORLD provides a real multimedia experience on the Internet. In case you're wondering how the programmers opened a new window without toolbars, look at the following code:

```
<SCRIPT>
<!-- //window.open ('world-view.html?'+window.location.search.sub-
string   (1,window.location.search.length),'inside_offworld','tool-
bar=no,location=no,directories=no,status=yes,menubar=no,scrollbars
=no,resizable=no,width=635,height=428');// -->
</SCRIPT>
```

LiveVideo

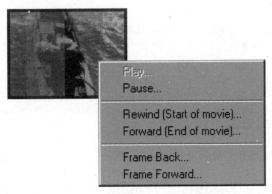

Figure 7-17. LiveVideo output on an HTML page.

With LiveVideo, Windows 3.1 and Windows 95 users can instantly view AVI movies that are either embedded in or linked to Web pages. Its viewer contains a complete set of controls including, Play, Pause, Rewind, Fast Forward, Frame Back, and Frame Forward, but can be displayed hiding these controls as shown in figure 7-17. The HTML to perform this task follows:

```
<EMBED
SRC="/comprod/products/navigator/version_3.0/multimedia/video/fla-
gloop.avi"
LOOP=TRUE
AUTOSTART=TRUE
HEIGHT=90 WIDTH=120
ALIGN=LEFT
HSPACE=10>
</EMBED>
```

LiveVideo plays video files in AVI format on Windows 95 and NT platforms. The format of the <embed> command follows:

```
<EMBED
SRC=[URL]
AUTOSTART=[TRUE|FALSE]
LOOP=[TRUE|FALSE]
WIDTH=[# PIXELS] HEIGHT=[#PIXELS]
ALIGN=[TOP|BOTTOM|CENTER|BASELINE|LEFT|RIGHT|TEXTTOP
MIDDLE|ABSMIDDLE|ABSBOTTOM]...>
```

EMBED. Use this tag to place AVI movies into your Web document.

SRC=[URL]. The URL of the source AVI file.

AUTOSTART=[TRUE|FALSE]. Setting the value to TRUE allows the AVI movie to begin playing automatically when the Web page is loaded. The default is FALSE.

LOOP=[TRUE|FALSE]. Setting the value to TRUE allows the AVI movie to play continuously until the user clicks on the movie to stop it from playing or goes to another page. The default is FALSE.

WIDTH=[# PIXELS]. Use this attribute to display the width of the AVI movie.

HEIGHT=[# PIXELS]. Use this attribute to display the height of the AVI movie. Standard sizes for movies are 90x120, 120x160, 180x240, and 240x320 (all size references are HEIGHT x WIDTH). These are all standard sizes using the 4:3 aspect ratio.

ALIGN=[TOP|BOTTOM|CENTER|BASELINE|LEFT|RIGHT|TEXTTOP|MIDDLE|ABSMIDDLE|ABSBOTTOM]. This attribute tells Netscape Navigator how you want to align text as it flows around the AVI movie. It acts similarly to the IMG tag.

Java and JavaScript functions include:

```
play() - Starts playing the source file at the current location.
stop() - Stops the currently playing video.
rewind() - Rewinds the currently loaded video.
seek(frame-number) - Sets the current frame of the video to the given
frame number.
```

Live3D

Live3D extends Navigator 3.0 into the 3D realm. With this VRML (Virtual Reality Modeling Language) viewer, you can experience a rich new world of 3D spaces and interact with text, images, animation, sound, music, and video. As I write this page Live3D is available with Netscape Navigator 3.0 for Windows 3.1, Windows 95, Windows NT, and Power Macintosh. Versions for 68K Macintosh and UNIX are under development. If you don't have the most recent version, which has Live3D as one of its bundled components, then it may be downloaded from the Live3D site at http://home.netscape.com/comprod/products/navigator/live3d/download_live3d.html.

Live3D, whose viewer is an integral component of Netscape Navigator, lets you access distributed 3D spaces rendered at maximum speed with adaptive rendering, background processing, hardware acceleration, and GZIP data compression. You will not be able to make it out in the black and white photo in fig-

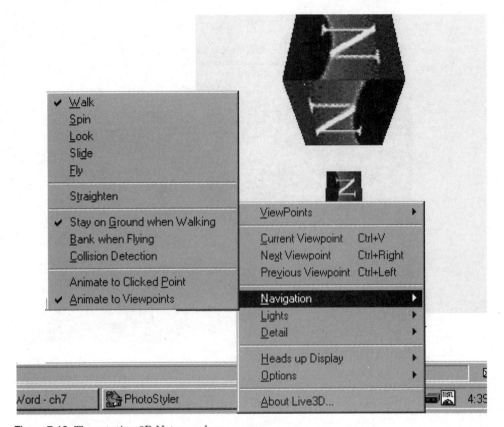

Figure 7-18. The rotating 3D Netscape logo.

ure 7-18, but the Netscape logo is rotating with glints of light reflecting off the cube. I right-clicked on the image to see what kind of image file it was and was surprised to see the menu that popped up as seen in the figure. This was when I realized that Live3D was part of the version of Netscape I had just downloaded.

Live3D worlds can be full of objects with rich, lifelike behaviors. A Live3D world is navigated by letting walking, flying, or pointing. Selectable camera viewpoints, collision detection, and optional gravity add flexibility and realism to navigation. Live3D offers full integration with LiveMedia for streaming audio and video in 3D space.

Live3D has a great sampler site located in Netscape's Cool Worlds site at //home.netscape.com/comprod/products/navigator/live3d/cool_worlds.html. The image is figure 7-19 shows an Italian café. You move your mouse to move into the virtual reality world.

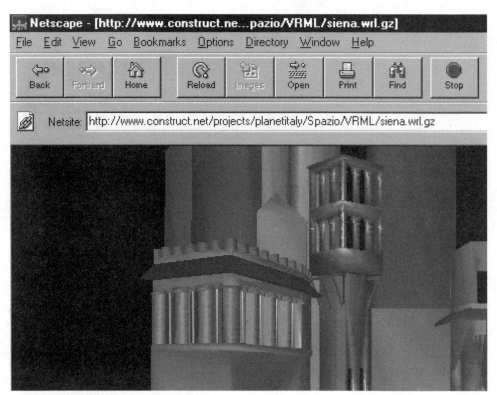

Figure 7-19. The Italian cafe.

Live3D is a VRML product. VRML is an open, extensible, industry-standard scene description language for 3-D scenes, or worlds, on the Internet. It's worth a few pages, at this time, to review just how one goes about creating a VRML world.

Using VRML

There are three ways to create a VRML world:

1. Create and edit a VRML text file by hand
2. Use a conversion program to convert an existing non-VRML 3-D file to VRML
3. Use an authoring package to create models and position them within a world

Because VRML is still a very new technology, chances are high that even if you use an authoring tool or converter to create your VRML world, you will need to modify it slightly by hand. Accordingly, it is helpful to familiarize yourself with the basic VRML concepts and syntax.

Once you have created your VRML world, you can embed it within an HTML document by using the <EMBED> tag. Using the <EMBED> tag to place a

VRML world in an HTML document is similar to using the <IMG> tag to place a 2-D image in an HTML document. For example, the following example embeds a VRML file called example.wrl into an HTML document:

```
<EMBED SRC="example.wrl" WIDTH=128 HEIGHT=128
BORDER=0 ALIGN=middle>
```

Shapes in a VRML world are made of polygons. The more complex a shape, the more polygons are required. A cube, for example, is typically comprised of just twelve polygons, since each side is made of two triangles. In contrast, a seemingly simple sphere requires more than 200 triangular polygons. As more objects are added to a world, the polygon count for that world increases. Each time a user's viewpoint changes in the VRML world, the browser has to redraw the scene. The more polygons the world contains, the longer the redraws take. Therefore, low polygon counts are one way to increase the user's navigation speed.

VRML allows the textures to be mapped onto shapes. Textures used in a VRML world may increase its size considerably. This will affect both download and redraw times. Therefore, if textures are used, small textures are desirable as one way to keep download times low and navigation speed high. Also, textures used in VRML worlds will require fewer client resources if they use fewer colors.

VRML is really beyond the scope of this book. The Netscape site has a good list of resources you should check out if you are interested in this subject: //home.netscape.com/comprod/products/navigator/live3d/vrml_resources.html. You might also want to find a copy of the Ultimate Sourcebook of Multimedia published by McGraw-Hill, which I edited. It contains extension information on this subject.

Like LiveAudio and LiveVideo, Live3D is embedded into your HTML using the following syntax:

```
<EMBED SRC=[URL] ...>
```

It can be embedded into Java and JavaScript using the following parameters:

`LoadScene(SceneURL, Frame)` Loads a new scene in the specified frame. If the frame is NULL, the URL is loaded into the _current Frame.

`SetBackgroundImage(BackgroundImage)`. Specifies the background image for the current scene. Supported image formats include PNG, RGB, GIF, JPEG, BMP, and RAS.

`GotoViewPoint(ViewPoint, nAnimationSteps)`. Animates the camera to the named viewpoint over nAnimationSteps.

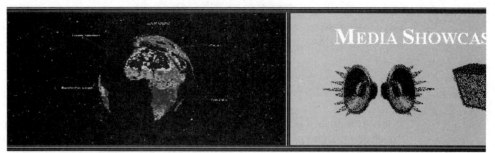

Now Netscape Navigator lets you combine 3D worlds, in-line audio, and in-line video all on one page. What's mo create links between them. For example, you can spin a 3D globe, zoom in on the globe, and select a city that is li and video clips in a different frame. To experience the integrated features of Live3D, LiveAudio, and QuickTime V page, download Netscape Navigator 3.0.

First, make sure your monitor is set to display 16-bit color or higher to ensure proper palette control. To get starte cursor in the left-hand VRML frame and click your right mouse button until the Live3D pop-up menu appears. Un select Navigation Bar. A navigation console should appear in the bottom of the frame.

Figure 7-20. Combining audio, video and VRML on one page.

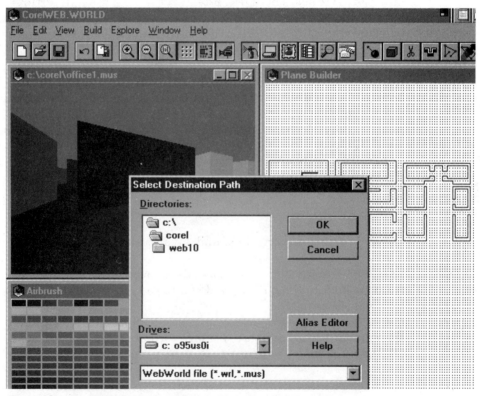

Figure 7-21. CorelWEB.WORLD can be used to create VRML worlds.

`SpinObject(Object, Pitch, Yaw, Roll, nLocal)`. Spins the named object around the specified axes. Rotations occur in World Coordinate Space if nLocal is FALSE; otherwise, rotation occurs around the object's geometric center point.

`AnimateObject(Object, URL)`. Animates an object. The animation file is specified in the URL. Supported animation files include Autodesk's VUEformat.

`Morph Object(Object, num_vertices, fCoords, nFrames, nMorphType)`. Morphs the specified object. Morphing occurs over nFrames with interpolation between the object's original vertices to the target fCoords. nMorphType is one of LOOP, ONCE, BACKFORTH.

`HideObject(Object)`. Hides an object.

`ShowObject(Object)`. Makes an object invisible.

`DeleteObject(Object)`. Deletes an object from the scene graph.

`SetObjectAnchor(Object, Anchor)`. Changes the anchor for the named object. The anchor may be a relative URL.

Java and Javascript callbacks:
`onAnchorClick()`.. Called when an anchor has been clicked.
`onMouseMove()`. Called whenever the mouse moves over the plug-in window.

You may combine Live3D, LiveAudio, LiveVideo and QuickTime all on one page. In figure 7-20 you see that the window is really split, using frames, into separate windows. Each uses the <EMBED> tag to embed the webcasting element into the HTML.

There are several packages that let you easily model 3D worlds. Corel's CorelWEB.WORLD provides an easy-to-use interface, complete with a plane builder, a set of textures, and a telephoto zoom lens that lets you zoom in and out of the world you're creating. Once you get the hang of it, it doesn't take you long to create a VRML file as shown in figure 7-21. You also have the ability to "publish" the file to a VRML standard format such as WRL, which is compatible with Live3D.

Netscape Multimedia Plug-ins

The Netscape site has a wide variety of plug-ins for those who are interested in making full use of audio and video over the Internet .Each of the following plug-ins can be downloaded directly from http://home.netscape.com/comprod/products/navigator/version_2.0/plugins/audio-video.html, but it's still worthwhile to visit each individual site to see what makes that particular plug-in tick.

Apple QuickTime
(http://www.quickTime.apple.com/dev/devweb.html)

The Apple QuickTime plug-in lets you experience QuickTime animation, music, MIDI, audio, video, and VR panoramas and objects directly in a Web page. The Apple QuickTime Plug-in's "fast-start" feature allows you to experience QuickTime content while it's downloading. It works seamlessly within firewalls. This plug-in is available for Macintosh 68K, Power Mac, and all Windows platforms.

CineWeb
(http://www.digigami.com/CineWebPress.html)

CineWeb brings real-time, streaming audio-video to the Web using standard movie (AVI, MOV, and MPG) and audio (WAV, MID, and MP2) files. Just say no to proprietary video codecs, per-user licensing fees, and special server software. Now everyone can afford to put independent TV and radio-style content on the Web. Used with Digigami's Weblisher and MegaPEG, CineWeb turns Netscape Navigator into a multimedia authoring tool so easy to use that anyone familiar with Microsoft Word, Corel WordPerfect, or Lotus WordPro can quickly create corporate training systems and multimedia marketing tools. This plug-in is available for all Windows platforms.

ClearFusion
(http://www.iterated.com)

ClearFusion is a streaming Video for Windows AVI plug-in. It enables any Video for Windows AVI file to be viewed inline as it's received. AVI files are easily included within HTML documents. Small and simple animations in AVI format can liven up a Web page. Larger AVI files present no more "download downers" because film clips are seen as soon as they begin to arrive and can be replayed at full speed. Plus, you can cancel the process at any time. ClearFusion doesn't mind firewalls — AVI files are streamed over standard HTTP connections and no special servers are needed. This plug-in is available for Windows 95 only.

Crescendo Plus
(http://www.liveupdate.com/cplus.html

The second generation of the Crescendo music plug-in family is now available. Version 2 delivers higher-quality stereo MIDI music to the Web. The free Crescendo plug-in has a cool new look with a CD-like control panel and digital counter. The Crescendo PLUS plug-in adds live real-time streaming (no download delays) and "sticky" client-side preferences. Plug-ins are available for Macintosh 68K, and all Windows platform.

Echospeech
(http://www.echospeech.com)

Add high-quality compressed speech to your Web pages with Echospeech. It was designed from the start as a multimedia-quality speech coder. This plug-in is available for all Windows platforms.

Flashware
(http://www.precept.com/release/fwserver_viewer.htm)

FlashWare, Precept's RTP Multimedia Networking software, includes a Netscape Navigator plug-in for inline, real-time audio and video broadcasting. FlashWare is used by developers to create intranet applications such as LAN TV, corporate communications, computer-based training, distance learning, process monitoring, and telemedicine. Plug-ins are available for Windows platforms.

InterVU Mpeg Player
(http://www.intervu.com)

The InterVU MPEG Player provides streaming MPEG audio-video downloads for Netscape Navigator 2.0 or better. It allows any industry standard MPEG audio-video file to be played within a Web page without using specialized MPEG hardware decoders on the user's computer, and without proprietary video servers. The InterVU MPEG Player provides a view of the first frame of the video right in the Web page, streaming of the video while downloading, and full-speed cached playback from the computer's hard drive. The full-quality, video and audio, of the originally recorded file is retained. Plug-ins are available for Macintosh 68K, Power Mac, Windows 95 and Windows NT.

MacZilla
(http://maczilla.com)

MacZilla is a Navigator 2.0 Macintosh plug-in that does (almost) everything: QuickTime; ambient MIDI background sound; WAV, AU, and AIFF audio; MPEG; and AVI. Having its own plug-in component architecture, MacZilla can extend and update itself over the Net with the click of a button. Plug-in is available for the Macintosh 68K only.

MIDPLUG
(http://www.yamaha.com.jp/english/xg/html/midhm.html)

The Yamaha MIDPLUG module for Netscape Navigator offers the impact of sound and music accompaniment for animation, ads, text — anything that can benefit from the power of sound. Compact MIDI data means maximum speed and efficiency on the Internet, with no extra equipment required. MIDPLUG features a built-in Soft Synthesizer with 128 GM-compatible voices, 8 drum kits, and even reverb. External MIDI playback equipment such as an XG sound module or daughtercard can be connected if required. Plug-ins are available for Macintosh, Power Mac, Windows 95 and Windows 3.1.

MovieStar
(http://www.beingthere.com)

The MovieStar plug-in gives your Netscape Navigator 2.0 browser the ability to view QuickTime movies from a Web site using MovieStar Maker, a multimedia editing application also available for download, webmasters can optimize QuickTime movies so Navigator users can view the movies while they download. Full technical information is provided for webmasters so they can configure movies for autoplay, looping, and many other settings. This plug-in is available for Windows 95 and Macintosh 68K.

RapidTransit
(http://monsterbit.com/rapidtransit)

RapidTransit decompresses and plays music that has been compressed up to 40:1 but still sounds good. RapidTransit provides full 16-bit, 44.1 kHz, CD-quality sound at compression rates of 10:1 or better. This plug-in is available for Windows 95, Windows NT and Macintosh 68K.

RealAudio
(http://www.realaudio.com)

RealAudio (which we discussed at length in Chapter 5) provides live and on-demand real-time audio over 14.4 kbps or faster connections to the Internet. RealAudio Version 2.0 is available for download now, with a powerful plug-in for Netscape that lets you easily customize and deliver audio from your Web site. Plug-ins are available for Macinotsh 68K, and all Windows platforms.

Talker
(http://www.mvpsolutions.com)

Your Web site can talk to Macintosh users with MVP Solutions' free Talker plug-in. The Talker plug-ins speech synthesis technology uses much less bandwidth than recorded audio. You can change the words your Web page speaks simply by editing a text file. The new version of Talker lets Web pages talk (and sing) using many different voices. A plug-in is available for Macintosh 68K.

Toolvox
(http://www.voxware.com)

Add high-quality speech audio to your Web pages. Your existing HTTP server can stream audio. ToolVox delivers 53:1 compression ratios. Plug-ins are available for Macintosh 68K, Windows 3.x and Windows 95.

TrueSpeech
(http://www.dspg.com)

The TrueSpeech Player plug-in version 3.20b enables embedded plug-in control functions in your Web page for style, ease, and simplicity. The plug-in is installed automatically with the Player, and works with Netscape 2.0 and later versions. Start, stop, and rewind buttons are small and unobtrusive. This plug-in was originally part of version 3.10b of the TrueSpeech Player for Windows 3.x, though that version was not real-time, as is version 3.20b. The plug-in has an optional autostart command and a loop option for repeat playback. This plug-in is available for Windows 95 and Windows NT.

VDOLive
(http://www.vdo.net)

VDOLive, which we discussed at length in Chapter 6, compresses video images without compromising quality on the receiving end. The speed of your connection determines the frame delivery rate: With a 28.8 kbps modem, VDOLive runs in real-time at 10 to 15 frames per second. A plug-in is available for all Windows platforms.

ViewMovie
(http://www.well.com/~ivanski/viewmovie/docs.html)

ViewMovie is a Netscape Navigator 2.0 plug-in that supports viewing and embedding Apple QuickTime movies in Web pages, including using movies as link anchors and image maps. There is a plug-in available for Macintosh 68K.

VivoActive Player
(http://www.vivo.com)

The VivoActive Player, a streaming video plug-in for Netscape Navigator, is a simple, fast way to get video clips on your Web page. Video for Windows AVI files are compressed up to 250:1, and the resulting VIV files can be viewed with the VivoActive Player as they download. VivoActive videos are transmitted using HTTP, so anyone who can view your Web pages can see your video. Plug-ins are available for Macintosh, Power Mac and all Windows platforms.

Now that we've discussed all the major tools, let's take a peak at some of the lesser luminaries of the webcasted Internet. For that, turn to Chapter 8.

Note:

The information in this chapter has been provided with permission from Netscape.

Netscape Communications Corporation has not authorized, sponsored, or endorsed, or approved this publication and is not responsible for its content. Netscape and the Netscape Communications Corporate Logos, are trademarks and trade names of Netscape Communications Corporation. All other product names and/or logos are trademarks of their respective owners.

Netscape images are Copyright 1996 Netscape Communications Corp. All Rights Reserved. The images may not be reprinted or copied without the express written permission of Netscape.

Chapter

8

More Webcasting Tools

Although this book has spent quite a lot of time discussing the products of Progressive Networks, Microsoft, Netscape and VDOnet, there are other companies that sell webcasting products. This chapter will survey other tools out there in the marketplace.

Be forewarned, however. These products work at varying levels of quality.

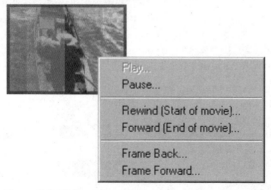

Figure 8-1. Webcasting toolset.

Some of the plug-in sizes are large and some smaller. I might be stating the obvious, but this needs to be taken into account if you are making an effort to choose a product on which to standardize.

I downloaded each and every one of these products. This chapter is not a series of product reviews, so I won't get into my opinion here. I will share with you the fact that I did have trouble with some of the products. In one case I downloaded the Netscape 32-bit version of a plug-in only to be told that I needed the 16-bit version. When I downloaded the 16-bit version I was told I needed the 32-bit version. Sort of like a dog chasing his tail. The same product worked like a charm on my laptop. Go figure. Another product worked just fine on my laptop, but seemed to consume every last morsel of memory. I couldn't paste into my word processor and the rest of my Windows 95 session dragged.

If you're serious about moving into this arena do the following:

1. Download all of the software discussed in this book onto multiple PCs: Pentium, 486, 14.4 kbps, 28.8 kbps, etc.
2. Test each piece of software on each platform using both Netscape Navigator and Microsoft Internet Explorer.

Just remember, having fancy webcasting on your site is one thing. Having your users get it to work is an entirely different matter.

VivoActive

Vivo Software (http://www.vivo.com/) was founded in 1993 by a team of experts in video and audio signal processing technology. Vivo develops and markets VivoActive software as shown in figure 8-2, the only commercially available solution for producing and viewing low-bandwidth, on-demand streaming media (audio and video) over the World Wide Web. Vivo's patented compression technology also is licensed to PictureTel Corp., which uses it as the basis for its PC-based videoconferencing products.

Figure 8-2. VivoActive product set.

VivoActive is touted as being the world's first serverless streaming video product, providing excellent video quality even at very low bit rates. Since there's no server component, the high cost and complexity of providing streaming video are eliminated. Now, even over 28.8 modems, Web surfers can watch uninterrupted streaming audio/video content that pretty much starts to play when they click. There are two parts to the VivoActive product line — the VivoActive Producer and the VivoActive Player.

Vivo performs this feat of serverless magic with their audio/video compression tool called the VivoActive Producer. There are two versions of the VivoActive Producer — one that runs on IBM-compatible PCs under Windows 95 or NT — and one that runs on PowerMacs. The Windows 95 or NT version compresses Video for Windows (AVI) files into a much smaller VIVO formatted (VIV) file. Similarly, the PowerMac version of the VivoActive Producer compresses QuickTime (MOV) files into VIVO formatted files.

The VIVO format uses the international video and audio compression standards from the world of low bit-rate videoconferencing, namely H.263 video compression and G.723 audio compression. H.263 is based on Discrete Cosine Transform algorithms, which are much more efficient than fractal or wavelet algorithms. For example, a 30 megabyte .AVI file containing roughly 30 seconds of video can be compressed to under 100 kilobytes by VivoActive Producer.

Once the original AVI file is converted to a VIV file, the Web site developer simply uses the HTML <EMBED> command to embed the VIVO file into the Web page, the same way he or she would embed a GIF or JPG file. So the HTML document, and the VIVO video file it references, can live on any old Web server, not just some special video server. And with one copy of the VivoActive Producer, you can compress and distribute all the video content you want, to as many people as you want.

There are free VivoActive Players for a variety of browsers (http://www.vivo.com/dload.htm) and platforms (plug-ins for Netscape Navigator on the Macintosh, Windows 95, Window NT, Windows 3.1, and an ActiveX control for Microsoft Internet Explorer on Windows 95 or NT) which perform the video and audio decoding on your machine "on-the-fly." The video is streamed from the Web server via HTTP over TCP, just like the rest of the page, so it goes through all firewalls and doesn't require special UDP ports to be opened. The only thing a Web server administrator has to do is add a new MIME type table entry to associate VIV files with VivoActive video.

VivoActive Producer

A popular application for digitizing and compressing videos on PCs is Video for Windows which carries the file extension AVI. VivoActive Producer (trial version for Windows 95/NT and PowerMac at http://www.vivo.com/download/dld-prod.htm) software lets you further compress an AVI file by a factor of hundreds of its original size, while maintaining high video and audio quality. Videos created with VivoActive have the file extension VIV and a Multipurpose

Internet Mail Extension (MIME) format. MIME is a standard for sending multimedia and binary data over the Internet and simplifies transmission of VIV files.

For $495 you get a serverless digital video production tool that uses standard digital video formats (AVI and QuickTime); provides video compression; ratios of 200:1; streams video directly from any Web page; uses HTTP protocol safely across firewalls; uses standards (H.263/G.723); lets you stream at frame rates at compression ratios you determine.

Steps For Adding VIVO Video to a Web Site

There are six basic steps to adding VIVO video to a Web site: Gathering video content, capturing to digital video format, editing the digital video, converting digital video to VIVO format, creating the HTML pages, and testing your results. Depending on whether you are creating new video content or working from a video library, the steps in this process can vary.

1. **Gathering Video Content:** If you are creating new video to include on your Web site, it is important that you take certain elements of the filming process into consideration. Some material will work better when compressed than others. For example, if you plan to shoot video of a person giving a speech, consider what this person is wearing. A solid shirt will work better than a striped shirt.

2. **Capturing to Digital Video Format:** Once you have a video tape containing the content for your Web site, you need to capture this into a digital video format stored on your computer. To do this, you need an audio/video capture card. Some newer computers are being sold with these cards included. If you have a computer, but do not have a capture card, they are easy to find at any computer store or by searching on the Internet.

To capture the video, you connect your VCR or video camera to the capture card. The VCR or camera should have line-out jacks for audio and video. These lines connect to the line-in jacks on the capture card. If your card and camera offer S-Video connections in addition to the standard line-in/out connections, you will get better quality using S-Video.

Most capture cards are sold with capture software, or video editing software to allow you to perform the video capture. You need to make some decisions in the software about different settings that will affect the quality of the video you create. Some typical settings are as follows:

Audio Format:
Choose 16 bit, 8 kHz, mono. The VivoActive Producer will accept any mono audio setting, but the digital audio format is converted to 16 bit, 8 kHz, mono before it is converted to the standard G.723 audio. Choosing this format will give you the best audio quality, and the conversion will complete more quickly.

Video Format:
The VivoActive Producer will accept any Video Format although some formats result in larger files than others. Most video capture cards have several formats to choose from. Choose whichever format is recommended for your capture card.

Video Resolution:
The VivoActive Producer supports 176x144 (QCIF) resolution. If your capture card supports this resolution, then this is the best choice. If your card does not support this resolution, then the VivoActive Producer will take care of resizing the image automatically. Choose the closest setting available.

Compression:
Although the VivoActive Producer will accept compressed digital files, it is best to capture your source as an uncompressed file. Avoid using Cinepak or Indeo compression since these formats will compromise the quality of the video. Choosing uncompressed will result in a better quality image.

Frame Rate:
To determine the best frame rate for your video, you need to consider the connection rate at which the videos on your Web site will be viewed, and the type of content you are using. If your video contains a person giving a speech, then lip synchronization is important. You want to see the person saying every word. To achieve this, you should choose a frame rate of at least 10 frames per second (fps). If your video content contains a high motion subject like a race car, a lower frame rate (7.5 fps) will provide you with a better quality image. Of course, if you are planning to use videos in an Intranet environment where the connection rate isn't an issue, you can choose 15-30 fps for all videos. When working on a site that expects 28.8 kbps modem users, stick with the 10 fps for head shots and 7.5 fps for high motion guidelines.

3. **Editing the Digital Video**: If you are capturing the video file from a video tape, you may find that it is difficult to start and stop the capture process at the right spot. You could keep trying with hopes that your quick fingers will eventually get it right, or you can edit the video using a non-linear editing tool. There are many products available that will allow you to edit your videos (see the resources list at the end of Chapter 10). These products allow you to remove frames, merge audio and video together, add subtitles, as well as a whole list of video options. The options available and ease of use will depend on the product that you select.

4. **Converting Video to VIVO Format**: The VivoActive Producer allows you to convert a standard digital video file into a format that you can embed in your Web page. Instead of the user having to download a video to play it, the VIVO

file will automatically play when a user visits your site. The conversion process in the VivoActive Producer is quite simple. The bit-rate is the amount of the file that will be transferred over the modem line each second. Bit-rate is measured in kilobits per second (kbps). A higher bit-rate results in a larger file with sharper quality.

So why not always choose the highest bit-rate possible? Remember you are dealing with the Internet. If you expect users to connect to your site using a 28.8 kbps modem, it will take a long time for them to view your videos. If your VIVO file has a bit-rate of 56 kbps, a user connected with a 28.8 kbps modem will not be able to download and view the video at the same time. They will experience a delay at the beginning of the video as information is downloaded into memory. Depending on the length of the video, they may also experience an interruption in the middle while more of the information is downloaded into memory. Try to select a bit-rate that is going to be slightly lower than the connection rates that you expect to your site. The VivoActive Producer offers many bitrate settings ranging from 14.4 kbps to 115.2 kbps.

The frame rate controls how smooth the motion of the image will be. The frame rate slider in the VivoActive Producer has settings that are based on the actual frame rate of the video you are converting. There are 6 settings which represent fractions of the actual frame rate from 1/1, 1/2, 1/3, 1/4, 1/5, 1/6. So, if the frame rate of your original video is 15 fps, then the options on the second slider will be 15, 7.5, 5, 3.75, 3, 2.5 (fps). Choose a frame rate that is going to give you good motion for your video, but still leave you with good quality along with the bit-rate you are selecting. You want to maximize the bits per frame, so if you are creating videos for users connecting to your site using a 28.8 kbps modem, here are the suggested settings:

Motion Bit-rate Frame Rate
Talking Head (low) 21.6K 10 fps
Action (high) 21.6K 7.5 fps

5. **Creating an HTML Page to Include a VIVO Video**: Including a VIVO video in your HTML page is quite simple. You can use the code listed below into your pages. You will only need to change the path and file name of the actual video. Here is the Object tag code needed to embed a VIVO video:

```
<OBJECT CLASSID="clsid:02466323-75ed-11cf-a267-0020af2546ea"
   WIDTH=176 HEIGHT=144
   CODEBASE="http://www.vivo.com/ie/vvweb.cab#Version=1,0,0,0">
   <PARAM NAME="URL" VALUE="filename.viv">
   <PARAM NAME="VIDEOCONTROLS" VALUE="on">
   <PARAM NAME="AUTOSTART" VALUE="false">
   <EMBED SRC="filename.viv" width=176 height=144 autostart=false
   videocontrols=on>
</OBJECT>
```

The above Object sequence will work for both Netscape Navigator 2.0 and Internet Explorer 3.0 Beta 2 or higher browsers. How does it work? The browser will come to the Object tag. If you are using Netscape, everything is ignored except for the EMBED tag which requires that the user has downloaded and installed the VivoActive Player plug-in from www.vivo.com.

If you are using Internet Explorer, it searches for the Class ID in your Windows 95 registry. If the Class ID is found, then the Parameters are sent to the VivoActive Player control. If the Class ID is not found, then the Codebase is accessed and the VivoActive Player for ActiveX is automatically installed on the user's machine. Parameters recognized by the VivoActive Player are:

`Autostart`
The Autostart parameter allows you to specify whether the video should play automatically when a page containing a VIVO video is accessed, or if the user must click on the video control for the video to begin playing.

`Videocontrols`
The Videocontrols parameter specifies whether the video controls appear on the video.

You can embed a VIVO video into any element you wish just like a GIF or JPG file. The limitation is one VIVO per page. If you have video content that you would like to show on a single page, tables may be a good alternative. Tables will allow you to show a list of video descriptions down the first column and show the corresponding video in the second column.

There is a MIME Type associated with the VIVO file. Your Webmaster will need to know information about the VIVO MIME Type so your VIVO files will be recognized. If you use a leased server from an Internet Service Provider, they will be able to handle this for you. The information you need is:

`AddType video/vnd.vivo for .viv extensions`

If your server does not have this information, you will get a MIME Type error when trying to view videos.

6. **Testing Your Results:** Since there is no server software required, you can test your videos locally either by opening the VIVO file directly into Netscape, or opening the HTML page which accesses the VIVO file locally. Once you verify that the page layout and video quality are acceptable, simply FTP the HTML page, any associated images, and the VIVO file to your server.

Remember that you will have visitors to your site using all different connection speeds. By testing your new pages at modem speeds, you can see how fast your visitors will view your pages and your videos. This additional testing may help you to determine better video settings to use for bit-rate and frame rate in the future. If you notice that with a modem connection, you are waiting a long time to view your videos, try a lower bit-rate in the future. If you notice that the videos start really quickly, but the image looks blurry, try a lower frame rate in the future.

Vosaic

Vosaic (http://vosaic.com/) uses standards compliant technology to integrate streaming video and audio with the Web. Their product scales from 28 kbps to T-1, is MPEG adaptive and operates at any frame rate between 5 fps — 15 fps.

The Vosaic video browser is integrated as a plug-in into the Netscape and Spyglass Web browsers. It is provided as an ActiveX control for the Internet Explorer 3.0 beta 2. The video browser is available in two flavors: one for the Pentium processor and one for the 80486. The plug-in features real-time download and display of:

1. MPEG 1 and 2 video
2. MPEG layer 1 and layer 2 audio
3. H.263 video
4. GSM and half rate GSM audio
5. G723.1 and half rate G723.1 audio

Vosaic also has a plug-in which is DirectX enabled. If you have high-performance graphics hardware capable of video acceleration, DirectX will allow you

Figure 8-3. Vosaic's video library.

Figure 8-4. Vosaic controls.

to smoothly expand videos to full size. Vosaic has a great video library as shown in figure 8-3, which is worth perusing if you're trying to decide which videocasting product to invest in.

A full set of control buttons enables you to play and stop, and fast forward or rewind through the video as shown in figure 8-4. Detachable video windows allow you to expand the image to any size you want. Video hyperlinks embedded within the video stream make objects within the video itself clickable — click on a video hyperlink to go off to another related page.

The Vosaic video server is available for the Windows 95 and NT platforms, the Macintosh Power PC platform, as well as Linux, SGI and SUN Solaris UNIX. Vosaic's Video Datagram Protocol (VDP) efficiently transmits continuous media over the Internet. The video server manages large stores of video and audio files. Tools are provided for building your own video database.

The server software has the following features: PC NT or UNIX compatibility; manages large video and audio files; video and audio clips are frame addressable; video and audio meta-information management, for support of flexible access and efficient reuse of video and audio material; admission control — access to videoserver is evaluated so that new request will not degrade current connections being served.

The video is transmitted over the Internet using a network bandwidth friendly algorithm that avoids congestion. It uses VDP: A Video Datagram Protocol that operates end-to-end; the standard UDP network protocol; a best effort, adaptive flow control; a control loop that adapts to network conditions; and adapts to client side CPU conditions.

Currently the video used is of MPEG-1 format, and the audio is MPEG layer I or layer II format. Also the video and audio are separate, even for the same movie. Vosaic requires this because in case of the network congestion, the audio is given higher priority to get through while video frames will be dropped. The following are the parameters of the video and audio you see from the Vosaic site:

Mpeg Video:

Picture Size: 320x240, 240x180, 160x120
Frame rate: 5 f/s — 15 f/s, a few with 30 f/s
Bit rate: 20 kbps — 600 kbps
Digitizing process: Most of the movies are captured using the capture tools on SGI and then converted to MPEG using an encoder from Berkeley.

Mpeg Audio:

Sample rate: 44.1 KHz
Bit rate: 32 kbps
Digitizing process: Most of the audio clips are captured using the capture tools on SGI (capture and sound editor) into AIFF format and then converted using MOVIEMASTER and a program called MUSICIN. The SOUNDFILER on SGI is also quite useful in converting between audio formats.

It is worthwhile to note that Vosaic hosts the Continuous Media Enhanced Web Discussion Forum which can be accessed from the following site: http://www.vosaic.com/html/forum.html.

Xing StreamWorks

The Xing StreamWorks player (http://www.xingtech.com) has the following capabilities: real-time streamed playing which permits you to play audio and video streams from the network with no wait for download; it is based on the international MPEG standard for digital audio and video on a multimedia PC without requiring expensive hardware add-ons; it works as a helper application for Web browsers such as Netscape's Navigator and Microsoft's Internet Explorer; it is capable of up to full screen, full color, full motion video with CD quality, 44 KHz, audio; it enables scaleable data rates — from 8.5 Kilobits to 2.0 Megabits, including ISDN and popular 14.4 kbps and 28.8 kbps modems; available for Macintosh, Windows, and X-Windows.

The StreamWorks player can be downloaded from the following site: http://www.xingtech.com/sw_now.html. The Xing content guide is also worth perusing. It is located at http://www.xingtech.com/content/sw2_content.html. Figure 8-5 shows how the StreamWorks player looked during the Emmy awards as Florence Henderson interviewed yet another Emmy contender.

The Xing StreamWorks Server provides a scaleable solution that is designed for existing local and wide area networks (intranets) and the Internet. StreamWorks Server works in unison with StreamWorks Player to coordinate

Figure 8-5. The Streamworks player.

playback and handle problems that are typical of existing networks. Given the scaleable nature of StreamWorks Server, it can support users connected at any data rate, including the 14.4, 28.8, and ISDN connections that are typical of the Internet. With the addition of a StreamWorks Transmitter, StreamWorks Server becomes a live broadcast center capable of delivering live video and audio to a large simultaneous audience.

Attributes of the StreamWorks Server include: MPEG-based; scaleable delivery — stream scaling allows a single source stream to be delivered at multiple lower data rates; topology Independent — Ethernet, ATM, ISDN, PPP, etc.; live and on-demand flexibility — delivers pre-recorded files on-demand from disk or live feeds from StreamWorks Transmitter; available for UNIX (SGI IRIX, Solaris for SPARC, Linux), and Windows NT; according to the vendor approach uses only 3-5% network overhead, much more efficient than traditional video/audio servers; PlusPACKs add additional power and flexibility.

PlusPACK includes both LiveFile and propagation capabilities. LiveFile enables virtual live feeds (simulated live broadcasts) from pre-recorded files. LiveFiles minimize server hardware requirements while also allowing audience extension through propagation. StreamWorks propagation adds the ability to reach very large audiences by propagating StreamWorks feeds across multiple Servers.

Supported stream formats include:

MPEG System Streams
Video Support: Delivers first MPEG-1 video stream
Audio Support: Delivers first MPEG-1 audio stream, or delivers MPEG-1 private data streams containing an MPEG-2 audio stream or an LBR audio stream

MPEG-1 Video Streams
Frame Types: I, P, B
Resolution: 32x32 to 384x240 (NTSC) or 352x288 (PAL)
Frame Rates: 23.976, 24, 25, 29.97, 30
Bit Rates: up to 500 kilobytes per second
Variable bit rates supported (no random access
Aspect Ratios: ignored

MPEG-1 or MPEG-2 Audio Streams
Layers: I and II
Bit rates: all
Modes: mono, stereo, dual channel, joint stereo

LBR Audio Streams
Bit rates: all

Pricing for the server is shown in figure 8-6.

XingMPEG Encoder

XingMPEG Encoder ($89, available for sale from CompuServe: Go xing) creates fully compliant MPEG-1 streams from digital audio and video source files. This capability allows XingMPEG Encoder to work with many different source files from video capture cards, video editing software and other popular multi-

Bandwidth	Server	PlusPack	Propagation Server
128K	$795	$200	$400
512K	$1495	$400	$750
1.54M	$3500	$875	$1750
10M	$4950	$1250	$2500
45M	$9950	$2500	$4950
Unlimited	$14950	$3750	$7500

Figure 8-6. StreamWorks pricing.

media tools. The built in playback controls allow for easy review of your finished MPEG files using the included XingMPEG Player software or your own MPEG playback hardware.

It has a variety of features including: full quality optimization. It uses all available MPEG-1 features including motion compensation with multilevel motion estimation, automatic bit-rate control and complete intra (I), predicted (P) and bidirectional (B) frame support; supports Popular Multimedia tools; it can directly encode AVI and WAV files created using tools like Adobe Premiere, FAST FPS-60, InSync Razor and many more third-party products; it comes with predefined format settings which lets you start encoding immediately using optimized settings for Single Speed CD-ROM, Whitebook and other popular MPEG formats; its support for the Whitebook standard enables creation of audio and video material for VideoCDs, CD-i Movies and Karaoke CDs.

StreamWorks Transmitter

StreamWorks Transmitter gives you live network encoding with a simple, turn key system. An audio transmitter is priced at $2500 while both audio and video will cost $6500.

StreamWorks Transmitter is a dedicated hardware/software system that brings together universally recognized standards and protocols for real time MPEG encoding and live network transmission across any IP network (Internet, intranet, WAN or LAN).

Specifications for the Transmitter are:

Audio Input
Type: Unbalanced line level input
Connector: 1/8" Stereo Mini Jack

Video Input
Type: NTSC or PAL composite analog signal
Connector: RCA Jack

Network Output
MPEG-1 System Streams
Standard: One MPEG-1 video stream and one MPEG-1 audio stream
Extended: One MPEG-1 video stream and one MPEG-1 private data stream containing an MPEG-2 audio stream or an LBR audio stream

MPEG-1 Video Streams
Frame Types: I, P, B
Resolution: 32x32 to 352x240 (NTSC) or 352x288 (PAL)
Frame Rates: 23.976, 24, 25, 29.97, 30
Bit Rates: 64 to 3000 kbits/s

MPEG-1 Audio Streams (Layer II)
Per Channel Bit Rates: 32, 48, 56, 64, 80, 96, 112, 128, 160 or 192 kbits/s
Modes: mono, joint stereo
Joint Stereo Bands: 4, 8, 12, 16
Sample Rates: 32, 44.1, 48

MPEG-2 Audio Streams (Layer II)
Per Channel Bit rates: 8, 16, 24, 32, 40, 48, 56, 64 or 80 kbits/s
Modes: mono, joint stereo
Joint Stereo Bands: 4, 8, 12, 16
Sample Rates: 16, 22.05, 32, 44.1, 48

LBR Audio Streams
Bit rates: 8, 9, 10, 11, 12, 13, 14, 15 or 16 kbits/s
Modes: mono
Sample Rates: 8

Network Connection
Type: Auto-config Ethernet (coax or twisted pair)
Connector: 10 Base-T or BNC

Monitor Connection
(monitor not included)
Type: VGA monochrome
Connector: 9 pin D-sub

Keyboard Connection
(keyboard not included)
Type: Standard keyboard
Connector: 5 pin DIN

Power Connection
110 or 220 Volts AC, 250 Watts

InterVU

InterVU's MPEG player is an example of what is known as a pseudo-streaming technology. Pseudo-streams typically start playing back a file after enough of it has been downloaded to ensure a complete and stutter-free playback. Other differences between a streamer and a pseudo-streamer are that a pseudo-streamer plays the file only from the beginning to the end rather than being able to start anywhere within the file and that the file itself is downloaded to the client rather than remaining on the server.

InterVU's (http://www.cerf.net/intervu/prevu.html) goal is to make high-speed, high-quality, cost-effective video delivery available over the Internet.

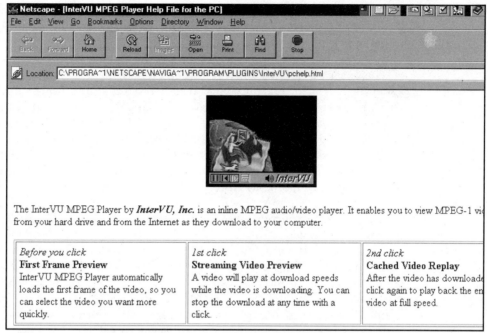

Figure 8-7. InterVU player.

InterVU's patented Client-Network Video Distribution Solution embraces today's Internet (TCP/IP) and Digital Broadcast Television Network (MPEG) Standards.

InterVU's Client application (the InterVU MPEG Video Player which is available for download from http://www.cerf.net/intervu/player/player.html) provides direct plug-in compatibility for leading Internet browser companies (e.g., Netscape Communications). A plug-in is available for Windows 95/NT and the Macintosh.

The InterVU MPEG Player by InterVU, Inc. is an inline MPEG audio/video player. It enables you to view MPEG-1 videos from your hard drive and from the Internet as they download to your computer.

InterVU has a unique approach to displaying audio/video as shown in figure 8-7. Another nice feature, from an end-user's perspective, is that, unlike proprietary formats such as RealAudio, InterVU's use of MPEGs means the video can be easily downloaded to the end-user's PC.

Before you click: First Frame Preview. InterVU MPEG Player automatically loads the first frame of the video, so you can select the video you want more quickly.

1st click: Streaming Video Preview. A video will play at download speeds while the video is downloading. You can stop the download at any time. .

2nd click: Cached Video Replay. After the video has downloaded, click again to play back the entire video at full speed.

The InterVU MPEG Player implements several strategies for pacing and synchronizing its video playback. It helps to understand these strategies when you are designing video content to achieve maximum quality and visual impact.

When the InterVU MPEG Player plays a video stream, it does not know if there is sound in the video until sound data is encountered. For this reason, you may sometimes see the unknown sound symbol (a speaker icon overlaid with a question mark) momentarily before seeing the sound symbol and hearing sound.

Until sound is encountered in the stream, the InterVU MPEG Player uses an unsynchronized strategy. This means it plays every video frame in the stream. If you have a fast machine (or low-bandwidth video), the InterVU MPEG Player will have spare processing time and will wait between frames so they are displayed at the right speed. If your machine is slow relative to the video bandwidth, the InterVU MPEG Player is designed to display every frame, even if this means the video plays slower than specified in the video stream. Consequently, on fast machines the InterVU MPEG Player will play at the right speed, on slow machines it will play as fast as it can but that might be slower than the video specifies.

When sound is encountered in the stream, the InterVU MPEG Player switches to a synchronized strategy. This means that some video frames may be dropped in order to ensure that the video is delivered at the right speed. Most often this is unnoticeable, but occasionally may result in images that seem to "pause" momentarily while playing. A consequence of playing sound and video together is that the sound decompression places an additional load on processing power, and can reduce the video quality as the InterVU MPEG Player tries to compensate by devoting more processing time to the audio decompression.

While using a synchronized strategy (when sound is present in the stream), the InterVU MPEG Player detects the processor load dynamically and alters video quality on-the-fly by dropping video frames as needed. If, in order to stay synchronized with the sound, video quality drops below a certain threshold, the InterVU MPEG Player will stop playing sound altogether, and reverts to an unsynchronized strategy for playing video (as described above). At this point a red X will appear over the speaker icon. You can force the InterVU MPEG Player to try again to play sound with video by pressing the Reload or Refresh button on your Web browser. The InterVU MPEG Player will start playback from scratch, attempting to play both sound and video.

If the InterVU MPEG Player is not able to process video fast enough to keep up with the sound, you may occasionally hear gaps. If the number and frequency of the gaps are too great, it will drop sound altogether. In either case, this is an indication that the video is pushing the limits on time and space (of your machine or network).

HTML Coding

An easy way to have an MPEG file play by itself in a Netscape window is to use the standard HTML reference:

`<A REF="http://www.yoursite.com/coolvideo.mpg">Link to MPEG</A>`.

To add the InterVU MPEG Player to your Web pages, you use the EMBED tag which allows documents of varying data types to be embedded into an HTML file. This command has three required attributes, SRC, WIDTH, and HEIGHT and if you've read this book straight through you'll already be familiar with the syntax:

`<EMBED    SRC="Sample.mpg",    WIDTH=174,    HEIGHT=134,    CONBAR=NO, LOOP=YES>`

At the risk of being repetitive, I will repeat here the format of the <EMBED> tag:

`SRC=<URL>` The URL, or Internet location, of the source MPEG document. This file must have a MIME type of video/mpeg or video/x-mpeg for this product. This parameter is required.

`WIDTH=<size in pixels>` The WIDTH attribute specifies the width of the displayed image of the embedded MPEG document in pixels. You'll need to add 10 pixels to the width of the video in order to show the frame around the displayed image. If DOUBLESIZE or HALFSIZE attributes are also used, you will have to use double or half of the actual video size, respectively, in your calculation (details below). If WIDTH is greater than the size of the video plus the frame, then the excess will be displayed as a white border surrounding the Player. If WIDTH is less than the size of the video plus the frame, then the Player will be cropped and centered within the remaining area. This parameter is required.

`HEIGHT=<size in pixels>` The HEIGHT attribute specifies the height of the displayed document in pixels. You'll need to add 29 pixels to the height of the video frame in order to show the control bar of the InterVU MPEG Player. If the CONBAR=NO attribute is set, then only 10 pixels would be added. If DOUBLESIZE or HALFSIZE attributes are also used, you will have to use double or half of the actual video size, respectively, in your calculation. If HEIGHT is greater than the size of the video plus the frame, then the excess will be displayed as a white border surrounding the Player. If HEIGHT is less than the size of the video plus the frame, then the Player will be cropped and centered within the remaining area. This parameter is required.

`AUTOPLAY=<YES>` The AUTOPLAY attribute is an optional parameter. If set to YES, the video starts playing automatically when the "Web page" is selected or viewed. The default is NO. Specifying AUTOPLAY=NO (or by not including the AUTOPLAY parameter) will cause the first frame of the video to be displayed when the page is loaded. The user must then start the video manually.

`PLUGINSPAGE=<URL>` When a page is viewed that needs a plugin not found on the client, a special icon is displayed in place of the plug-in. The first time the unknown plug-in type is invoked, a dialog box is automatically opened. This dialog box contains two buttons: Plugin Info and Cancel. Clicking on Plugin Info causes Navigator to open a URL. The URL is either the location specified in the PLUGINSPAGE attribute in the EMBED tag, or if the attribute is not used, the Netscape page that lists current plug-ins. The URL generally contains information on obtaining the plug-in or the ability to download and save the plu-gin in the correct location on the client. InterVU encourages content providers to include the PLUGINSPAGE attribute with a value of "http://www.intervu.com" in their HTML pages to make it easier for users to access the InterVU MPEG Player.

Additional optional parameters:

`FRAMERATE=<Number>` You may use this attribute to decrease the frame rate for the MPEG file being displayed. Use positive integers from 1 to 25, representing how many frames (or separate video images) are played per second. The smaller the number you enter, the slower the video will play. It is best to adjust the number entered in the parameter until you get the result you would like. Please note that sound is dependent on the file playing at its normal rate. So if the FRAMERATE option is used, the file will play without sound.

`LOOP=<Number>` If you would like the video to loop, you may use this attribute and enter the number of times you would like it to loop. Each time the start button is pressed, the video will play the specified number of times.

`DOUBLESIZE=<YES>` This attribute configures the InterVU MPEG Player to play the video at double the encoded size. The default value is NO. The DOUBLESIZE attribute may not be used with HALFSIZE in the same EMBED statement. The HEIGHT and WIDTH attribute values must be changed when this attribute is used.

`HALFSIZE=<YES>` This attribute configures the InterVU MPEG Player to play the video at half the encoded size. The default value is NO. The HALFSIZE attribute may not be used with DOUBLESIZE in the same EMBED statement.

The HEIGHT and WIDTH attribute values must be changed when this attribute is used.

CONBAR=<NO> You may disable the "controls" bar of the InterVU MPEG Player with this option. When the control bar is disabled, just click on the video to start/stop the video. You will need to recalculate the number of pixels you add to the original video size so the display area will not show space for the control bar. The control bar's height is 19 pixels, so instead of adding 29 pixels, you will only need to add 10 pixels. The default value is YES.

FRAMES=<YES> This attribute is required if you are creating a Web page with Netscape FRAMES. For viewers using a Mac, the video will autoplay. For all other viewers, the FRAMES attribute will be ignored, and the video will play according to how you set the AUTOPLAY attribute (where the default is NO).

PALETTE=<FOREGROUND> This feature is not available for the Macintosh version at this time. The PALETTE option configures how colors are displayed when the InterVU MPEG Player is viewed on machines that are running in 256-color mode. Leaving this to default as FOREGROUND allows the InterVU MPEG Player to take control of all 256-colors and obtain the best possible image quality for displayed movies; other images embedded within the browser window may suffer slight degradation in quality. If PALETTE is set to BACKGROUND, then Netscape is allowed to retain control of all 256 colors. This will result in slight degradation in the quality of the displayed movie, and may improve surrounding images, however results vary widely depending on image content. This setting is ignored when the client is running in color modes greater than 256-color. In those modes, best color fidelity is achieved at all times regardless of the PALETTE setting.

Tools for Encoding MPEG

InterVU does not make any tools for encoding MPEG. They have their favorite vendors, though. There are several cards available for MPEG encoding. Each has certain benefits. For example, a company called Vitec Multimedia, (http://vitechts.com/) in Sarasota, Florida has one product that will give you considerable flexibility in encoding size — thus bandwidth — and costs approximately $700. Unfortunately, this card has no ability to encode sound. Their other product will encode both video and sound for around $1000.

Data Translation (http://www.b-way.com/) offers their Broadway product for under $1000. A higher-end option, is from Sigma Designs (http://www.realmagic.com/). Their encoder card is called Real Magic Producer. It comes with powerful video editing software by Adobe but its cost will definitely make your wallet sting (~$5000).

There are also software-only video encoding systems, but they are very slow. There are several available for free from various Web sites, such as The MPEG Plaza (http://www.visiblelight.com/mpeg/).

ClearVideo Decoder

In addition, see the end of Chapter 10 in this book for a list of audio and video resources.

The ClearVideo Decoder, from Iterated (http://www.iterated.com/) is a video viewing tool that works within standard Video for Windows (AVI) and QuickTime multimedia frameworks.

The ClearVideo decoder, or player, runs on a Windows 95 or Macintosh platform and can be downloaded for free from the Iterated site at http://www.iterated.com/ClearVideoDecoder/download/.

To create video that uses the ClearVideo decoder you'll have to cough up $995.

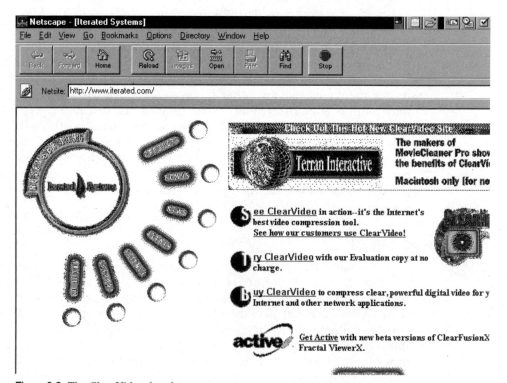

Figure 8-8. The ClearVideo decoder.

Quasi-webcasting Products

There are a host of products on the market that have near-webcasting types of functionality. A list of the more interesting ones, at least to me, follow:

CU-SeeMe

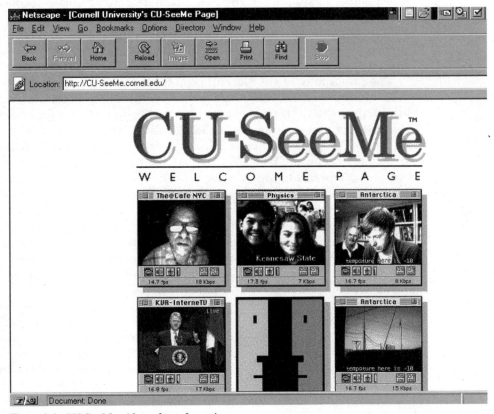

Figure 8-9. CU-SeeMe video teleconferencing.

CU-SeeMe is a product of Cornell University (http://CU-SeeMe.cornell.edu/). It is probably one of the first and best known of all video teleconferencing products.

It was developed by the CU-SeeMe Development Team of the Advanced Technologies and Planning group of the Network Resources division of Cornell Information Technologies in cooperation with the members of the CU-SeeMe Consortium.

CU-SeeMe is a free videoconferencing program (under copyright of Cornell University and its collaborators) available to anyone with a Macintosh or Windows and a connection to the Internet. With CU-SeeMe, you can videoconference with another site located anywhere in the world. By using a reflector, multiple parties at different locations can participate in a CU-SeeMe conference, each from his or her own desktop computer.

CU-SeeMe supports up to eight "windows" to other "parties" on your own computer screen. The CU-SeeMe Reflector (for more information, see http://CU-SeeMe.cornell.edu/Reflector.html) was constructed out of necessity, there being no support in the Macintosh TCP/IP facilities for multicast. You need to use a CU-SeeMe reflector to have a multiparty conference using CU-SeeMe software on the Internet. CU-SeeMe reflectors provide the ability to send multicast but not to receive. Without reflectors only point-to-point connections connecting two CU-SeeMe users are possible at this time.

The philosophy of the Cornell project was to start immediately with available, affordable hardware and deploy it as rapidly as possible. The goal was to stimulate creative thinking and create a wide base of user experience. By opening Internet videoconferences to Macintosh users, the CU-SeeMe team hoped to accelerate the adoption and usefulness of desktop conferencing, including live video. Because CU-SeeMe uses simple but efficient video frame-differencing and compression algorithms, it opens networked videoconferencing capability to users of lower-cost desktop computers, and enables broader participation in desktop video technology. During 1993 this grassroots development strategy was realized as interest in CU-SeeMe grew rapidly with training and user support from the New York State Educational Research Network (NYSERNet). NYSERNet spread the word among Internet users by providing one of the first "public" reflectors encouraging users to try the technology and test their connections.

Working with Dick Cogger in the summer or 1992, Tim Dorcey wrote the original version of CU-SeeMe. His overview of the project, CU-SeeMe Desktop Videoconferencing Software, was published in CONNEXIONS, March 1995.

Using the developers own words: "WARNING: Although being improved with each version, CU-SeeMe is not a mature production software—USE AT YOUR OWN RISK." At this time CU-SeeMe runs on the Macintosh and the PC Windows platform using an IP network connection.

With CU-SeeMe each participant can decide to be a sender, a receiver, or both. CU-SeeMe is intended to provide useful conferencing at minimal cost. Receiving requires only a Mac or PC with a screen capable of displaying 16 grays and a connection to the Internet. Sending requires the same plus a camera and digitizer which can cost as little as $100 to add on.

Requirements for sending and receiving video on a Windows platform include: a video capture board that supports Microsoft Video For Windows; a video camera to plug into the video capture board; a Windows Sound board that conforms to the Windows Multimedia Specification (Sound Blaster or better); full duplex audio is very desirable.

CU-SeeMe can be downloaded from its site at: http://CU-SeeMe.cornell.edu/get_cuseeme.html for the Macintosh environment and http://CU-SeeMe.cornell.edu/PC.CU-SeeMeCurrent.html for Windows users.

An enhanced (i.e. non-university version of the product) CU-SeeMe is available from White Pine (http://goliath.wpine.com/cu-seeme.html). This means that you have to pay for it (about $69), but the product is more stable and the company provides some support.

CUSee-Me has been used for everything from speeches, lectures, and even a film. Party Girl, a 1995 film, was shown at the Seattle International Film Festival. Information about the film and its Internet debut can be found at http://www.polis.com/firstlook/party/default.html.

Voxware

Voxware (http://www.voxware.com) provides streaming audio — without a server. The ToolVox Player 2.0 receives and plays the incoming VOX audio stream. It operates as a Netscape Navigator or Microsoft Explorer plug-in or helper application and activates automatically when incoming audio is detected. A unique feature of the ToolVox Player is its ability to speed-up or slow-down speech playback without changing the pitch or character of the original voice. Voxware's ToolVox Player 2.0 features a redesigned user interface and supports Netscape's LiveConnect, which allows Web developers to control speech playback from JavaScript and Java applets. The combination of LiveConnect compatibility and ToolVox's low bandwidth makes it possible to synchronize audio playback with graphics, animations, and streaming video, thus achieving performance not possible with higher bandwidth solutions.

ToolVox is a software tool that makes it simple for Web authors to add high-quality voice files to Web pages. At the core of each of Voxware's products is its unique MetaVoice coding technology. MetaVoice is a patent-pending system that creates an accurate, mathematical model of human speech, rather than the conventional system of compressing the audio waveform itself. This efficiency means Voxware codecs can deliver high-quality speech in a third the bandwidth of many voice codecs on the market today, and with far less server congestion and CPU overhead.

MetaVoice works by creating separate models of different vocal aspects: one creates a template of the user's vocal characteristics (spectral shape), and the other records the user's vocal articulation and frequency. In simple terms, spectral shape represents a vocal map or voice print of the vocal characteristics people use to recognize the voices of friends, celebrities, etc. Articulation and frequency are measurable, objective vocal elements such as pitch and volume.

MetaVoice is also specifically modeled after the human voice, which differs in many ways from other audio signals. Human speech is simpler in form than music created by multiple instruments, and an instrument's pitch may change much more quickly than a speaking voice. By tailoring its underlying model to voice alone, MetaVoice uses a fraction of the data required by general audio encoders to deliver comparable speech quality.

MetaVoice is designed to ignore ambient noise, such as traffic in the background, delivering cleaner sound and reducing the amount of data analyzed by the compressor. MetaVoice also takes advantage of a variable-bit-rate coding system, which processes only as much information as is needed to reproduce the speech signal. Fixed-rate systems process the same amount of data at all times, even during silent periods. Since not all applications support variable-rate coding, MetaVoice can also operate at a fixed rate. MetaVoice achieves

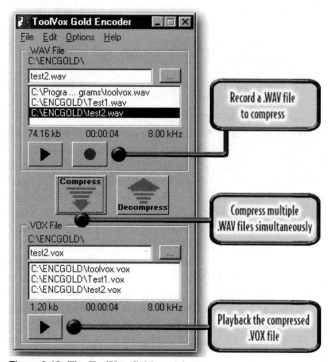

Figure 8-10. The ToolVox Gold encoder.

ratios as high as 100:1.

The Encoder is used to create highly compressed voice files, which are added to Web pages using standard HTML tags. The major difference between the ToolVox Gold version and the ToolVox Basic version is the functionality and features.

The ToolVox Gold Encoder features improved sound quality using Voxware's new RT29HQ codec, batch compression and the ability to embed MIDI files, for streaming background music with voice clips. ToolVox Gold also includes Voxware's VoiceFonts transformation technology which can completely transform the speaker's voice. Over thirty VoiceFonts are packaged with the Gold Encoder including cartoon-like characters, echoes, robots, and more.

The ToolVox Gold Encoder creates a compressed VOX file which is embedded on the Web page. No special server software is needed, and there are no arbitrary limits on the number of simultaneous listeners. Features include: high quality — ToolVox's low bandwidth minimizes breakup caused by congested Internet connections and slow modems; real-time streaming — playback begins immediately even while other HTML elements are downloading; no special server is required — ToolVox Gold works with any HTTP server; ease of integration — embed voice files using standard HTML tags. ToolVox does the rest; minimal demands on Web server — transmission of one minute of speech is equivalent to the download of an 18 k graphics file; no firewall con-

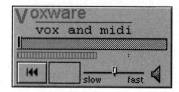 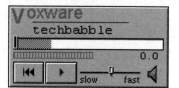

Figure 8-11. The ToolVox player.

flicts — if you use Netscape Navigator and can view a Web page you'll hear crisp and immediate voice playback.

The ToolVox Gold Encoder (figure 8-10) also offers Voxware's unique VoiceFont technology which can transform the speaker's voice. Over thirty VoiceFonts are packaged with the ToolVox Gold Encoder, including cartoon-like characters, echoes, robots, and more. The ToolVox Gold Encoder runs on Windows 95, Windows NT, and Mac OS.

The ToolVox Player 2.0 is available for free download (figure 8-11). Two versions of the ToolVox encoder are available. ToolVox Basic (1.0) is available to download free of charge. ToolVox Gold 2.0, now available for purchase, features an enhanced version of the Encoder based on Voxware's new RT29HQ codec. ToolVox Gold has extra features for developers and Web designers, including improved sound quality, batch compression, and an easy-to-use graphical interface. Users can even embed MIDI files, for streaming background music with voice clips. ToolVox Gold also includes VoiceFonts, which let a single user create multiple voice characters.

Macromedia Shockwave

No discussion of webcasting tools would be complete without mentioning Macromedia's Shockwave. .Macromedia (http://www.macromedia.com/shockwave/) is a well-known multimedia product company that has dominated the market.

Macromedia Shockwave has become a standard for the creation and playback of fully interactive multimedia on the World Wide Web and corporate intranets. Macromedia software tools:

Macromedia Director (http://www.macromedia.com/software/director/)
Authorware (http://www.macromedia.com/software/authorware/)
FreeHand http://www.macromedia.com/software/freehand/)
SoundEdit 16 (http://www.macromedia.com/software/sound/)
xRes (http://www.macromedia.com/software/xres/)

are standard products for professional multimedia producers. Shockwave is Macromedia's solution for delivering multimedia content on the Internet, with much of it being originally designed for one of Macromedia's multimedia tools.

Each of the tools listed above support plug-in Shockwave Xtras, which optimize your content for Web delivery. This means you are empowered to create the most dynamic, responsive, and professional Web experience available online: animations; interactive multimedia; streaming intranet applications; CD-quality streaming audio; zoomable vector graphics.

Essentially, you use one or more of Macromedia products to produce multimedia-enabled content (e.g. sound, video, animation) and then deliver it to the Web via Shockwave. The Shockwave player has over 12 million downloads to date, and is preinstalled on numerous Macintosh and Windows computers, making it the most accessible and widely used multimedia technology on the Web. Macromedia Shockwave players are free and available from www.macromedia.com/shockwave/download.

Since it is not Shockwave, but Macromedia's individual multimedia products that create the content, how to webcast using this product is really beyond the scope of this book and is actually deserving of its own book. However, it is still worthwhile to spend at least a bit of time in explaining how this set of tools can work webcasting miracles on your site.

Macromedia Freehand is an illustration, page layout, image creation and editing, 3D graphics and animation program. The Authorware Interactive Studio is a complete environment for creating and publishing interactive information that features hypermedia, database support, and data tracking. While these tools are impressive and can be ported to the Web, the real power behind "Macromedia on the Net" is the Director Studio product. The Studio is used to create diverse media elements and combine them to tell a story, share information, collect user data, and assess learning.

Director 5.0 is the industry standard for creating and distributing interactive applications. Director 5 makes it easy to import and integrate elements from the products included in the Director Multimedia Studio, and then orchestrate those elements into high-impact interactive applications. The interface in Director includes the cast, a database of graphics, sounds, color palettes, Lingo scripts, text, video, the score which is a frame-based control window with over 48 channels; and the script, the editor for natural-language Lingo scripting.

Macromedia combines most of these tools together in The Director Multimedia Studio package which includes:

Director 5, the authoring tool for multimedia and the Internet
SoundEdit 16 version 2 plus Deck II 2.5 (Macintosh), the desktop tool for audio production
Sound Forge XP (Windows), an award winning general purpose sound editor.
Extreme 3D 1.0, a powerful 3D solution for design and multimedia
xRes 2.0, a creative tool for hi-res images
Shockwave for Director

Platforms supported are: Windows 95, NT, 3.1, or Macintosh OS to deliver files on Windows 95, NT, and 3.1; Macintosh OS; and the Internet using

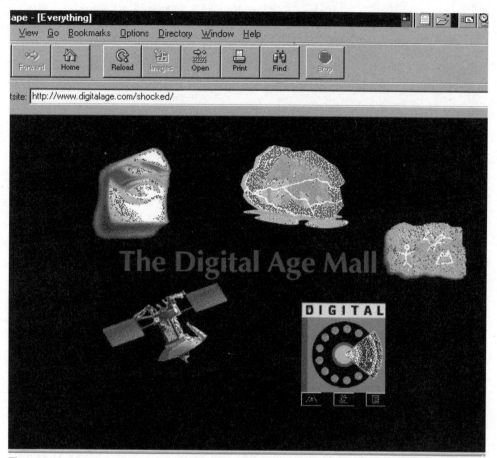

Figure 8-12. Macromedia Studio lets you create stunning multimedia sites.

Shockwave.

The end result is the ability to create stunning sites that look more like CD-quality than Net-quality as shown in figure 8-12. Sound, animation and a wonderful ability to handle text is accomplished through Director. You can't see it from the figure, but as I pass my cursor over an image or text, more information is fluidly displayed.

Once the Macromedia-enabled content is created, it is "shocked" and can then be embedded into an HTML page with the, now familiar, <EMBED> tag:

```
<EMBED   SRC="../images/ultra.dcr"  WIDTH="512"  HEIGHT="350"BGCOL-
OR="#000000">
```

Director and Shockwave are really a world unto themselves. Requiring equal parts animator, graphic designer, music producer and movie directory — it's the whole ball of wax.

But not all the functionality is in Director, Shockwave offers much navigational and control capabilities too. For example, you can use it to stream audio files (SWA files) of long duration, such as interviews or other material that will play for longer than 10 minutes. Macromedia's scripting language will have to be mastered as shown below:

```
on exitFrame
    --gCurrentPart : the number of the current file
    --gNumParts : the number of the last file in the sequence
    global gCurrentPart, gNumParts
    --if the current part is finished (state = 5, done) then
    --get the next 'part' of the sequence of parts
if the state of member "SWA file" = 5 then
    --reset the stream.
            Stop (member "SWA file")
            --check to see whether this was the last part
            --if it IS the last part, do nothing
            if gCurrentPart = gNumParts then
            nothing
else
            --If it is NOT the last part, then you need to get the NEXT part.
            --If you name your SWA files numerically, all you need to do is
            --increment a variable (gCurrentPart), then set the URL using this.
            --Then play the next .swa file.
            set gCurrentPart = gCurrentPart + 1
            set the URL of member "SWA file" = gCurrentPart & ".swa"
Play (member "SWA file")
            end if
    end if
go to the frame
end
```

Macromedia products are high-end and high-price. However, the company recently announced Backstage Designer ($99) which let's you use point and click methods to add multimedia to your page. It supports Shockwave, Java and even discussion groups along with image editing, icons and animated text.

Chatting and Collaboration on the Internet

Both the chapter on Netscape and the chapter on Microsoft were loaded with discussions of these vendors' webcasting tools. You probably noted that each of them has entered the chat market as well.

More Webcasting Tools 235

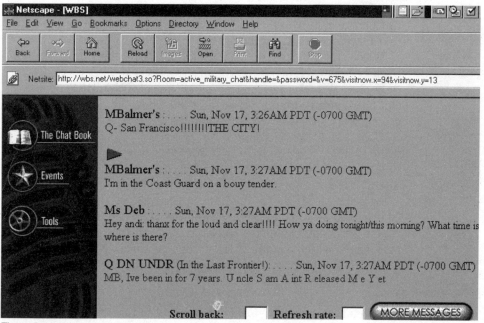

Figure 8-13. wbs.net chat room.

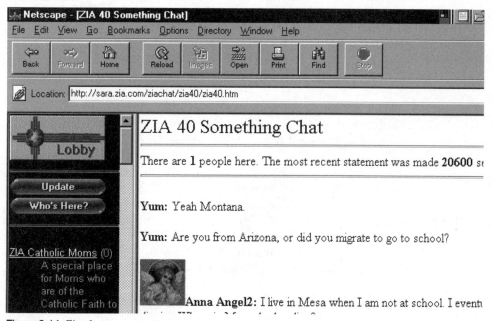

Figure 8-14. Zia chat.

While chat is not as exciting as streaming audio or streaming video, it still fulfills the requirements of a broadcasting medium — except in this case it's text instead of multimedia.

While the majority of chat aficionados are just plain folk wanting to "make friends with each other" and more than one person has noted that the majority of chat sessions are just so much drivel, if handled properly, chat sessions can be structured to be something like those moderated discussion panels you see on television every Sunday morning.

Companies like Nintendo and Sega hold chat sessions in which they take input from customers to help them write new games. More than one magazine lures authors to "moderate" panels which discuss every issue from technology to childcare as shown in figures 8-13 and 8-14.

Netscape and Microsoft are not the only vendors who offer chat software. There are a variety of other companies who are making inroads into this popular area. Like any other webcasting product, you'll have to evaluate several and decide which among them is the one suitable for your needs. Issues to consider are whether or not to use a product that requires downloading a plug-in and how supportive the vendor is.

The following is a list of chat vendors to research:

ComputerLink	Secure Communicator	http://www.idirect.com/secure/
HiJiNX	InterFACE	http://www.hijinx.com.au
Ichat, Inc.	Ichat	http://www.ichat.com
Internet Direct	Internet TeleCafe	http://www.telecafe.com/telecafe.
The Palace Inc.	The Palace	http://www.thepalace.com
Quarterdeck	Global Chat	http://www.qdeck.com/chat/
Tribal Voice	PowWow	http://www.worlds.net

You probably also noted that Microsoft's NetMeeting and Netscape's CoolTalk came with collaborative whiteboard and application sharing. Those wishing to research other collaborative products are directed to:

Attachmate	CrossTalk	http://www.attachmate.com
	OpenMind	
Avalan Tech	Remotely Possible/32	http://www.avalan.com
Farallon	Look@Me	http://www.farallon.com
	FlashNotes	
	Timbuktu Pro	
ForeFront	RoundTable	http://www.ffg.com
FTP Software	OnNet for Windows	http://www.ftp.com

Chapter 9

The Telecom Connection

Introduction

No book on webcasting would be complete without a discussion of telecommunications. Webcasting has the potential of chewing up precious bandwidth. Even as I write this book (Fall of 1996), when few are actually delving into this new broadcasting medium, the Internet is slowing down considerably.

This slow-down is the result of a tremendous increase in the number of users accessing an increasing number of Web sites. Today those Web sites are hosting minimal audio and video content. What will happen in the future when everyone jumps on the webcasting bandwagon?

Transmission of digitized webcast content places heavy requirements on the underlying networks. In particular, continuous media, such as sounds and motion video, require both high bit-rates (that is, high transmission capacity in terms of bits per second) and limited "burstiness" and transmission delays. Improvements to the network, such as fiber optics and new switching technologies, create new possibilities in the area of networked multimedia transmission. In the next few years, we are likely to see significant improvements in network bandwidth and quality of service. Industry analysts predict that bandwidth on the Internet will continue to grow at a steady rate, specifically in the area of mid-band communications. (Mid-band is the area in the communication spectrum where ISDN and cable modems reside.)

These enhanced telecommunication tools will continue to push the envelope of performance on the Internet and will enable end-users to consume more services that need high processing power, such as audio and video. In the broad-band spectrum, improvements in Ethernet configurations and in high-end technologies such as ATM would make transmission of video better and more reliable.

Television as Precursor to the Information Revolution*

Over the past decade, television has dramatically changed America's living habits. 193 million US homes now have television. That's 98% of US households. So television is virtually universal in the United States. About two-thirds of the homes have more than one set, and about the same number are connected to cable.

Americans spend nearly half their free time watching television. According to Nielsen, the average TV set is on around 7 hours a day, and the average American watches TV between 3 to 4 hours a day.

The only activities that take up more time than watching TV are work and sleep. At almost any moment every evening, over one-third of the US population is in front of a television set. That's a massive market. Nearly all of these people are at home while watching TV, not at the mall. But, of course, they are not all watching the same channel. This huge TV audience is made up of a multitude of moving targets.

Sight, sound and motion combine to make television the most powerful means of mass communication. That unique combination makes TV the most effective — and the most cost-effective — medium for direct marketing. As has been proven by the shopping networks, TV can move mountains of merchandise, very rapidly.

Communications is fast moving toward digitization. One change, now just getting under way, is converting phone and television transmission systems from analog to digital.

Digital signals offer many advantages over analog signals — including greater precision, less distortion, elimination of ghosting, more special effects, and more opportunities for two-way communication.

Digitized voice, data and video can all be transmitted the same way, over the same lines. That's one of the key reasons why the television, telephone and computer industries are all doing mating dances with each other (i.e. NBC and Microsoft).

Right on the heels of digitization is digital compression. Digital compression is analogous to what orange juice processors do when they remove the water, ship only the pulp, and then the water is added back in at the consumer's home.

Recently-developed computer chips automatically remove the digits that represent the repeated parts of successive video frames. To restore the complete picture, related chips in the receiving set put the redundant digits back in. A single analog TV channel takes up a fixed slice, or bandwidth, of the government-rationed frequency spectrum. With digital compression, up to 10 channels can be transmitted within the same bandwidth.

Eventually, all new TV sets will have built-in digital reception and process-

---

*This section was excerpted from Technology Trendlines, ed. Jessica Keyes. 1995. Van Nostrand Rheinhold. *The Information Superhighway — Separating Hype from Reality* by Joseph M. Segel.

ing capabilities. Before that happens, there will be a new generation of converter boxes that will process digital data and convert it to analog signals that are viewable on present-day TV sets. This is already beginning to happen with the introduction in 1996 of such devices as WebTV which is a decoder box and remote control which enables Internet connection through your TV.

Fiber-optic cables exponentially increase capacity. In the meantime, cable companies and phone companies are racing to rewire the country with fiber-optic cables. Fiber-optic cables can carry thousands of times as much digitized information as standard telephone wire or coaxial cable. It's claimed that a single fiber-optic cable can transmit the entire contents of the Encyclopedia Brittanica in one second.

There are, however, two bottlenecks — (1) the lower-capacity wires that run from the pole to the home, and (2) the wires within the typical home. This is much more of a problem with phone wires than with coaxial cable. The full capacity potential of fiber-optics will not be realized until the far future, when those last few feet are rewired. Meanwhile, combining fiber-optic trunk lines with phone company switching equipment and cable company home connections will enable consumers to tap a substantial portion of the increased capacity and also to enjoy improved transmission quality and reliability.

The next step is HDTV — High Definition Television. HDTV is now being transmitted on a limited basis in Japan. Within a few years, HDTV should get rolling in this country, paralleling and merging with the digital revolution.

HDTV will make large TV pictures almost as sharp as a photograph. You will see much more detail, with better colors, so it will be more pleasurable to watch television. The result will surely be a further increase in the amount of time that the average person watches TV.

For the past decade, there have been more cable networks than channel capacity to carry them. Channel scarcity has been a big problem. Within the next 3 to 5 years, that situation is likely to be turned upside down, with far more channels than programming available.

Channel scarcity will thus gradually change into channel abundance, as capacity opens up, the major occupiers will be:

Video on Demand

You will be able to select a movie from a large library of old and new movies and have the movie start on your TV set at a time of your choosing. That should certainly be an appealing option for many consumers, especially those who now go out to a store to rent videotapes. Several competing video-on-demand systems are in an advanced stage of development and testing. There are still some rough edges to be worked out, but video-on-demand is definitely coming.

Video Malls

There will surely be an expansion of televised shopping channels. Macy's, Nordstrom and Spiegel have already announced their intention to enter this business. The more big names on television, the more people will begin shopping this way.

Special-interest shopping channels will also be tested, and some may be successful. Right now, for example, QVC is like a department store where only one department is open at a time. In the future, with multiple channels, it's possible that QVC will be more like a mall, where you can click on a QVC sporting goods channel or a QVC photo equipment channel, and so forth.

Games and Voting

Several companies are developing interactive games for the new television environment, In the future, kids will be able to play Nintendo-like games against a central computer or with other viewers across the network — that is, until their parents get the communications bill. However, downloaded games may partially solve that problem.

Voting won't take up much channel capacity, but it's another service that will be offered in the future. It's possible that voting from your home by clicking on a remote control will expand from voting on issues to actually voting in elections.

Reruns Rather than Original Programming

What you're not likely to see is much expansion in the way of elaborately-produced entertainment programming. It just costs too much, especially in a new environment where the ratings will probably be lower as a result of audience fragmentation.

Educational Programming — A Sleeper

Very little has been written about the possibility of using expanded channel capacity for educational programs — probably because there is not much commercial potential in it.

But think about the possibilities. If only it could be financed, we could put the most talented teachers and professors on TV, with channels categorized by subject matter. We could have educational programs for every grade level, and even a television university. What a marvelous way to uplift the educational level of great numbers of Americans.

Sadly, the teacher unions would probably consider it a threat and oppose it. And the viewership might be dismal. But it would be nice to see it happen.

Special Interest Niche Channels

There are a number of special-interest niche channels that have already started — such as The Travel Channel, a food and cooking channel, a comedy channel, a couple of game-show channels, a couple of live courtroom channels, a computer channel. Others are in the wings, just waiting for channel capacity to open up.

Audience fragmentation will be a problem for all channels, especially the general-interest channels. As the Information Superhighway grows in breadth, the increased number of choices will seriously fragment the total audience, creating a viewership problem for all channels and a ratings problem for those who sell advertising.

The major broadcast networks deny the danger. But as viewing choices increase, ratings for traditional broadcast networks and local TV stations will probably continue to slide downhill. If that happens, reductions in advertising revenue are likely to follow. Some broadcasters will undoubtedly be resourceful enough to find ways to survive and prosper. Those who do not adapt will surely become casualties of progress.

The TV of the Future

Everyone knows how to turn on a TV set — with one or two clicks of a remote control — and how to select the channel they want to watch.

Everyone knows how to dial a phone to call an 800 number and place an order. So, present-day systems are about as simple as they can be. People are very comfortable with the way TV and phones work. If a new system requires more steps to do essentially the same things, consumers may resist it.

It would be to the peril of creative geniuses to forget that people always gravitate toward doing things in the easiest possible way.

Consumers are generally satisfied with the range of choices now on cable TV. Fairly or unfairly, the main complaint with cable TV is not lack of choices, but the cost of service.

If new services are very easy to use, very inexpensive and very appealing, consumers may buy them. Focus groups and limited-market tests seem to indicate that is the case. But there's no crying demand on the part of consumers for additional services or for interactive TV.

It's not consumer demand, but to a large extent the specter of having a huge number of channels available, and not enough programming to put on them, that has spurred the communications and entertainment industries to develop new services.

However, it should be noted that there is a corps of very bright businesspeople — such as Barry Diller, John Malone and Bill Gates — who are totally convinced that interactive services will be gobbled up by the public, in big numbers.

Text and non-moving pictures won't satisfy the public. Moving images are more appealing than still images, and listening is more appealing than reading. Those are two powerful reasons why every text-based and still-picture based interactive television experiment in the past has failed. That's also why no computer terminal-based service has ever generated anywhere near the volume of retail merchandise orders that the televised shopping channels have achieved.

Few people will be interested in a television interface that reminds them of a computer. To gain maximum acceptance, the visual appearance of interactive services needs to be more television-like than computer-like.

Ideally, an interactive shopping program should produce full-motion demonstrations of the selected products, but doing that in a practical and economical manner is yet to be developed.

Television viewers are naturally passive. Some system developers and their software programmers seem to assume that consumers are itching to be converted from passive to interactive TV watchers.

Being computer-literate doesn't change human nature. Our younger generations are more comfortable using computers than older people. But that doesn't mean that they would prefer to do something with a computer-like interface that they can do in a more natural way. Ordering merchandise with a computer-like interface is not as much fun as playing games.

The Wired World*

Over the next ten years bandwidth to consumers and businesses will increase by two to three orders of magnitude while continuing to cost about the same as current telecommunications service. The reality of this basic economic fact is going to reshape our society as surely, and as completely, as the Industrial Revolution reshaped the western world in the 1850s.

But information isn't the only important thing. The speed at which it's delivered is as important as the quality of the information itself. Imagine turning on your faucet and watching your sink fill in four seconds. Now imagine turning on the same faucet and watching a whole swimming pool fill up in the same time. And finally, imagine that all that extra water doesn't cost you anything extra! That's what high bandwidth service will give you: lots of information, fast, at the same rate you're being charged for your phone service or cable TV service.

There are five major groups of players in the telecommunications game. Each of the groups has its own identity, strengths and weaknesses. Each brings to the table an existing infrastructure of equipment and corporate identity. Some groups are prepared to make the transition to the new telecommunications world, while others are not. Some will have to re-engineer their companies, while others are unprepared to do so. We will discuss each of these market players in turn, to give you an idea of where they stand.

The players are the RBOCs, the long-distance carriers, the wireless communications companies, the cable television companies, and, perhaps somewhat surprisingly, the power companies.

RBOCs are responsible for only local telephone service. In the decision to break up Bell Telephone, eight new companies were created, the RBOCs and

---

*This section was excerpted from Technology Trendlines, ed. Jessica Keyes. 1995. Van Nostrand Rheinhold. *The Wired World* by Andrew Forbes and Fred Seelig.

AT&T. The seven RBOCs were each limited to providing telephony services within a specific area, or region, hence the eponymous name.

RBOC management, company philosophy, switching equipment, and home access circuits were largely inherited from the old Bell Telephone Company. It has only been recently that each RBOC's management team has seen itself in true competition with other RBOCs. The telephone company industry's pace is much slower than parallel electrical engineering industries, but this too is changing as the reality of market competition is sinking in. A positive asset which RBOCs have is its top-quality switching equipment, and its massive investment in both telephony hardware and software. The RBOCs know communications technology down into their very bones.

Interspersed with the RBOCs are the so-called Ma and Pa Bells, small local exchange carriers that fill in the gaps where RBOCs do not provide service. Between the RBOCs and Ma and Pa Bells almost every home in the US has the option of phone service. Ma and Pa Bells traditionally have had poorer service and poorer grades of equipment, which came as a result of being undercapitalized. These companies may be acquired by RBOCs. But they are generally not located in high-revenue communications-intensive areas.

Long-distance carriers are also an amalgam of old Bell Telephone and independent companies such as MCI, Sprint, GTE, and WilTel. AT&T Long Lines became simply AT&T. It is responsible for overseas connections and major cross-country telephone trunks. The overseas connections are a hybrid of undersea oceanic cable (both metallic and fiber optic) and geostationary satellite.

What distinguishes the long-distance companies from the others is that they are used to working with high-bandwidth signals. As computer-to-computer communications and video-on-demand services increase, it is high-bandwidth technology which will dominate. So long-distance companies can exploit their knowledge of high-bandwidth technologies into the coming Information Revolution. It remains to be seen if they have the corporate resolve to do so.

Wireless communications providers include cellular telephone and paging companies. Although some are independent business entities, most are not. Some are owned by RBOCs, some by long-distance companies. Their owners are gambling on the wireless market being a future source of revenue. Wireless access reaches two kinds of users: mobile and non-traditional remote users.

The mobile community is dominated by business users. Non-traditional users include farmers, who use cellular telephones from their tractors to radio back to the farmhouse, and schoolchildren in major metropolitan areas, whose pagers are used by working parents to coordinate after-school schedules.

How can wireless companies be expected to adapt to compete in the future? The two kinds of wireless providers are divided on this issue. The wireless cellular telephone companies have increased their presence in major metropolitan areas. They have switching and access infrastructure, and they connect to local and long-distance companies. They are well-positioned to grow. Paging companies are not.

They have the wrong kind of physical link structure geostationary satellite to earth surface (one-way only), the wrong kind of switching equipment (typically, not high-bandwidth telephone company equipment) and the wrong kind of information content (one or two lines of text, maximum). In short, paging companies are dead ends in the evolutionary tree of the global information network of the future.

Cable television companies' historical business roots are in one-way entertainment dissemination, not in two-way information transmission. Their genesis as humble earthbound competitors of satellite Direct Broadcast Service (DBS) companies such as Home Box Office did not hint at what they are today: a potent force challenging local telephone companies for the future of local access to the new Information Superhighway or GII.

What cable companies have is bandwidth, raw bandwidth. The ability to transmit 10 Mb/sec of data over a line into the house is a capability telephone companies would kill for. They also have access to a large percentage of homes. At the time of this writing, it is estimated that sixty-five percent of the homes in the US have cable service, and ninety-five percent have the option of cable service. What cable companies don't have is well, lots of things.

They do not have a reputation for reliable service. They do not have, in any sense of the phrase, a capable switching system, or anything remotely resembling a telephone company's central office (the last switching office before a call is routed to a user's home phone). They do not have two-way information flow, nor does their equipment allow them to have home-out transmission. They do not have much penetration into the business market.

The Wired Home

Almost every home in the US is wired for A/C power. This means that the power companies own a right of way to almost every home in the US They do not currently use these rights of way for telecommunications infrastructure, although they are investigating the possibility of doing so. There are two reasons why electrical power companies are regarded as players in the telecommunications world of the future. First is the obvious advantage of already existing access to homes and businesses, as well as access through major metropolitan areas. This access is simply not available any more. Second is that optical fibers can be run in the same cable, or strung next to a high-voltage power line, with no interference between the two signals.

Light signals in optical fiber are relatively immune to high-voltage electrical lines. This means that optical fiber can be strung over the entire electrical grid, using the same access enjoyed by electrical companies, and can be switched and run right into a home or business with no additional access considerations. Although power companies may seem like dark horse candidates to be future telecommunications leaders, the single huge factor called access makes them a very real and important player.

Each of the players: RBOCs, long-distance carriers, wireless companies, cable companies, and power companies evolved to meet a specific set of restricted challenges. In all five cases, the challenges, and the solutions, were to one degree or another regulated by the U.S., state, and local governments.

But the US government is rewriting the regulations. The net result will be to throw open the local telephony, long-distance telephony, wireless, and cable television markets to all comers. Almost all the companies in all five groups would like to be active in all the markets that Congress is opening. But there are hurdles that each of the players will have to clear to succeed.

The RBOCs must replace old wiring with new wiring. Phone service wiring that runs into most homes and businesses is six-wire twisted pair, i.e., three sets of twisted pairs of wires per telephone line. Even with the most advanced compression and modulation techniques, twisted pair is capable of the transmission of a very limited amount of bandwidth, on the order of tens to hundreds of kilobits per second. Plain old telephone service (POTS) wiring is simply incapable of delivering the two to three orders of magnitude worth of increased bandwidth that will be required to transmit at video rates. To compete, RBOCs are faced with a major rebuild of their networks.

The cable companies wired up the US with coaxial cable. The potential bandwidth of coax cable is several orders of magnitude greater than that of twisted pair. Unfortunately, the cable systems are broadcast systems. The cable television signal runs from the cable system hub out to all the homes the system serves. It's a one-way system. To summarize, current cable video systems have no switching and offer only one-way service. To compete, cable companies, like the RBOCs, are faced with a major rebuild of their networks.

Since the commercial introduction of cellular technology, the wireless companies have built systems that provide coverage to a majority of people in the US. The problem that these companies have is somewhat analogous to the problems facing the RBOCs. But while the RBOCs can solve their bandwidth problems by installing more and better cable the wireless companies face a different problem. Spectrum is a finite resource.

There are new modulation and compression techniques that increase the effective digital bandwidth of a fixed amount of spectrum, but these new technologies are not currently in commercial use. Current cellular service can handle voice and low bit rate computer to computer data, but it is not meant for high bit-rate traffic. Future cellular systems which are capable of higher bit-rates would require replacing all base stations and handsets with new equipment. Thus once again, to compete, the wireless companies are faced with a major rebuild of their networks.

The power companies are, where telecommunication services are involved, operating in a vacuum. They have no investment in existing telecommunications infrastructure, and have no experience operating telecommunications services. If they want to be telecommunications competitors, they are faced with building telecommunications networks from scratch. They, more than any other group, are faced with not just a rebuild, but a first-level build to create a network.

In some respects, the long-distance companies are in an enviable position.

They do not have a major investment in home and business telephony services infrastructure that requires a major rebuild. On the other hand, they do not have a telecommunications path to every home and business either. They do, however, have money to spend and experience with telephony networks. This would make them inclined to purchase, or to partner with, one or more of the companies in the other groups. Their ideal partners would provide right of way, switching infrastructure, and a local business presence, while the long-distance companies would provide capital and telephony systems experience.

The telecommunication industry is currently in the throes of merger mania. Since every player is faced with major capital expenditures to be competitive, each is trying to find partners to share expenses. After the mergers, there will be a time for consolidation and competition. Following that, we will see an industry-wide shakeout leaving three to five major telecommunications firms. Regardless of which firm "wins," the competition and deregulation will result in a high bit-rate telecommunications system at low rates to telephones, televisions, computers, cellular phones, and to wireless devices of all kinds. The combination of high bandwidth and low rates will hasten the coming of the Information Revolution.

This idea has been addressed by technological visionaries over the last decade. Its most public spokesman has been Vice President Al Gore, who has called this convergence of technology the Global Information Infrastructure, or GII. Having articulated the vision, however, is not the same as creating it. What force will propel the GII into existence?

The answer to that can be stated in a single two-word phrase: *marketing communications*. Advertising pays a majority of the cost of producing newspapers and magazines. Viewers pay nothing to watch broadcast television situation comedies. Marketing communications subsidize almost every mass market method of content delivery. It is important to understand that marketing communications will pay most of the costs associated with building the GII.

Building the GII

Because all the major players understand that the GII will be financed by marketing communications, the GII will be designed to facilitate the delivery of marketing communications to consumers. The impact of that statement cannot be underestimated. It costs money — lots of it — to wire houses and businesses, to build fast, wide-bandwidth switches, and to build in network intelligence for the GII.

The GII will allow information consumers to have access to an unimaginably rich variety of information. Consumers will want to get the information, they will even be willing to pay for it, but not if the rate has to be so high as to completely fund the building of the GII infrastructure. But this cost can be shared by GII advertisers. Advertisers will barter their ability to advertise in a new medium, which allows them to choose a target audience very precisely and use pointcast advertising techniques, for the consumers' ability to get information at an affordable cost.

There will two kinds of GII businesses: access providers, and content providers. Access providers will be the firms that are a consumer's gateway into the GII, and content providers will be the firms that provide the reason consumers use the GII. All the telecommunications firms mentioned previously will be access providers. They may dabble in content, but the main thrust of their business will be access provision.

The main source of marketing communication income for access providers will be in targeted advertising. The consumer is targeted based on information the advertiser and access provider have about that consumer. Such information is apt to be indirect in nature. A consumer profile can be built from such indirect information. Building such a customer profile, and then building a database of customer profiles by region, income, etc., allows an access provider to pointcast his or her marketing communications more effectively.

How will the access provider learn about each consumer? The access provider will track every action that a consumer takes while on the GII. What channels are viewed? What did this consumer order in the past? With which companies did this consumer have transactions in the previous year? Because information about every activity of each consumer will be valuable, access providers will offer consumers bundled services.

Access providers will try to persuade consumers to buy their telephone, television, computer, and wireless (voice and data) services as a bundle. By bringing together all access points into the GII into one billing center, the access provider can track all the ways a consumer uses the GII. This allows the access provider to build a more complete picture of a consumer than if, for example, it was only to be involved in providing telephone, but not computer, service.

In return for this information the access provider will offer consumers savings on bundled services. Financed primarily by the income from presenting marketing communications to consumers, access providers will build and maintain the GII. A parallel effort will be occurring as content providers build infrastructure to offer up specialized libraries of information. Recall that content providers are information "sources," and the consumers are information "sinks," and that the GII is in between, conveying information between sources and sinks.

What is a content provider? To answer that question requires a brief review of the endpoints of the GII. Consumers will be able to interact with the GII in a myriad of ways. They will be able to use their television, their computer, their telephone, their cellular phone, their wireless personal digital assistant, and if current research pans out, even their home thermostats and major appliances. In other words, almost any object that uses or generates data will potentially be on the GII. This suggests that the phrase content provider is a generic term for accessible data of almost any type.

Some content providers will make textual data and scanned photographs available, a virtual on-line library service. Some will sell audio/visual material e.g. movies, old TV shows, music videos, news clips, archival speeches.

Some will operate virtual reality multi-user multimedia games. Some will administer mailboxes that store and play back messages, regardless of the original form of the message and the current playback device. Some will sell houses, automobiles, and catalog merchandise. Universities will offer on-line, remote graduate school programs. Building management firms will adjust heating and air conditioning levels remotely, even into separate areas of the same building. Banking will be able to be done from your home computer. So will stock transactions, airline reservations, hotel and business meeting reservations, teleconferencing, voting, and working.

Because marketing communications will build and maintain the GII, the cost of equipment to operate as a content provider will be minimal. In fact, it will be in the best interest of the access providers to encourage content providers to be on the GII. The larger the number of content providers, the more reason consumers will have to use the access provider's services.

Thus, the end state of the GII will be a telecommunications world of access providers and content providers. How is today's mélange of RBOCs, long-distance companies, cable companies, wireless companies, power companies, and potential content providers going to transform themselves into the GII? The answer is with partnerships, mergers, and outright purchases of each other.

The telecommunications industry today has no integrated approach to telecommunications. The networks that provide these services are not integrated because they are usually not owned and operated by the same company. That's going to change as the industry moves to the concept of access providers.

Access providers will take a horizontal business model approach. When a set of consumers in the same region buys their telephone, television, and wireless services from a single access provider, the only path to those consumers for interactive marketing communications is through that access provider. Content providers will know that one access provider has information regarding all means of communications used by a particular consumer. Therefore they can be assured of a complete picture of the behavior and purchasing profile of that customer. This enhances the value of the access provider in the flow of information about the consumer. The owner of access will be the holder of the keys of the kingdom.

The partnerships, mergers, and purchases that roll across the telecommunications industry will be aimed at building firms capable of offering bundled services. Long-distance companies will merge with RBOCs and/or wireless communications firms and/or cable companies and/or power companies. The result will be a handful of huge horizontal firms.

The US telecommunications industry will eventually coalesce into three to five access providers. A logical question would be "how many access providers will there be world wide?" The "Global" portion of the GII is not a meaningless word — the GII will be a telecommunications network that spans the globe. Other governments will want to control their citizens' access to the GII, much like citizens' passport control physical movement across national boundaries. Therefore, there will be at least one access provider for each country on the GII. So the total number of access providers world wide will be somewhere between two hundred and fifty and one thousand.

The initial architecture of the GII will be many content providers connected to a single access provider, in a hub-spoke arrangement. This means that your access provider will be connected to local or regional content providers, such as local banking services, businesses, and video entertainment services. As time goes on, there will be continuing innovations in the manufacturing and storage of content. At first the access providers will build and maintain content storage systems, but as the cost and difficulty of content storage drops, independent content providers will start to come on-line. Each access provider will set up a network of content providers.

It will be in the best interests of the access providers to have exclusive rights to a content providers' content, but it will be in the best interest of the content providers to be on as many access provider networks as possible.

Mergers will affect content providers as well as access providers. As the number of content provider networks shrinks to double digits and then single digits, most major content providers will be on all of the remaining networks. In fact, it's likely that as the number of networks begins to stabilize that there will be gateways between each of the remaining networks. This will, for all practical purposes, give consumers access to almost all content on all networks. The access provision will become very transparent. The consumer will only be conscious of the wealth of information available, and not the location of the source of that information. The Information Infrastructure will indeed become Global in nature. Everybody will have access to all information.

How many content providers will there be on the GII? There will be hundreds of millions of content providers world wide. It's estimated that there are currently more than fifty thousand computer bulletin boards in the US. So there are already fifty thousand content providers in the US alone. More importantly, there are fifty thousand content providers for a presentation channel (computers) that most people find confusing and difficult to use. As additional presentation channels (televisions, personal digital assistants, thermostats, etc.) come into popular use the number of content providers will go through a period of exponential growth.

The Universal Box

To discuss content provision in detail requires taking a small detour to the idea of the universal "in-box." A universal in box is an electronic device, physical or virtual, which is connected to the GII, and which can store incoming content regardless of the type or format of that content. Text, fax, still photo, audio, audio/visual, multimedia, it should store all of it and make the content available for playback, regardless of the playback presentation channel. If the presentation channel is a TV set, then the contents of the universal in-box are transmogrified to be displayed on a TV. If the presentation channel is a computer, then the contents of the universal in-box are transmogrified to be displayed on a computer. A universal in-box should store any kind of content for playback on any presentation channel.

Obviously, it will not be possible for a universal in-box to convert all types of content for playback on all types of presentation channels. But it will be possible for most types of content to play back on most types of presentation channels. This is why the concept of a universal in-box is important to any discussion of content provision. Content format, as a rule, will be presentation channel independent. Content providers will create content that can be used by as many presentation channels as possible.

Initially there will not be a content provider network. The access providers will set up content storage equipment and solicit content producers for content to sell to the access provider's customers. This means that the content available through an access provider will be presentation channel specific. It also means that early access providers will be involved in content provision. Movies and television shows will still be targeted for televisions, text and still photos for computers, and voice for telephones or portable handsets. As the cost of content storage equipment drops, content providers will start to set up their own content provision systems. This will be agreeable to access providers, because it gets them out of the content business and lets them concentrate on access provision.

As the access providers begin to establish content networks, the early content providers will still create presentation channel specific content. Film studios and television sitcom producers will provide audio/visual content servers. On-line computer services and bulletin boards will provide text and still photos. Phone companies will provide voice mail services. But there are outside forces at work that are going to change the way content providers do business.

Presentation channels are going to start evolving at a furious rate. The functionality currently defined by the words telephone, fax, VCR, computer, television, and personal digital assistant are going to merge, mix, and match in new and interesting ways. Some computers, such as the Apple Macintosh Aptiva, already have television reception capability built in. Television image capture is possible while you watch. Interactive set-top boxes attached to televisions make them more computer-like, as well. What is less obvious is that telephones are going to become more computer-like. Personal digital assistants are going to get personal communications services and become like phones. As interactive television comes on-line one of the first new services consumers will be offered is a fax in-box. Just as the phone company now operates voice mail boxes, in a year or two they will be operating fax boxes. Consumers will be able to view their in-bound faxes on their computer or television.

The presentation channel will become much less important than the content being presented. This means that over the next few years content providers will begin to concentrate less on the presentation channel and more on content, and on creating content that is reasonably channel independent.

As the access providers and the content networks continue to merge, the number of content providers available to consumers will grow dramatically. How are consumers going to find information on the GII when there are hundreds of millions of content providers?

Consumers will use software based intelligent agents. Intelligent agents will search the GII for information the consumer desires. Intelligent agents will filter the incoming data, limit the data to what the consumer wants to see, and format the data for the consumer's current presentation channel. The consumer's intelligent agent will interact with the access provider's marketing communication system to make sure that there is a match between the consumer and specific marketing communications.

The Internet

Where does the Internet fall in all of this? The Internet and the emerging commercial content networks are currently at opposite ends of the spectrum. The Internet is currently an open, decentralized, content provision network with many access providers. The emerging commercial content provider networks will be, in their early stages, proprietary closed networks with a single access provider per network. Both have features attractive to the other that will eventually result in their merger.

The Internet already has, for all practical purposes, more content than any one person could use in a lifetime. The Internet is experiencing explosive growth at the current time, both in users, content providers, and sheer quantity of content. What the Internet does not have is a clear way for content providers to profit from the provision of their content. The Internet is currently a wide open environment where most users feel they should not have to pay for content, or for that matter, respect trademark, copyright, and libel laws.

The emerging commercial content networks will, at first, have a limited amount of content (compared to the Internet.) But from day one they will have the mechanisms in place to track content usage and reimburse content providers. Their systems will have centralized control of users, content providers, and the interactions between users and content providers. Most importantly, the commercial networks will enable the presentation of marketing communications, the main source of financing for the GII. The convergence of the two types of systems will be the true GII.

What are some of the first order effects that the GII is going to have on our society? The GII is going to enable telecommuting. The same infrastructure that enables interactive shopping, video malls, and on-line ordering will enable video dial tone, and audio/visual teleconferencing, and wide area networks that reach into employees' homes and computers. Any job that does not require physical contact with co-workers or customers, or only requires an occasional face-to-face meeting, will be a candidate for telecommuting. Telecommuting employees no longer need live near their employers. An obvious class of candidates for telecommuting are software developers. They already use computers comfortably, and are used to the concept of information networking and e-mail, so telecommuting will not be a major adjustment in work lifestyle.

The GII will impact the educational system. GII services will enable home schooling. Tele-education will allow children's education to be tailored to the needs of each and every child. Math and reading skills can be sped up or slowed down to meet each child's individual requirements. Children with Attention Deficit Disorder can be taught from their homes. Handicapped or disabled students will be able to receive a full day's schoolwork at home. Students can receive supplemental tutoring at home, as they need it. Tele-education will mean that students in remote locations will no longer face long daily bus rides. In fact, no child will face long daily bus rides. When a quality education exists on every television or computer screen, where the children are located when receiving that education becomes much less important.

The GII is going to normalize the standard of living around the world. High technology enterprises will have as their available labor pool the entire networked world, not just local talent. They will hire skilled workers irrespective of physical location. This will be a dual benefit: companies will make use of a floating pool of globally available talent, and employees will be able to live where they want to, rather than having to live near their employer. US companies are already making use of programmers in Russia, India, and southeast Asia.

The Case for Internet Access Via Cable TV*

As Vint Cerf, one of the founding fathers of the Internet, points out, "The information superhighway model, with low-speed access to a high-speed backbone, is flawed. My experience with data networking is that sometimes it makes sense to back out of the driveway at 900 miles per hour. We need to support both low-speed and high-speed access. For that reason, narrowband, 128 kbps integrated services digital network connections are not bad, but developments like cable TV-provided 10 Mbps Ethernet links are even more interesting."

The capacity of the Internet will continue to grow, as will the user systems connecting to it. Multimedia and client-server based applications, such as digital libraries, telecollaboration, concurrent engineering, and visualization will proliferate. Taking video or audio material, digitizing it, and sending it over the Internet, will benefit greatly from cable. Videoconferencing over the Internet to the home PC or to the desktop will become possible. Cable TV can make high-speed access to the multimedia Internet of tomorrow a reality today.

Over the last few years, cable operators have been gearing up to offer interactive data, telephony, video-on-demand, and other services in addition to traditional entertainment. To meet the needs of such services, cable TV networks have been evolving into a hybrid combination of coaxial and fiber optic cable, referred to as a hybrid fiber coax (HFC) architecture. This architecture uses a digital fiber backbone and a distributed star, tree and branch topology, as opposed to the totally analog tree and branch system. One advantage of this

---

*This section was excerpted from the Ultimate Sourcebook of Multimedia, ed. Jessica Keyes. 1997. *Internet Access via Cable Television: High Speed Access to Multimedia on the Worldwide Web* by Lynn Jones.

approach is increased network bandwidth with improved reliability due to fewer amplifiers and other active components. This approach also lets cable operators use a build-as-you go approach, capitalizing on their existing coax infrastructure and building fiber further out into the system as more bandwidth is needed. The newer HFC systems are 750 MHz networks which can carry up to 110 channels.

Data networks use devices such as repeaters, bridges, and routers to extend, as well as segment, local area networks. A repeater, whether in a LAN or in a cable TV network, connects two segments of network cable. It retimes, regenerates, and forwards a digital signal. Repeaters, however, can only extend a high-speed LAN a few thousand yards.

Bridges are used to connect two networks which use the same network signaling and the same media access-control protocol, such as Ethernet. Routers are used to connect two different types of networks, in this case to route IP datagrams.

Routers are also used to connect LANs to WANs, and make up the Internet backbone. A backbone is a central network to which other networks are connected.

It is important to remember that in the same way that a Local Area Network is a network of computers, the Internet is essentially a network of networks, consisting of thousands of computer networks interconnected by routers. It is also important to make a distinction between an Internet backbone router and a router on the community Ethernet network, or on the customer LAN.

The advantage to the user of accessing the Internet via cable TV is that he does not need his own leased line in order to get high-speed 10 Mbps access to the Internet. In the past, these speeds, since they required a dedicated leased line, were out of reach for all but large corporations. By connecting businesses, institutions, municipal offices, and home users into a community-wide network over cable TV, performance can be improved by three orders of magnitude while cost is reduced.

ECnet

Electronic Commerce Network (ECnet of Phoenix, Arizona) was one of the first data networks set up over cable television. The network was developed as a collaboration between Times Mirror Cable Television, Digital Equipment Corporation, and Arizona State University. ECnet connects together manufacturing companies in the Phoenix area for the purposes of concurrent Computer Aided Design (CAD), video conferencing, electronic whiteboarding, and access to the Internet. Companies using the network include McDonnell Douglas, Tempe Precision Aircraft, and Modern Instruments.

In cable television, the antenna picks up signals from the airwaves, satellites, or microwave transmitters, and sends them to a central site called the headend. The headend consists of equipment that receives the radio frequency (RF) signals and transmits them out over the distribution network. The term headend is used to refer both to the building where the equipment is located, as well as the equipment itself. The backbone of the ECnet network is a 100 Mbps FDDI (Fiber Distributed Data Interface) fiber ring, which connects four headends. Connected to each headend is a community Ethernet network, comprised of one to three companies. Each company site itself houses its own LAN, which may be comprised of hundreds of users. Bridges are used to connect the LAN sites to the community network.

The physical media in the network include dedicated fiber in the backbone, shared AM fiber for the headend trunks, and coax. The fiber ring is supporting distances as great as 36 miles between headends, while the longest fiber/coax headend trunk extends over 15 miles to a customer site. The network operates downstream at 336-342 MHz, and upstream at channel T8 (11.75 MHz — 17.75 MHz).

Access to the Internet is provided by Arizona State University. Security is provided which includes 24 hour/7 day monitoring, file encryption, protocol monitoring, automated alerts, and lockouts.

Hawaii Public Schools

The Hawaii public school district includes 360 schools located on six islands. This unique geography has perhaps contributed to the Hawaii Department of Education being on the leading edge of networking technology.

Oceanic Cable, a Time-Warner subsidiary, Digital Equipment Corporation, and Convergence Systems, Inc., a Digital reseller, have collaborated on the Hawaiian school network.

The Hawaiian schools original network consisted of a T3 (45 Mbps) microwave backbone, 28 T1 (1.5 Mbps) leased lines, which didn't meet the needs of the school system. "Leased lines are expensive and they don't really provide us with the bandwidth we need for the applications we'd like to run on the network. We needed a high bandwidth, high-speed network. With the telephone company, that would have meant a T1 line for every school, which would have been very expensive," said Kyunghak J. Kim, director of network support services for the state of Hawaii's department of education.

Hawaiian schools are using the Internet for collaborative learning with schools on the mainland, accessing images from weather services, maps, and information from libraries and universities. "The main thing ChannelWorks has provided students is the ability to effectively communicate with other students in other parts of the country and the world, and the capability to access resources available in other places," comments Kim. The ChannelWorks solution has sped up Internet access considerably at Hawaii's schools: sending a message from the University of Hawaii to the mainland and back can now be completed in seven or eight seconds — which is 100 times faster than what was possible on phone lines.

How to Set Up A Community Ethernet to Internet Network

Setting up a community Ethernet to Internet network involves a cooperative effort between the community, the cable operator, and often an Internet service provider. Although the idea for starting such a network may come from individuals or institutions in the community, it is the cable operator who actually creates the network and the business of offering Internet service to the community. It is important that the community and the cable operator work together to understand each other needs, motivations, and constraints.

Setting up a cable television network for Internet access involves both business and technical issues for a cable operator. To begin, a business case must be completed to show the cost of network implementation, the projected market, and the economic return for offering data and Internet access services in a community. The scope, schedule, and budget for the network must be defined. A project team, project manager, installation team, and site contact for each site must be identified, and a project plan prepared.

Network Planning and Design

The next step is the network design and network map. The design must include network layout, site locations, amplifiers, channel assignments, network components, leased lines, etc. The basic requirements to set up a community Ethernet to Internet network are:

one forward and one reverse channel
one bridge or brouter per site
one translator at the headend (not required for a dual system)
diplexors (either sub-, mid-, or high-split)
an Internet point-of-presence (i.e. access to a backbone router
on the Internet) either via a user site on the network, or via the headend

Several decisions need to be made during the network planning phase. The services of an Internet consultant or Internet Service Provider may be used during the network planning and installation phase of the project to help answer these questions and devise the network plan.

1. Which sites will be in the same Closed User Groups? Security can be provided via a system of closed user groups, as implemented in the UniLINK protocol. Using this system, users are assigned to one or more user groups. Ethernet data from one bridge or brouter can only be read by another bridge or brouter if it is a member of the same user group. This system allows multiple users to share the same RF channel, but operate as if they are on different networks, essentially creating multiple logical networks on one physical network
2. Which sites will be on the same IP network?
3. What are the security and firewall requirements, and where should firewalls

be located?

4. Where will the connection to the Internet be located? Will it be in the headend or at a user site?

5. If the Internet connection will be at the headend, who will install and manage the connection?

6. Who will procure, assign, and manage the IP addresses?

7. Who will secure the leased line connection to the Internet Service Provider? What line speed is required? How much will it cost? How will it be paid for?

8. Who will manage the data network?

9. Who will supply help desk support? What is the problem reporting procedure? What are the service hours? What are the problem escalation procedures?

10. What is the monthly service charge? What are the billing procedures?

11. When should the cable plant be certified? As early as possible in the project planning, a certification of the cable plant should be done. The certification of the cable plant is an important first step. A detailed checklist is used to ensure that all requirements are met so that the network will function properly.

12. Who will provide network management — the cable operator or a third party? As a network grows in size, so does the need for network management. The plans for network management should be put in place during the planning and design phase.

Chapter

10

Audio and Video Production Values

This book is not intended for professional movie makers and/or broadcasters. However, some of their expertise would be worthwhile to discuss. This chapter delves into some of the things that make good webcasting.

There are some basics that I'd like to discuss right up-front. Some people have it. Some people don't. What I mean is that you should select with care those folks who will be your spokespeople online. Some people's voices are more suited to recording than others. Professional announcers are paid not only for their reading abilities, but also for their pacing, dynamics, inflection, and most importantly, vocal tone. Bear this in mind when choosing the person behind the microphone.

You might also want to surf over to http://www.broadcast.net/, which is a great jump-off point for broadcast enthusiasts.

Guidelines for Digital Video

There is no commonly-agreed upon methodology to create digital video. Since the hardware and software involved is continually evolving, the digital video maker will have to keep on his or her toes to make sure that the videos produced are always on the "cutting edge."

The following discussion depicts a fairly common sequence of events that take place in the creation of a video on a PC (before encoding). Since the computer brings the creation process into the nonlinear age, none of these steps really has to follow in exact sequence. Assuming that the storyboarding process has been completed, the following steps can occur.

Gathering Source Material

Production facilities and personnel may be employed to create new footage for editing and manipulation, or stock footage may be gathered. The effects of the non-linear editing process is obvious here because it allows editors to play "what if" with the story line in an unprecedented manner. Thus additional footage may be shot at this stage, and more footage may be required later if the story line is allowed to evolve. The computer itself is capable of generating text, graphics and even 2D and 3D animations.

Digitizing

Before any editing can take place, the source video must be converted into digital form by the computer and stored on disk. This process is known as *digitizing*.

Video input can come from many kinds of input devices, from consumer-quality VHS machines to traditional high-end tape equipment. However, the quality of the digital image is directly dependent on the quality of the medium from which it comes. While there are several methods of digitizing, they all depend on the quality of the source device. Thus the rental or purchase of a high-quality deck should be factored into the overall cost of equipment. Still frames to be included in the production can be created in the PC or brought in through a high-quality scanner.

Editing Nonlinearly

The nonlinear editing process has many advantages. Most software products handle the editing process by facilitating the creation in an off-line model of the final video, rather than by actually compositing the video themselves on-line. This model contains information about how the video is to unfold over time. Various video clips are trimmed and then sequenced together with intervening transitions, wipes and keys. Rather than manipulate the video files themselves, the model contains information about the files and pointers to them.

Since the computer is a general purpose tool, it can be used for more than just the editing process. Static graphic elements can be assembled by means of professional-quality graphics programs, text can be generated, and 2D and 3D animations can be created. Changes to all of these production elements can be made right up to the last minute.

The computer allows the editor to create and store a model of the video project without creating the actual video. Since this model can also be duplicated, and the duplicate can be altered without altering the original, it is possible to create several different models or previews of the same project.

After the creation process has ended, the resulting video model must be used to create or render an actual video. During the rendering process the computer proceeds frame-by-frame through the model and performs all operations necessary to create a complete frame at the desired resolution and quality. This process can be quite time-consuming depending on the complexity of the model and the duration of the video.

Since many compositing and special-effect computations are very processor-intensive, three ways to speed the rendering process are to (1) purchase a faster computer, (2) accelerate your current machine, or (3) take advantage of multi-processor hardware and software to operate in parallel.

Broadcast-Quality Software

Software for personal computers and workstations now exists to create stills, edit video nonlinearly, create transitions, perform composites, render special effects, animate in two and three dimensions, and so on. See the end of this chapter for a list of resources in this area.

No one package can do it all, however, so it is important to research the capabilities of different software from different vendors. The minimum feature-set necessary to ensure broadcast-quality output is comprised of 24-bit color manipulation, subpixel positioning and anti-aliasing, Alpha channel support, and text generation that supports anti-aliasing of Postscript and TrueType fonts.

The most common representation of color in personal computers is familiar to video professionals as "component" video. Here, colors are composed of three channels: red, green, and blue. Each channel is represented by 8 bits (1 byte), for a total of 24 bits per pixel. Programs that generate 24-bit color output are essential to broadcast-quality work, because this color scheme can represent more than 16 million separate colors, more than the human eye can distinguish.

If your software has DVE-like features, subpixel positioning is essential for achieving smooth-looking motion of video layers and important for compositing. To achieve broadcast-quality motion, it is necessary to compensate for the computer's limited screen resolution. This is created by the illusion that the number of screen pixels per inch is much greater than it actually is. Subpixel sampling is the frame-processing method that creates this illusion.

Anti-aliasing becomes important when the edges of any graphic object are diagonal to any degree, when rectangular shapes are rotated, or when smooth curves are desired, as with character generation. Like subpixel positioning, it is a method of compensating for the limited resolution of the screen. It accomplishes this by removing "jaggies," thereby smoothing diagonal lines and curves.

The Alpha channel contains transparency information for each pixel. Many video professionals are surprised to learn that some PC-based graphics software, such as Photoshop, are more capable of creating and handling Alpha channel information than a more professional broadcast paint system. To the video professional, this transparency information is a key signal that defines which parts of the video frame are transparent, which opaque, and which semi-transparent.

The most common example of this may be seen on most newscasts. The character-generator used to overlay the type on the screen contains an Alpha channel. The layering device uses the Alpha channel to determine which parts of the overlay (the letters) will be opaque and which parts will be filled with the background image (a reporter standing in front of City Hall). Uses for this include compositing 3D, computer-generated graphic animations into 2D backgrounds.

Vivo's Recommendations for Video and Audio Capture

The basic shooting goals for compressed video are:

1. Limit the amount of picture content that changes from one frame to the next.

2. Limit the amount of textured detail in the picture (clothing, backgrounds, etc.)

The following list of tips naturally follow from these two basic goals. If possible, always use a stationary (tripod-mounted) camera, especially for "talking heads," office interiors, even outside location shots. This is probably the single most important factor for high-quality compressed video.

Plan for limited motion in and through the scene. For example, if you're shooting a talking head, put the person in a chair that can't rock back and forth. If your subject is particularly animated, shoot from farther back to reduce the amount of motion in the frame.

Have your subject wear bright colors. Red, pink, yellow, and light blue solids are good. Black and navy are bad — dark colors generate video "noise" which gets interpreted as changing frame contents and is thus unnecessarily encoded.

Have your subject wear solids instead of patterns. Herringbone, checks, stripes, and prints all contain complicated edge details that must be encoded and compressed taking precious bits away from the details you want to render, like facial expressions and moving lips. These color and pattern recommendations apply to background detail as well. It's much better to shoot your subject in front of a piece of uniformly colored seamless paper than sitting in front of a bookcase filled with books or a window covered by venetian blinds.

Plan for "settle time" after transitions (e.g. titles, screen shots, cuts). Say you're creating a training video and shooting screen shots of a computer application. You show the mouse clicking on a menu item, and a sub-menu drops down. The sub-menu will be a bit blurry when it first makes its appearance. Wait a few seconds for the text to clear up.

Use large, clear fonts for titles, credits, supers, computer screen shots, etc. The picture is going to be small to begin with and it will be difficult to read fine print in a compressed image. Larger text will make your viewers much more comfortable. Avoid rapid-fire "Music Video"-style cuts, dissolves, wipes, pans, zooms, special effects, etc. Images that aren't on the screen for more than a second or two won't have a chance to resolve themselves to clarity.

If you have the flexibility, short depth-of-field is preferable — soft, out-of-focus backgrounds are easier to code than sharply defined complicated details and textures. Choose a shorter shutter speed and a wider aperture to reduce depth-of-field. Don't use automatic exposure controls — maintain constant brightness. For example, while shooting an interior location, as people move into and out of the scene the background light level should not change. Changing background lighting levels will be interpreted as changes in frame contents and will be unnecessarily encoded. Brighter lighting gets coded better — avoid dark frame contents, large shadows, etc. Areas that are dimly lit can generate video "noise" which will be interpreted as changing frame contents and will be unnecessarily encoded.

Digitize video in uncompressed format. After connecting the video source to your computer's video capture board, capture digital video in uncompressed format. If your video is already compressed when you pass it to the VivoActive Producer, the VIVO file that results will not be of as high quality as it will be if the Producer operates on uncompressed digital video. Capture at a resolution of 176x144 if possible (VivoActive's display size, based on the H.263 video compression standard).

If you capture at another resolution (e.g. 320x240, 160x120) the VivoActive Producer will automatically scale your video up or down to achieve a 176x144 picture. Capture 10 to 15 frames per second (fps), or higher depending on the connection rate of your target audience.

Audio Considerations

Here are some tips for achieving high quality compressed audio:

Use a good microphone to reduce or eliminate background noise as much as possible. For "talking heads" use a wired (not wireless) clip-on lavalier microphone. In crowded areas, use a shotgun or boom microphone, as directional as you can.

Do not use a camcorder's built-in microphone. These generally pick up motor noise in the camcorder itself, in additional to omni-directional sounds in a noisy environment.

Set microphone gain properly. If the gain is too high, clipping or distortion may result. If it's too low, the audio may be too faint to be encoded properly or heard upon playback.

Understand the limitations of the G.723 audio compression algorithm. The audio heard at the far-end, when decompressed, will be of telephone "toll quality." The frequency range of the audio will be between 300 Hz and 3400 Hz. Don't expect to hear high sibilant treble or booming bass sounds. G.723 audio lends itself quite well to a single human speaker, not as well to music, and somewhat poorly to a simultaneous combination of speech and music.

Digitize audio at 8 kHz 16-bit Mono. When the time comes to perform audio capture from tape onto your computer, these settings work best for VivoActive's G.723 audio compressor. Avoid higher sampling rates, avoid 8-bit samples, and avoid stereo sampling.

Digital Editing — The Key to Digital Production

If your ambition is to come up with a piece of work that you might actually be able to sell, on a professional level, then the standards we're looking at begin with an onscreen image that is at least in the 800x600 region. British TV is 768x576, US slightly less. Anything else isn't real, won't sell, and will just waste your investment, unless this is just an expensive hobby for you.

You should look at a hardware/software kit that will give you full-motion video of 25 and/or 30 frames a second as well as 768x576. There's a lot of pretty boxes out there with big bright letters claiming Full-Motion-Video, but they only have very tiny letters confessing that you'll only fill a quarter of a TV screen with their end-result. And that isn't real, won't sell, and will just waste your money.

A major issue, before you go any further, is which hardware platform you will use. PC, Mac, or Amiga? Or something else, like a Silicon Graphics system? If you've already got a computer, then your choice is also pretty much made for you.

All professionals will tell you the same thing: "Silicon Graphics is the best for this kind of business, but they are quite expensive!" By the time you buy all the bits and pieces, especially the software, you won't get a lot of change out of $75,000 per work-station.

Nowadays, they're only partly correct: today's PCs and Macs can do pretty much anything that a Silicon Graphics can do, they may just take a little longer.

In reputation-terms, the Mac has been progressing steadily in this area for some time, but because they're mainly used by companies rather than individuals, their pricing is reflected in this: they cost more, though their dealers will do all they can to convince you otherwise.

The PC, however, being a Personal Computer, tends to be owned by individuals instead of companies. Individuals don't have the ability to throw money around the way some companies do, and they don't have the access to company borrowing facilities, and they don't have the same level of income. PC manufacturers realized this a long time ago, and most of the digital production equipment for the PC is priced accordingly.

If super-speed is the issue, and money doesn't matter to you, and you want a "Big Guy" image, buy Silicon Graphics. If super-speed is the issue, and you don't have that much money, then buy several computers, and network them up to speed up the work. It's still cheaper than Silicon Graphics. But if price is the issue, then go for the PC; all the top-end Mac kits will be PC-available by the time this is published, and so will the equally-good, but low-priced Amiga stuff.

Digital Software

It's easy! It's a breeze! But it can be agonizingly S-L-O-W-!!! (Not the learning:

but the amount of time taken by the software to do even the most basic FX.) Now this depends largely on your machine, and its configuration. More RAM helps, and anything less than a 486 DX 66 with a SCSI-drive will send you into fountains of frustration when it comes to running a Preview, or saving a file. This is not essentially because the software isn't up to it, it's because you're asking the whole system to do so much.

Try this in your own machine — just load up a picture, any picture that has a screen-size of 800x600, in 24-bit color. See how long that single frame takes to load up. Now think of a PAL Video-sequence 15 seconds long, (375 frames) and another sequence 10 seconds, (250 frames), with a simple Cross-Fade transition between the two that lasts for 3 seconds (75 frames). You are asking your computer to deal with 550 "normal" frames, and 75 frames which have to be "processed" for the Cross-Fade.

If the result is too slow for comfort, you might want to try a video acceleration card such as the Truevision Targa 2000 board — which claims to accelerate the main functions in Video-Editing by as much as 700%!!!

Leaving aside speed, which is really down to the performance of the host system, the major considerations for a video-editing system have to be:
- Can it do everything that a tape editing system can do? and if so,
- Can it do them cheaper?

So what is a "properly set-up system" then? PC or Mac, it needs the fastest processor, as much RAM as you can afford, and the biggest, fastest disk-drive you can lay your hands on. A big monitor helps too, because you are editing, not just linking strings of still-frames. That means that you're selecting "Takes" for the way they fit together, for the way the whole sequence will "Flow" once you're done. And that means that you want to be able to see detail in every frame.

You must setup your computer to give you the very best monitoring capabilities when you play back video. If you're linking clips of video together, you must be able to see them playback in the most natural way, as close to finished video quality as you can get it. If that means buying a faster hard disk, buy it. If that means buying a faster graphics card, buy it. You cannot judge your edit if you are watching a halting, jerky movement, with those infuriating vertical rolls dribbling down the screen!

The system must have satisfactory sound on board, and it must output to a VCR, which in turn displays on a monitor of its own, with good quality sound-monitoring as well. Use an old hi-fi from a rummage sale if you have to! Don't rely on the speakers in a TV!

And, because digitized audio-video files take up a ton of space, you need to worry about disk space and file compression. You also need to keep in mind that compression causes image degradation.

Adobe, or U-Lead are the two leading image editing software packages. Both are easy to use, both are over-loaded with features that you'll probably never use, and both come with manuals that nobody ever seems to read. But the truth of the matter is that a computer-based edit suite is far more than just that. It is also a Special FX suite, and a full post-production facility.

Imagine you're watching through the day's shoot and you need a right-hand view of the leading man turning to face the bad guys, to match their left-hand response. Take two was by far the best, but for some reason, the lighting was just a little bit too dim. Creative use of the Filter FX can boost the brightness, tweak the color, and adjust the contrast just enough to compensate for what was wrong. Without touching a camera or paying an actor or crew you've, in effect, gone back and re-shot the unusable scene and set different light levels! Either of the two edit software packages let you set the key colors, and use the Plug-ins of an Image Editor. You can also matte out a background, and superimpose the remaining foreground action on top of another sequence.

You can put anything behind your foreground. If your foreground happens to be an actor, talking to the camera, you could "place" him in front of a background clip of a Hawaiian Island sequence, or move him to Hong Kong, or the Tower of London. With a computer, you can use 3D modeling software to build the interior of a space craft, or a Martian landscape. In conventional production terms, you're incurring design costs, construction and painting, props, and studio hire as well, and they all take up time.

The computer lets you build virtual sets and locations, and they only take a few days, and only cost you the price of the software, and maybe a design artist, if you can't do it for yourself. So digital editing is the doorway to digital production. You can set motion-paths, create 3D FX, and create morphs that will impress the fussiest movie fans! All with one package.

Then there's the audio. The most you're going to get on the fanciest tape system will be four tracks, unless you spend a ton of money, buy a whole sound-studio, and then spend more money synchronizing this to your video studio. Digital systems now offer you hundreds of channels of audio to work on, and all the FX processing you can think of.

What Does This Really Mean

A new generation of movie makers, and video producers, that's what it means. People who understand how to create their own virtual locations, in photo-realistic 3D, who understand how to plan their shots in relation to their virtual sets, in relation to the editing they're already seeing in their mind's eye, which links with the music they're already anticipating. People who will be planning an entire production in the virtual dimension.

The images that they will create onscreen will start, not on bits of paper, or in their head, but in the computer, and there they will remain, where they can be improved, and perfected, or amended, until the finished result is ready to come out to tape or film.

And they will come out to film. A year ago, resolutions of 4,000 x 4,000 were considered huge, but now the software that builds the sets and locations will go up to 8,000 x 8,000, above what's needed for Cinemascope.

Beginning now, a new breed of "Auteur" movie/video-maker is evolving. People who "see" their entire production in this virtual dimension will now be able to execute their vision, single-handed, if that's their wish.

Applications and Design Considerations in Using Audio in Webcasting

Several different types of audio output — speech, music and sound effects — can be incorporated into audio on the Internet. To use each type effectively, developers need to learn more about how each of the types can be used to improve their content.

Speech

Two types of speech are available for use: digitized and synthesized. Digitized speech provides high-quality, natural speech, but requires significant disk-storage capacity. Synthesized speech is not as storage intensive, but may not sound as natural as human speech.

Speech is an important element of human communication and can be used effectively to transmit information. One advantage of using natural speech is the power of the human voice to persuade. Another advantage is that speech can potentially eliminate the need to display large amounts of text.

Music

Music is also an important component of human communication. It is used to set a mood or tone, provide connections or transitions, add interest or excitement and evoke emotion. Music, especially when combined with speech and sound effects, can greatly enhance the presentation of text and visuals.

Sound Effects

Sound effects are used to enhance or augment the presentation of information. Two types of sound effects are natural and synthetic. Natural sounds are unadorned, commonplace sounds that occur around us. Synthetic sounds are those that are produced electronically or artificially.

There are two general categories of sound effects: ambient and special. Ambient sounds are the background sounds that communicate the context of the screen or place. Special sounds are uniquely identifiable sounds, such as the ring of a telephone, that complement narration and/or visuals.

Narration

To produce high-quality recorded speech, a script should be written and professionally recorded. To provide balance, both female and male narrators should be used. Nonprofessional narrators, such as corporate officers may be used to provide credibility. When content needs to be explained or information needs to be delivered accurately, a professional can be relied upon to follow the specifications of the script and deliver a professional-sounding audio track.

To be effective, a narrator should:
1. Vary intonation to motivate, explain, provoke, exhort or empathize
2. Use a conversational tone
3. Be amiable, candid, sincere and straightforward
4. Avoid sounding arrogant, pretentious, flippant, disrespectful, or sarcastic
5. Avoid a lecturing tone

When you are recording narrative speech, be sure to eliminate background or ambient sound unless it is used to provide a realistic environment. On occasion, incorporating ambient sound can be effective, since it can be used to help establish a mood or to increase the feeling of reality.

Developing the Speech

Good writing techniques are essential to the development of successful webcasting programs. Thus, to integrate speech as an effective tool, developers must learn to write an effective narration as part of a program script. General guidelines for this activity can be gathered from the techniques used for scriptwriting for other media:

1. Write the way people speak
2. Use language the audience can understand
3. Write as if the narrator were teaching or speaking with one person
4. Write in a clear, straightforward manner
5. Write in short sentences that can be spoken in a single breath
6. Use second-person pronouns — you and your
7. Use contractions and other simplified forms that are used in speech
8. Emphasize clarity and simplicity
9. Omit needless words
10. Avoid slang
11. Avoid oral presentation of figures and statistics
12. Use humor when appropriate
13. Present information in small chunks
14. Emphasize the objectives or goals of the webcast
15. Interpret what the user is seeing rather than simply describe it
16. Make the visuals and narration go hand-in-hand; usually the visuals tell the story and the narration interprets, explains or elaborates
17. Adhere to time limits and length requirements
18. Understand the capabilities and limitations of Internet hardware and software, especially as related to the use of speech

Narration should be read aloud and then revised if it sounds awkward, stilted or boring. To raise the level of user interest, quotes, conversations, conversations and case studies could be included in audio scripts.

Selecting Music

Few articles or books have been written that provide detailed information or guidelines about the effective use of music in interactive programs. Some suggest that incorporating music begins with identifying the function of the music and making it an integral element of the script. Thus, the use of music needs to be considered as the program is being visualized and the script written. Generally, music can be used to:

1. Establish mood
2. Set pace
3. Signal a turn of events
4. Indicate progress and activity
5. Provide transitions and continuity
6. Evoke emotion
7. Accompany titles or introduction information
8. Emphasize important points
9. Support visual information
10. Add interest, realism and surprise

Music can have a wide variety of effects on its listeners. It is not only "background" but also works in conjunction with the visual message or provide interest, excitement, tension and realism. Since music plays an important story telling role, it should fit the pace and mood of the presentation and appeal to the audience's lifestyle, taste and workplace position. Guidelines to accomplish this are:

1. Make music an integral part from the start, rather than try to find music to "go with" imagery later
2. Choose a music style that conveys the mood you wish to create
3. Convey personality through instrumentation
4. Use recurring themes as musical signatures to help the audience feel familiar with a characters, place or segment
5. Use tempo, dynamics and pitch to establish energy levels
6. Use different styles of music and instrumentation to suggest time periods, cultures, locations and sense of place
7. Use musical genres to communicate to specific audiences: e.g., big band sounds for older audiences, or rap, metal, or pop for teenagers
8. Know when to hold them, when to fold them. Music should not compete with the narration or overwhelm the message of the program

Selecting Sound Effects

Natural, ambient sounds are an integral part of our daily lives. We use them to help us interpret and assess our surroundings. For example, we listen to the thunk of a car door to find out if it has closed properly.

Sound or non-speech audio can provide different types of messages, including alarms or warnings and status or monitoring messages. Alarms and warnings are sounds and signals that interrupt and alert a listener. These sounds, such as fire alarms and police sirens, normally are loud and easily identifiable. Status and monitoring messages are sounds that give us information about ongoing tasks. The click of the keys on the keyboard is an example of these typically short sounds. Status and monitoring sounds fade rapidly from the listener's awareness and are significant only when they indicate a change; for example, when the sound does not occur.

There are several other categories of sound:

1. Physical events. We can identify whether a dropped glass bounded or shattered
2. Invisible structures. Tapping a wall helps us to locate where to hang a picture
3. Dynamic change. As we pour liquid into a glass, we can hear when it is full
4. Abnormal structures. We can tell when our car engine is malfunctioning by its sound
5. Events in space. We can hear someone approaching by the sound of footsteps

Not only can sound effects provide specific information about an environment or setting, they can also be used to accomplish the following tasks:

1. Create atmosphere
2. Add realism
3. Emphasize important points
4. Indicate progress or activity
5. Increase interest
6. Establish mood
7. Cue or prompt users
8. Increase users' motivation

Three significant considerations should govern the use of sound effects:

1. They must be clear and easily identifiable
2. They should not overwhelm the primary message
3. They should be appropriate to the intended audience

General Guidelines

1. To maximize the use of audio, analyze carefully the target audience, delivery environment, and content
2. Clearly define why and how audio will be used
3. Whenever possible, integrate audio into the whole program, and do it from the start of the project
4. Develop detailed scripts or storyboards

5. Allow users to control the audio
6. Make sound effects meaningful
7. Use the highest-quality audio possible, given the storage constraints of the internet
8. Collaborate with others who have experience using different types of audio
9. Learn more about the use of sound, especially music

Audio Hints

The staff of Progressive Networks (RealAudio) have become experts at squeezing the best sound out of the limited bandwidth of the Internet. Here's some of their words of wisdom, which is also discussed in Chapter 5:

1. Use a Good Original Source.

A high-quality audio source is probably the single most important variable in determining your final audio quality. They start with satellite signals, audio Compact Discs, or Digital Audio Tapes. When creating sounds from scratch, they use professional-quality microphones. You can make sound files from low-quality analog cassettes, tiny condenser microphones, or anything else — but the hiss and distortion in the resulting sound file will have a substantial adverse effect on clarity after the file is encoded.

You should always encode from 16-bit (not 8-bit or mu-law) sound files. They also recommend digitizing at a 22050 Hz sample rate.

2. Set Your Input Levels Correctly.

Setting correct levels is absolutely crucial. When creating your original sound file, the input level should be set to use the full range of available amplitude, while avoiding clipping. Clipping is audible as a high-frequency crackling noise and is what happens if you try to send too much input to your soundcard (or any other piece of audio equipment).

When digitizing with your sound card, first do several test runs and adjust your input level so the input approaches but does not exceed the maximum level. You can adjust this on the mixer page of your sound card utilities. Look for the Input Levels or Recording Levels option. Most mixer pages have some sort of visual display where you can see how much sound is coming in. Make sure there are no peaks above maximum. These are generally indicated by a red light somewhere. Be conservative with your levels; you never know when someone will get excited and speak much louder, or when a great play at a sports event will make a crowd roar. Differences in volume levels can be evened out later.

Sound files that do not use the full amplitude range will produce poor-quality encoded files. If the amplitude range of an existing file is too low, you can use your audio editor's Increase Amplitude or Increase Volume command to adjust the range before encoding the your levels automatically.

Note, however, that better quality will be achieved if the levels are set correctly at the time of recording. The good news is that once you set your input levels correctly, they generally will not need to be reset. If you are reasonably consistent with your recording practices, you'll save yourself a lot of trouble in the long run.

3. Use High-Quality Equipment.

High-quality equipment will produce better results and save you a lot of headaches in the long run. Every piece of equipment in the audio chain, from the microphone to the soundcard to the software, will have an effect on your encoded files. If you intend to make sound a big part of your web site, you should invest in professional quality audio equipment. This need not be a crippling investment, but it does mean you will have to purchase from a professional recording equipment dealer, not your local computer/hi-fi/gadget store.

4. Select Appropriate Material.

If you want to encode music for transmission over 14.4 kbps phone lines, remember that the simpler the source, the better chance that the encoded version will be faithful to the original. There isn't enough bandwidth in a 14.4 line to do a harmonically complex signal (like a full orchestra) justice. Many folks have used music successfully in their 14.4 clips as background, where fidelity isn't as important an issue.

5. Correcting DC Offset.

Sometimes when files are digitized, something known as *DC offset* creeps in. This is when the digitized waveform is not correctly centered around the 0 volts axis. Most of this is due to improper grounding of soundcards. Some soundcards are worse than others; to see how bad your soundcard is try recording silence. You should in theory see nothing in you waveform window, but you'll probably see a flat line just slightly above or below the 0 volts axis. This is DC offset.

This can wreak havoc when you attempt to process your waveform, and can add a low rumbling sound to the encoded file. Luckily most editors have a built in facility to take care of this. Some call it 'Centering the Wave' and are automatic; others allow you to adjust DC offset manually (+/-). In this case you'll have to find out precisely what your DC offset is by running a 'statistics' command or something similar. Then you'll have to correct it. For instance, if your average DC offset is 45 you'll want to offset the wave by -45.

Obviously if you are doing a live broadcast, you'll have to live with whatever DC offset you have. Proper balanced wiring between all your audio components will help minimize this as well as any ground loops.

6. Noise Gating (or Expansion).

Noise Gating, or downward expansion, eliminates unwanted background noise which becomes audible during pauses in the audio (e.g. when an announcer pauses, or there is a gap between programs). Signals above a certain volume level are left alone, but below this level the signal is turned down or even off, depending on how heavy the gating or expansion is. Setting up a noise gate or expander is straightforward. Most budget compressors have a noise gate built in.

To use noise gating, set the threshold control so that the gating or expansion occurs when there is no desired audio, but not so high that the beginnings of words or music that you want to hear are chopped off. It takes a bit of time, but remember to err on the side of caution just in case the next person in the program has a softer voice.

If your gate or expander has a range control, set this to around 5 to 10 dB. This means it will turn down the "noise" sections a little, but not turn them off altogether. That way you'll hear if the gate is cutting something off that you want to hear, and you can then readjust the threshold setting accordingly.

7. Compression.

One of the side effects of digital encoding is artifacts — sounds that weren't there before encoding. These can be heard sometimes as rumbling or distortion in the signal. These artifacts appear at a relatively constant low level, whether the original soundfile was loud or quiet. Louder files tend to mask these quiet artifacts. So it is recommended to feed the encoder a loud signal. However, we are limited by the loudest section of the file being encoded. If we could turn down the loudest section, we could turn the overall volume of the soundfile up. A compressor helps us accomplish this.

Compression reduces the difference between the loudest and quietest sections of the incoming signal. Sections that exceed a user-defined threshold are turned down. Now that these loud sections have been turned down, we can turn the overall volume of the soundfile up. How much the sections are turned up or down depends on how much compression you use.

How much compression should you use? The exact settings will be determined by experience and by referring to the manual that comes with your equipment or software. However, for speech if is recommended that you use moderate to extreme compression (4:1 to 10:1).

8. Equalization.

Equalization (or EQ) changes the tone of the incoming signal just as you can on your home stereo or car radio. This is done by "boosting" (turning up) or "cutting" (turning down) certain frequencies. Using EQ, we can boost frequencies that we like (where the important content is) and cut frequencies where noise or unwanted sound is. By doing this, we can give the encoder a big hint about which sound information to keep. Encoding discards a lot of the high end, or treble information. This can make files sound dull. To compensate for this, it helps to boost the middle frequencies or midrange. This will also make speech sound more intelligible.

Most good mixing boards will have a midrange EQ knob. Sometimes you can choose which frequency to boost, other times this is preset at the factory. If not, or if you are using a graphic equalizer or audio processing software, you'll want to boost at around 2.5 KHz.

If your equipment does not have a mid-frequencies EQ knob, you can obtain a similar result by turning the low and high EQ knobs down and then turning the overall volume back up (note, though, that this is not as effective as boosting the *mids*, which attacks the problem at its source).

The amount that you should turn up the midrange depends on your EQ equipment and source file. A little experimentation is necessary. Try adding some *mids* to a short section of a piece to be encoded and check it with the RealAudio Player. If it is a bit muddy or hard to understand, try adding a little more. You can keep going until the knob won't turn anymore, or until the result starts to sound too harsh.

For digital audio encoded at 14.4 kbps it is important to try and make the voice as full as possible in the middle frequencies. This is where the majority of speech information is contained. What we are trying to do is lift the voice away from any background noise.

Some signals can be improved by rolling off (turning down) the bass frequencies as well. Side effects of encoding are sometimes audible as a lower voice "shadowing" the original. This is particularly noticeable with women speakers. When this effect is too prominent, try rolling off the bass and encoding the result. The artifacts will not disappear, but sometimes they will be quieter. Be careful not to make the voice sound too thin or brittle.

For audio played back at 28.8 kbps, much more of the fidelity of the original recording is retained so you won't need to worry about EQ as much. It still helps to boost at around 2.5 KHz to compensate for the high frequency loss, but boosting too much will make music sound thin and tinny.

9. Normalization.

Normalization is a process included in most audio recording software whereby the computer calculates exactly how much it can turn up the volume of a file without distortion. Because we always want to feed the encoder the loudest files possible, this is a very handy function. This is why you can afford to be fairly conservative with your recording input levels, and then let your program's normalization function take care of the rest. Normalization should be the last thing you do. If you normalize your file, and then add some EQ, you'll end up with distortion.

Digital and Audio Resources

The following list of resources will help you get started on the road to creative audio and video production. Note, however, that many of these tools are multimedia oriented. There's a reason for this. You have to create your video from something. Aside from live action, what better source than the multimedia productions you create right on your very own computer.

Digital Video

928Movie

A single-slot ISA or VL bus Windows and multimedia accelerator that delivers up to six times the performance of ordinary VGAs and visibly improves the quality of CD multimedia titles by scaling up video clips to full-color, full-screen movies.

VideoLogic Inc.
245 First St.
Cambridge, MA 02142
617-494-0530

Rapier 24

A two-page graphics processor that brings workstation class 24-bit true color performance to Windows Autodesk and TIGA applications. It provides resolutions from 640 x 480 to 1,152 x 882 and allows users to select from a wide range of third-party multisync VGA and Apple monitors.

VideoLogic Inc.
245 First St.
Cambridge, MA 02142
617-494-0530

SynchroMaster 300AV

A synchronizer, switcher, fader and dissolve unit for data display projectors. It provides instantaneous clean cuts between two computer sources of up to 1,280 x 1,024 pixel resolution, as well as fade and dissolves.

RGB Spectrum
950 Marina Village Pkwy
Alameda, CA 94501
510-814-7000

Vivid 3D

A sound enhancement system for video games and multimedia. It creates dynamic 3-D sound from only two speakers.

NuReality
2907 Damier St.
Santa Ana, CA 92705
714-442-1080

DigiTracker

This uncomplicated digital tracker combines a multiple-sensor motion tracker (up to 30 sensors) with a 3-D digitizer that allows for easy creation of 3-D models. Mesh files can be created by simply positioning the stylus on any point on a model and pressing a button to enter the coordinate.

Visual Circuits
3309 83rd Ave. North
Brooklyn Park, MN 55443
612-560-6205

LiveWindows

A collection of routines to provide real-time display and scaling of live video within a window or multiple windows on the VGA screen. The card plugs into a 16-bit slot and connects to a VGA card with a feature connector.

Software Interphase
82 Cucumber Hill Rd.
Ste 258
Foster, RI 02825
800-542-2742

Super Video Windows — ISA

A professional-quality frame grabber and video windowing board that accepts up to three composite or S-VHS inputs from camera, VCR or videodisc and displays full-motion video in a scalable window.

New Media Graphics Corp
780 Boston Rd.
Billerica, MA 01821
800-288-2207

Video-It!

A high-performance video-capture card, featuring real-time capture and compression. Available in ISA, CPI and VESA Local Bus version, it can display live video-in-a-window at any graphics resolution.

ATI Technologies Inc.
33 Commerce Valley Dr. East
Thornhill, Ontario, Canada L3T 7N6
905-882-2600

VideoSurge

A full-motion, 24-bit color video display and capture board that has the ability to do chroma-key and luma-key effects and forms the basis of any video processing studio. Features include three independent audio and video sources, audio pass-through and optimal support for 24-bit VGA color.

AITech International
47971 Fremont Blvd.
Fremont, CA 94538
800-882-8184

Audio/Video Key-PC Presentation Kit

This add-on comprises two external interfaces that connect a DOS computer to a wide range of audio/visual hardware. With the included presentation software, HSC Interactive, AudioVideo Key — a portable multimedia presentation system.

Comedge Inc.
2211 S. Hacienda Blvd. #100
Hacienda Heights, CA 91745
818-336-7522

Chroma Gold

This is a HiColor, 32,768 color VGA display adapter with NTSC composite output. It supports all VGA and SuperVGA modes with standard VGA outputs.

Ventura Technologies
4820 Adhor Ln. Ste M
Camarillo, CA 93012
805-45-4411

CVC

The CVC converts interfaced 15 HZ RGB analog video to studio-quality component video in selectable Betacam or Mll formats.

Visual Circuits
3309 83rd Ave. N
Brooklyn Park, MN 55443
612-560-6205

Delta VC

An integrated, PC solution for creating interactive and linear-play video program. It combines real-time MPEG video and audio compression technology with powerful interactive design and mastering tools.

Optimage
7185 Vista Dr. West
Des Moines, IA 50266
800-234-5484

Genie Scan Converter

Genie is an external portable box that converts PC graphics to TV video. Genie is a true 100 percent hardware scan converter; it requires no software and is truly plug and play.

Jovian Logic Corp
47929 Fremont Blvd.
Fremont, CA 94538
510-651-4823

TV Link

TV Link delivers precision computer images to any standard TV system. It handles VGA resolution up to 640x480 with as many as 16 million colors.

KDI/Precision Products Inc.
60 S. Jefferson Rd.
Whippany, NJ 07981
201-887-5700

Captivator ProTV

Coupled to VESA Media Channel (VMC) graphics systems, Captivator ProTV for VMC displays crystal clear TV pictures on a PC screen. The user has total control of the picture attributes (brightness, contrast etc.) through an easy to use control panel. The live-video window can be set to stay on top of the display, enabling the user to monitor the TV while working with another application. It's simple to install and use thus making it ideal for home use.

VideoLogic
245 First St.
Suite 1403
Cambridge, MA 02142
617-494-0530
Internet: usa@videologic.com

MPEG Player for VMC

Using VideoLogic's PowerStream video processor and associated proprietary SmoothScale algorithms to deliver sensational quality video, this peripheral equips today's PCs to take advantage of MPEG, the dominant standard for exceptionally high-quality digital video and audio. It features the highest quality video playback, full support for application developers, outstanding CD audio and easy installation.

VideoLogic
245 First St.
Suite 1403
Cambridge, MA 02142
617-494-0530
Internet: usa@videologic.com

MovieLine

Full-featured, low-cost, MovieLine enables users to create dynamic presentations etc. with digital effects and animation. MovieLine includes Movie Machine Pro with Motion-JPEG Option, Adobe Premiere, Animator Pro and XingCD MPEG encoding.

Fast Electronic
393 Vintage Dr.
Foster City, CA 94404
800-864-MOVIE

Alladin Media Printer

Alladin integrates a seven-input digital switcher, fully programmable 3-D DVE and bundles a graphics software package for paint, character generation, #-D modeling and animation.

Pinnacle Systems Inc.
870 W. Maude Ave.
Sunnyvale, CA
408-720-9669

Asii Switcher

This is a broadcast-quality plug-in switcher that utilizes the latest technology to provide various digital effects. PC control allows users to set up multiple events, allowing the editor to pre-select and store a series of digital effects.

Hotronic Inc.
1875 S. Winchester Blvd.
Campbell, CA 99508
408-378-3883

AmiLink CIP Desktop Video Editing Systems

This editing tool allows users true A/B roll editing with consumer industrial level video equipment and lets users upgrade to professional editing and still use their CIP equipment. It comes with extensive edit list tools.

RGB Computer & Video Inc.
4152 Blue Heron Blvd. West
Ste 118
Riviera Beach, FL 33404
808-5635-7876

Edit-San

This is a low-cost A/B Roll system that provides the professional features requested by most editors. It lets users create tape logs right from the editing software and then build edit decision lists directly from the tape logs.

TAO Inc.
PO Box 1254
Roll, MO 65401
800-264-1121

The Executive Librarian

This system features multiuser access for fast, full text searches of thousands of records. Pull lists are generated from query results and may be further edited, saved or e-mailed.

Imagine Products Inc.
581 S. Rangeline Rd Ste B3
Carmel, IN 46032
317-843-0706

Media Merge

A video editing software designed to edit video in Windows. It enables users to choose source material from popular video, paint, spreadsheet, animation, presentation, word processing or desktop publishing packages and combine it into a new video presentation.

ATI Technologies
33 Commerce Valley Dr. East
Thornhill, Ontario, Canada L3T 7N6
905-882-2600

Scene Stealer

Scene Stealer is a PC/AT circuit board and software for automatic scene detection and video logging, saving hours of logging drudgery. The on-board frame grabber examines incoming video to determine when a cut takes place.

Dubner International Inc.
13 Westervelt Pl
Westwood, NJ 07675
201-664-6434

Strassner SES-2000 Thru 3000

An editors wish list of artistic tools. These features provide the ultimate in off-line and online editing applications, and every Strassner system has, built in, the capacity for upgrading and adding new features.

Strassner Editing Systems
104-19 McCormick St.
North Hollywood, CA 91601
800-836-3348

Studio Magic

Enables users to display VGA output on any TV Screen. Second, it can capture full-size, full-color video images and store them on disk for later use. The heart is an online video production studio.

Studio Magic Corp.
1690 Dell Ave.
Campbell, CA 95008
408-378-3638

U-Edit

A very affordable news and video magazine edit controller. Based on the PC platform, U-Edit converts a user-supplied 286 or better into a frame-accurate 99 event editor.

Editing Technologies Corp.
11992 Challenger Ct.
Moorpark, CA 93021
805-529-7074

ScreenPlay 2.2

A audio/video editing package that offers 24-bit true-color playback and is able to run on Windows-based applications as well as Apple's Quicktime applications. It's fully licensed to allow people the right to distribute the ScreenPlay 2.2 Viewer and ScreenPlay formatted movies over the Internet.

RAD Technologies
745 Emerson St.
Palo Alto, CA 94301
415-617-9430

MediaSpace

A cost-effective means to add video wherever needed, this digital video board allows you to record, edit and playback in real-time. It includes Adobe Premiere and works with more than 100 video for Windows compatible applications.

VideoLogic Inc
245 First St.
Ste 1403
Cambridge, MA 02142
617-494-0530

Captivator: Video Capture Card

A low-cost video capture card that brings desktop video to office and home PCs.

Easily installed, this card enables high-quality video to be displayed in any size and in 8, 16, or 24-bit color.

VideoLogic Inc.
245 First St. Ste 1403
Cambridge, MA 02142
617-494-0530

Adobe Premier

The hot-ticket for Macs and now PCs.

Adobe Systems Inc.
1585 Charleston Rd., P.O. Box 7900
Mountain View, CA 94039
(800) 833-6687

CameraMan

CameraMan is a screen movie capture utility for Windows computers. Unlike screen capture utilities that can only capture static pictures of the screen, CameraMan records everything that takes place on the screen in real-time to a standard movie file.

Motion Works USA
524 Second St.
San Francisco, CA 94107
800-800-8476

D/Vision

Enables you to produce edited videotapes and multimedia video. Uses Intel's i750/Indeo digital video board. Enables instant revision and playback of editorial decisions. Good price for the power. Touts SupeRTV which is an enhancement of Intel's RTV (real time video); let's you "print" high-quality, full-screen video directly to videotape. There's actually two versions of this software. The basic system, which retails for under $500, is touted as being the lowest cost non-linear editing software on the market. The Pro version, retailing for slightly under $4,000, turns your PC into a professional video production studio. It even stores over 70 hours of accessible, on-line digital video.

TouchVision Systems Inc.
1800 Winnemanc Ave.
Chicago, IL 60640
(312) 989-2160

VGA Producer Pro

A VGA-to-NTSC genlockable encoder that enables you to transfer your multimedia work of art to videotape. Promises to be flicker-free.

Magni Systems Inc.
9500 SW Gemini Dr.
Beaverton, OR 97005
(503) 626-8400

DVA-4000

A family of full-motion digital video adapters for IBM PC/AT, PS/2 or Mac computers.

VideoLogic, Inc.
245 First St.
Cambridge, MA 02142
(617) 494-0530

Mediator

High quality computer graphics to video conversion system for Mac and VGA displays.

VideoLogic, Inc.
245 First St.
Cambridge, MA 02142
(617) 494-0530

Pro Movie Spectrum

This is a playback, capture and editing add-in board with bundled software. Enables users to bring synchronized, full-motion video sequences to the PC.

Media Vision
3185 Laruelview Ct.
Fremont, CA 94538
(800) 845-5870

Bandit

Bandit simplifies the process of transferring images between your computer and VCR or video camera. Bandit is a peripheral device which works in the Mac and PC environments by connecting to either a SCSI or serial port.

Fast Forward Video
18200-C West McDurmott
Irvine, CA 92714
(714) 852-8404

Bravado

Combines full-featured, on-board VGA with live NTSC or PAL video-in-a-windows and controllable pass-through audio in one board. Apparently a single-board multimedia presentation engine.

Truevision
7240 Shadeland Station
Indianapolis, Indiana 46256
(317) 841-0332

Super Still-Frame Compression

Reduces storage requirements for captured video through JPEG (8:1 to 75:1) compression.

New Media Graphics
780 Boston Rd.
Billerica, MA 01821
(800) 288-2207

VideoSpigot for Windows

Captures digital video from cameras, VCRs, laser discs, etc. Includes Microsoft Video for Windows which enables editing of motion video sequences for embedding in any application that supports Object Linking and Embedding (OLE). CinePak software compression lets you stores AVI files at a fraction of their original size.

Creative Labs
1901 McCarthy Blvd.
Milpitas, CA 95035
(800) 428-6600

Videovue

Ability to extract images from motion or still-frame video. Incoming video can be PAL, NTSC, composite or S-video.

Video Associates Labs

4926 Spicewood Springs Rd.
Austin, Texas 78759
(800) 331-0547

Intel Smart Video Recorder

One-step recording and Indeo compression allows a 50 MB 60-second clip to be stored in a relatively small 9MB.

Intel Corp.
2200 Mission College Blvd.
Santa Clara, CA 95052
(800) 538-3373

DigiTV

Built-in 122 channel cable-ready TV tuner, on-board 4-Watt stereo audio amplifier lets you watch TV through your PC.

Videomail, Inc.
568-4 Weddell Dr.
Sunnyvale, CA 94089
(408) 747-0223

Video Machine

Enables broadcast quality video editing right on the desktop.

Fast Electronics
5 Commonwealth Rd.
Natick, MA 01760
(508) 655-FAST

TelevEyes

An inexpensive tool for converting computer VGA to recordable composite video. Allows displaying computer screens on any standard composite video monitor or recording VGS screens to video tape.

Digital Vision Inc.
270 Bridge St.
Dedham, MA 02026
(617) 329-5400

WatchIT

This is an add-on board that allows you to watch TV on your PC. It runs under DOS or Windows using a pop-up remote control for TV adjustment.

New Media Graphics
780 Boston Rd.
Billerica, MA 01821
(509) 663-0666

PC Tele-VISION PLUS

This is a board that allows an IBM-PC compatible computer to display NTSC or composite video in a window of variable size on a VGA or Super VGA monitor.

50/50 Micro Electronics
1249 Innsbruck Dr.
Sunnyvale, CA 94089
(408) 720-5050

TapeIT

An inexpensive video encoding board which converts VGA signals to NTSC or PAL.

New Media Graphics
780 Boston Rd.
Billerica, MA 01821
(800) 288-2207

The Indy Workstation

I haven't listed any multimedia PCs here because all vendors seem to be offering them. This, however, is unique. Silicon Graphics is now offering a workstation with a built-in color video camera for under $4,995. Given the price of a multimedia-enabled PC nowadays, this workstation is worth a look-see. Remember, Silicon Graphics are the guys who brought you the special effects for Jurassic Park.

Silicon Graphics
2011 N. Shoreline Rd.
P.O. Box 7311
Mountain View, CA
(800) 800-7441

Media Add-in Boards

ViVA

This is truly a super board. It provides a low cost multimedia solution by combining audio, video and VGA all on one board.

Omnicorp
1734 W. Sam Houston Pkwy N.
Houston, TX
(713) 464-2990

MediaTime Adapter

A NuBus adapter that combines CD-quality audio with 24-bit real-time digital video and graphics display for the MAC.

RasterOps
2500 Walsh Ave.
Santa Clara, CA 95051
(408) 562-4200

Super VideoWindows

Enables playing of full motion video and stereo audio from a TV camera, VCR, still-frame camera, videodisc, computer hard disk. Allows scalability, freeze or frame/grab, combination of audio/video and VGA graphics.

New Media Graphics
780 Boston Rd.
Billerica, MA 01821
(800) 288-2207

Super Motion Compression

Captures clips of high quality video and stereo audio, compresses and stores them to hard disk and allows instant playback.

New Media Graphics
780 Boston Rd.
Billerica, MA 01821
(800) 288-2207

Video Blaster

Integrates video and audio from a wide range of sources — cameras, VCRs, and video discs, then combine them with VGA graphics. Cropping, scaling, masking and zooming capabilities. Includes a copy of Microsoft Video for Windows.

Creative Labs
1901 McCarthy Blvd.
Milpitas, CA 95035
(800) 428-6600

Sound

20-20 Sound Editor

A Windows program designed to deal with the audio part of multimedia presentation. Features include: fast, non-destructive waveform editing; powerful 8-tract audio file mixer, versatile multimedia browser, etc.

MKS Compu-Group Inc.
1730 Cunard St.
Lava Quebec Canada H7S 2B2
514-332-4110

Ballade for Windows

Record, play back and print out sheet music with this production package. Pick and choose from a variety of musical sounds and sound effects contained in the computer sound card.

Dynaware
950 Tower Ln. Ste 1150
Foster City, CA 94404
415-349-5700

Cakewalk Home Studio

Your PC can be turned into a multitrack recording studio with this innovative software package. Features include a virtual piano to record music with the keyboard or mouse.

Twelve Tone Systems
PO Box 760
Watertown, MA 02272
800-234-1171

The Editor Plus

Record one stereo sound file while listening to another with this software helpmate. It plays the file in the bottom waveform display window and records the new sound in the top window.

Digital Audio Labs
114505 21st Ave., Ste 202
Plymouth, MN 55447
612-473-7626

Knowledge Media Audio Plus

Audio contains public domain, freeware and shareware applications and data files, covering hundreds of sounds, sound effects and MOD files.

Knowledge Media Inc.
436 Nunneley, Ste B
Paradise, CA 95969
800-782-3766

MIDI Programmer's ToolKit for Windows

The MIDI Programmer's TookKit provides tools and documentation to assist Windows programmers in developing MIDI applications. All ToolKit features are found in a dynamic link library, which provides functions to easily access Standard MIDI files.

Music Quest Inc.
1700 Alma Dr., Ste 330
Plano, TX 17075
214-881-7408

Power Tracks Pro

A full-featured, integrated 48-track MIDI sequencer and music notation program for Window 3.1. Power Tracks Pro can record, play back and edit MIDI data.

P.G. Music Inc.
266 Elmwood Ave., Ste 111
Buffalo, NY 14222
800-268-6272

MusicPrinter Plus

A notation-based sequencer program that's chock full of such features as page view, automatic measure numbering, extended print to print, PCX files, accurate performance of artistic notation-rubato markings and more

Temporal Acuity Products
300 120th Ave. NE, Bldg 1, Ste 200
Bellevue, WA 98005
800-426-2673

Sound Impression

Manage MIDI data, waveform audio data (.WAV files) and CD audio with this full-featured program. Among its attributes are the ability to create scores for multimedia presentation using Wave, CD and MIDI audio, and interface that appears and operates like a stereo component rack, extensive OLE support etc.

Midisoft Corp
15379 NE 90th St.
Redmond, WA 98052
800-776-6434

AudioMan

A portable hand-held device with a built-in microphone, speaker, and 8-bit sound digitizer. Really built to let you add verbal notes to your work, rather than handwritten notes.

Logitech Inc.
6505 Kaiser Dr.
Fremont, CA 94555
(510) 795-8500

PortAble Sound

A Parallel port portable sound device with bundled DOS and Windows software.

Digispeech, Inc.
550 Main St.
Suite J
Placerville, CA 95667
(916) 621-1787

SoundXchange

Business level audio solution using a telephone instead of a microphone.

Interactive
204 N. Main
Humboldt, SD 57035
(800) 292-2112

Sound Blaster Deluxe
Sound Blaster Pro Deluxe
Sound Blaster 16 ASP

A variety of cards of every need. Creative Labs creates sound cards for those interested in gaming (Sound Blaster Deluxe) as well as those interested in 16-bit, CD-quality sound (Sound Blaster 16 ASP).

Creative Labs
1901 McCarthy Blvd.
Milpitas, CA 95035
(800) 428-6600

Wave Blaster

A MIDI add-on daughter board to the Sound Blaster 16 card. Wave Blaster provides realistic instrument sounds instead of FM synthesized sound.

Creative Labs
1901 McCarthy Blvd.
Milpitas, CA 95035
(800) 428-6600

Audioport
Microkey

Two products that let you take sound on the road. With Audioport you can both record and play sound, with microkey only play sound. Both devices are tiny and fit into the parallel port of your laptop computer. Uses 12-bit sampling and a 3:1 compression ratio for storage.

Video Associates Labs
4926 Spicewood Springs Rd.
Austin, Texas 78759
(800) 331-0547

Audioport

Antex's Audioport (not to be confused with Creative Labs' product of the same name) is an external device that offers broadcast quality digital audio. It interfaces with PCs via the parallel port and records or plays digital audio direct-to-disk.

Antex Electronics Corporation
16100 South Figueroa St.
Gardena, CA 90248
(310) 532-3092

AdLib Gold

This board is one of the standards in multimedia sound. Roughly equivalent to Creative Labs' Sound Blaster. Both of these boards are popular on the gaming side of the industry. Quality may not be what you're looking for in the professional arena.

AdLib Multimedia
(800) 463-2686

Port Blaster

A portable solution for "on-the-road" business or multimedia presentations. Works with a parallel port.

Creative Labs
1901 McCarthy Blvd.
Milpitas, CA 95035
(800) 428-6600

UltraSound

Can perform mixing of CD-audio, digital audio, synthesizers, a microphone and line input.

Advanced Graphics Computer Technology
Vancouver, British Columbia
Canada
(604) 431-5020

Microsoft Sound System

Built primarily to add verbal notes to Windows applications such as your spreadsheet or word processing document. Also has facility, ProofReader, that provides an audible proofing of numbers and Voice Pilot which enables users to execute commands by voice.

Microsoft Corporation
One Microsoft Way
Redmond, WA 98052
(206) 882-8080

Roland SCC-1 Sound Card

This card seems to be quite popular with those interested in recording high-fidelity music.

Roland Corporation
7200 Dominion Circle
Los Angles, CA 90040
(213) 685-5141

Audio Solution Board

Basically available through OEMs, IBM's Audio Solution Board supports Windows, OS/2 and DOS. Available either in ISA (Industry Standard Architecture) or Micro Channel bus versions (for IBM's own PS/2 series) this board enables 16-bit audio.

IBM
White Plains, NY
(800) 426-3333

Sound Galaxy

Offers 8- or 16-bit sound cards as well as multimedia upgrade kits.

Aztech Labs, Inc.
46707 Fremont Blvd.
Fremont, CA 94538
(510) 623-8988

Midisoft Studio for Windows

MIDI recording/editing software that delivers the power of a professional music studio to your multimedia PC.

Midisoft Corporation
15513 NE 52nd St.
Redmond, WA 98052
(206) 881-7176

Trax

Easy to use software for the MIDI beginner.

Passport Designs, Inc.
100 Stone Pine Rd.
Half Moon Bay, CA 94019
(415) 726-0280

Wave for Windows

Professional audio software for Windows.

Turtle Beach Systems
P.O. Box 5074
York, PA 17405
(717) 843-6916

Monologue

A software product for Windows that adds speech to your applications.

First Byte
19840 Pioneer Ave.
Torrance, CA 90503
(800) 545-7677

IBM Speech Recognition Family

Brings the power of speech to AIX and OS/2 workstations. Has an active vocabulary of over 20,000 words and a sophisticated language model.

IBM
Multimedia Information Center
P.O. Box 2150
Atlanta, GA 30301
(800) 772-2227

20-20 Sound Editor

An audio editing toolset for the IBM platform. Provides cut, paste, copy, an 8-track audio mixer and special effects.

MKS Compu-Group Inc.
1730 Cunard St.

Laval, Quebec
Canada, H7S 2B2
(514) 332-4110

Read My Lips

Not a George Bush record but software for the Mac that lets users record voice or sounds and attach digitized audio clips to documents.

Praxitel
Box 452
Pleasanton, CA 94566
(510) 846-9380

MCS Stereo

The complete interface to your computer's audio capability. Controls CD-ROMs, plays, records and edits .Wav files, and has an integrated database for all your audio sources.

Animotion Development
3720 4th Ave. South #205
Birmingham, AL 35222
(205) 591-5715

FluentLinks

This is a NetWare Loadable Module that enables multiple users to retrieve and play motion video and audio segments over industry-standard networks.

Fluent, Inc.
One Apple Hill
594 Worcester Rd.
Natick, Mass 01760
(508) 651-0911

ACS300.1 Computer Speaker System

Lets users hear digital audio sound with their computers. Users can plug this computer speaker system into any audio or video card to vastly enhance any business presentation etc. with the same level of recording quality as music CD.

Altec Lansing Multimedia
PO Box 277

Milford, PA 18337-0277
800-648-6663

AudioPrisma

A professional Digital Audio Workstation, integrated onto a single system board. Containing everything needed for complete audio editing and production for multimedia applications.

Spectral Synthesis
19501 144th Ave. NE Ste 100A
Woodville, WA 98072
206-487-2931

The CardD Plus

Specifically created for professional recording applications, this product delivers sonic performance equal to none. It comes complete with a Windows 3.1 driver and can be used with any Windows-compatible sound editing software.

Digital Audio Labs
14502 21st Ave. Ste 202
Plymouth, MN 55447
612-473-7626

SoundMan Wave

SoundMan Wave is a wave table synthesis board coupled with up-to-the-minute 16-bit stereo. Audio will no longer sound computer-generated but like real instruments.

Logitech Inc.
65505 Kaiser Dr..
Fremont, CA 94555
800-231-7717

Animation

Photorealism

That's what Strata calls their series of packages for the Mac. There's a bunch of them. Stratavision 3D is a 3D animation program; Stratatextures are collections of realistic looking materials which can be applied to objects.

Strata
2 W. Saint George Blvd.
Suite 2100
St. George, UT 84770
(801) 628-5218

ElectriImage Animation System Version 2.5

Speed and quality. The color jumps and shouts; images that can make you forget your watching Macintosh-generated computer graphics. This package is the only per-frame render anywhere.

Electric Image Inc.
818-577-1627, ext 224
sales@electricimg.com

Real3D

A full-featured 3D animation, modeling and rendering program for the Amiga. Enables objects to "rock and roll" and react to their environment with "intelligence."

RealSoft
544 Queen St.
Chatham, Ontario
Canada, N7M 2J6
(407) 539-0752

3D Studio

The superb animation product that made Autodesk a household name. Comes with over 500 MB of 3D objects, textures and animation. Not cheap, though.

Autodesk, Inc.
2320 Marinship Way
Sausalito, CA 94965
(415) 332-2344

Cyberspace Developer Kit

One of Autodesk's superb animation products. It's a complete toolset for 3D visualization and simulation. In other words, lets you create virtual reality applications.

Autodesk, Inc.
2320 Marinship Way
Sausalito, CA 94965
(415) 332-2344

Animation Works Interactive

Sophisticated animation system with interactivity support, multimedia extensions support and MCI support.

Gold Disk Inc.
5155 Spectrum Way, Unit 5
Mississaauga, Ontario, Canada L4W 5A1
(310) 320-5080

Creative Toonz 2D CEL

This is animation software for Silicon Graphics workstations. Enables animators to experiment with up to 32 different fill colors, add 3D animations, build a picture base of images, use of scanner of input.

Softimage Inc.
660 Newton-Yardley Rd.
Suite 202
Newton, PA 18940
(215) 860-5525

Liberty

A UNIX-based high-end graphics package coupled with animation tools.

Softimage Inc.
660 Newton-Yardley Rd.
Suite 202
Newton, PA 18940
(215) 860-5525

3D Choreographer

3D Choreographer is a model-based 3-D animation program for Windows. Users create animated sequences with pre-drawn people, 3-D shapes, etc. Each character is customizable and has an extensive library of predefined actions.

AniCom Inc.

PO Box 428
Columbia, MD 21045
800-949-4559

Animation Gallery

Animation Gallery contains more than 100 3-D animations for use with any presentation manager that handles Autodesk 3D studio (FLI) files.

Wizardware Multimedia Ltd
918 Delaware Ave.
Bethlehem, PA 18015
80-548-5969

Animation How-To CD

This intermediate-level book offers hands-on explanations that show users how to create dynamic moving objects. Each animation idea is explained, then the steps required to produce it are presented.

Waite Group Press
200 Tamai Plaza
Corte Madera, CA 94925
800-368-9369

Animation Paint Box

Animation Paint Box for Windows offers exceptional productivity tools for 8-bit animators. Features include the ability to resize a arrange of frames, extensive file conversion, ability to load a portion of a large animation, etc.

Azeena Technologies Inc.
PO Box 29169
Long Beach, CA 90806
310-981-2771

Animation Master

Animation Master, the three-dimensional motion picture studio, is a powerful and affordable spline-based modeling and animation program specifically designed for classic character animation. Features include: Inverse kinematics, time-based materials, image mapping etc.

Hash Inc.
2800 E. Evergreen Blvd.

Vancouver, WA 98661
206-750-0042

Caligari trueSpace

Caligari trueSpace for Windows enables users to easily create advanced 3-D graphics. In real-world 3-D perspective, users can twist and bend simple cylinders and spheres into sophisticated, organic shapes with free-form deformation and point-editing.

Caligari Corp.
1955 Landings Dr.
Mountain View, CA 94043
800-351-7620

Frame By Frame Graphic Animation System

Frame By Frame Graphic Animation Systems enable producers to capture VFW or Quick Time movies and computer graphics directly to Panasonic videodisc recorders for instant playback or full-screen, full-resolution video and animation.

Image Management Systems
239 W. 15th St.
New York, NY 10011
212-741-8765

MicroScribe-3D

Compatible with most currently available 3D graphics packages including AutoCAD, 3D Studio, Wavefront, SoftImage, Alias and Form-Z, this tool enhances 3D animations without heavy out-of-pocket expenses.

Immersion Corporation
2158 Paragon Dr.
San Jose, CA 95131
800-893-1160
immersion@starconn.com

Crystal Kaleidoscope

This 3D animation dream suite answers all you dreams and desires — multimedially speaking. It features Crystal TOPAS Professional 5.1, a extremely user friend 3D animation software.

CrystalGraphics
3110 Patrick Henry Dr.
Santa Clara, CA 95054
800-TOPAS-3D

Viewpoint Data Labs

The worlds largest 3D library available at one low price per title; no royalties, one low flat fee.

Viewpoint Data Labs
625 South State St.
Orem, UT 84058
800-328-2738

Photographic

Adobe Photoshop

Perhaps the most popular product in the photo-manipulation market. Enables user to retouch scanned photo and add significant amounts of creativity. Can make photo look like original artwork. Runs under MAC or Windows.

Adobe Systems Inc.
1585 Charleston Rd.
P.O. Box 7900
Mountain View, CA 94039
(800) 833-6687

Morph

If you've seen Terminator 2 then you know what morphing is. Basically you have a starting point and an ending point and then let the computer make the gradual transition between the two. You've also seen this done in one two many music videos.

Morph
Gryphon Software Corporation
7720 Trade St.
Suite 120
San Diego, California 02121
(619) 536-8815

HSC Digital Morph
HSC Software
1661 Lincoln Blvd.

Suite 101
Santa Monica, CA 90404
(310) 392-8441

Graphics

addDepth for Windows

A graphics application tool that adds 3-D impact to type and line art. Users enter text or choose their artwork and depth and perspective are added automatically.

Ray Dream Inc.
1804 N. Shoreline Blvd.
Mountain View, CA 94043
800-846-0111

Color Tools

Color Tools is a complete graphics solution for multimedia presentation. Color Tools provides a comprehensive set of line drawing tools, paint and effect brushes and enhancement capabilities for all types of presentation screens, information displays, training applications and more.

Time Arts Inc.
1425 Corporate Center Pkwy
Santa Rosa, CA 95407
707-576-7722

Creative License

Users can create and edit images, textures and backgrounds with this affordable graphics package. It contains a broad range of pressure-sensitive drawing and painting tools.

Time Arts Inc.
1425 Corporate Center Pkwy
Santa Rosa, CA 95407

Designer 4.0

Featuring a 32-bit graphics engine, this tools allows users unequaled precision, power and performance for illustration on a PC. Features include streamlined interface, precision symbol creation and editing with 29 drawing tools.

Micrografx Inc.

1303 E. Arapaho
Richardson, TX 75081
800-326-3576

Lumena

Lumena is a powerful raster paint, vector draw, animation and videographics software package for DOS-based systems.

Time Arts Inc.
1425 Corporate Center Pkwy
Santa Rosa, CA 95407
707-576-7722

Professional Ddraw

Professional Ddraw is a precision illustration program with built-in desktop publishing and high-end color control. A snap-top modifier palette allows precise size and placement of objects on the fly.

Gold Disk Inc.
3350 Scott Blvd, Bldg 14
Santa Clara, CA 95054
800-465-3375

Altamira Composer 1.01

A revolutionary image composition application for Windows that allows image elements to be automatically masked and anti-aliased through Dynamic Alpha technology and float as independent objects in an infinite stack.

Altamira Software Corp
150 Shoreline Hwy
Ste B-27 Mill Valley, CA 94941
800-425-8264

Chroma Tools

This is a file conversion utility for TARGA users. It converts TGA, PCX, GIF, TIF, BMP, MAC TIF, and VST images to TGA, PCX, GIF, TIF, VST, BMP MAC TIF and color/black and white PostScript. It supports all screen modes and includes multiple color reduction algorithms.

Videotex Systems Inc.
11880 Greenville Ave

#100
Dallas, TX 725243
214-231-9200

EasyCopy/X

This package offers an X Window-based tool for capture and production of high-quality, full-color images. It works independently of any application and provides an OSF/Motif-based user interface permits users to work directly from the command line. It also allows direct printing of images.

Image-in

A Windows-based editing tool that provides utilities for drawing, painting and editing or manipulating color, black and white or gray-scale images.

CPI Inc.
1820 Gateway Dr., Bldg. 3, Ste 370
San Francisco, CA 94404
800-345-3540

"Pixel Perfect" Graphics

A CD-ROM that contains more than 2,000 images in 11 formats in 300 dpi high resolution. Categories include Animals, Business, Computers, Food, High Tech, Holidays, States, Countries, etc.

Wizardware Multimedia Ltd
918 Delaware Ave.
Bethlehem, PA 18015
610-866-9613

Digital Morph

With an easy-to-use image manipulation tool users can now add exciting visual impact to their presentations with this sophisticated morphing tool. Users can morph form one still image to another or between moving images.

HSC Software
6303 Carpinteria Ave
Carpinteria, CA 93013
805-566-6200

Image Partner

A full-featured image processing and analysis program that offers high resolution with up to 1,024 by 768 by 256 gray-scale imaging displayable on Super/Extended VGA PC systems. Unique capabilities include video camera characterization, permitting users to understand and quantify the systematic errors in imaging systems.

Image Automation
7 Henry Clay Dr.
Merimack, NH 03054
603-598-3400

JAG for Windows

Concerned with the quality of digital images, JAG can be used to smooth out the stair-stepped edges in color and gray-scale graphics. It works with the popular paint, graphics, and image editing packages.

Ray Dream Inc.
1804 N. Shoreline Blvd.
Mountain View, CA 94043
800-846-0111

Picture Publisher 5.0

Picture Publisher is a professional image editing program that provides a combination of speed, functionality and ease of us. Features include: object layers, intuitive interface; Image Browser etc.

Micrografx Inc.
1303 E. Arapaho
Richardson, TX 75081
800-326-3576

3-D Modeling Lab

Crystal-clear hands-on examples enable users to learn 3-D modeling, rendering and animation for the PC. You can design 3-D images and animation for products, presentations, etc.

Waite Group Press
200 Tamal Plaza
Corte Madera, CA 94925
800-368-9369

Cheetah 3D

Render and animate complex 3-D images with this powerful multimedia tool. Standard rendering features include up to 10 parallel light sources with spectacular and ambient light controls. High-end features include multiple area rendering, bit map textures, etc.

Looking Glass Software
11222 La Cienga Blvd., Ste 305
Inglewood, CA 90304
310-348-8240

Envision

With unparalleled realism and rendering quality, this tool allows users to see their finished designs in photorealistic detail and 24-bit color. It renders any image and applies surface details, textures or finishes on any background.

ModaCAD
1954 Cotner Ave.
Los Angeles, CA 90025
310-312-6632

Fractals for Windows

With zoom box, menus and a mouse users can create new Fractals and control more than 85 different fractal types. Bundled with WinFract.

Waite Group Press
200 Tamal Plaza
Corte Madera, CA 94925
800-368-9369

Imagine

An 3-D image processing program that lets users create any kind of character with numberless effects applied to that character. Once users have snared the look that they have imagined, they can make those characters live through the extensive use of Imagine's animation capabilities.

Impulse Inc.
8416 Xerxes Ave. North
Brooklyn Park, MN 56544
800-328-0184

MacroModel

This package enables users to twist or bend 3-D objects. Since there is a version for the Mac as well as for the IBM PC platforms, images created on one can be easily transferred to the other.

Macromedia, Inc.
600 Townsend St.
San Francisco, CA 94103
(800) 288-8229

223 — The Stereo Paint System

A paint system that provides the ability to create true 3D, stereoscopic images. Also permits conversion of pre-existing 2D images into 3D Images.

Latent Image Development Corporation
Digital Media Group
111 Fourth Ave.
New York, NY 10003
(212) 388-0122

Adobe Illustrator

A powerful professional design tool. Enables designers to draw from scratch or work with existing images. Supports: 16.7 million colors, text, generate separations, custom views and page sizes, objects manipulation such as dividing, slicing and combining.

Adobe Systems Inc.
1585 Charleston Rd.
P.O. Box 7900
Mountain View, CA 94039
(800) 833-6687

Painterly Effects

UNIX-based set of filters that let you turn boring images into classical art.

Softimage Inc.
660 Newton-Yardley Rd.
Suite 202

Newton, PA 18940
(215) 860-5525

Media Clips

Wallace Music & Sound, Inc., provides original music and sound effects for software developers and publishers.

Wallace Music & Sound, Inc.
6210 West Pershing Ave.
Glendale, Arizona 95304
(602) 979-6201

Soundtrack Express

Compatible with all authoring and presentation tools, is an unlimited source of professional quality music for multimedia.

BlueRibbon Soundtracks Ltd
PO Box 8689
Atlanta, GA 30306
800-226-0212

Multimedia Music Library

A collection of more than 100 pop and orchestral musical sequences. Royalty-free.

Midisoft Corporation
P.O. Box 1000
Bellevue, WA 98009
(206) 881-7176

Killer Tracks

A series of music selections.

Killer Tracks
6534 Sunset Blvd.
Hollywood, CA 90028
(800) 877-0078

HyperClips for Windows is a CD-ROM volume containing hundreds of high-quality animation and sound clips designed to accent business, sales and technical presentations.

The HyperMedia Group
5900 Hollis St.
Suite O
Emeryville, CA 94608
(510) 601-0900

The DigiSound Audio Library

This library brings exciting, full fidelity sound to multimedia with professionally produced MIDI music, sound effects and DigiVoice clips.

Presentation Graphics Group
270 N. Canon Dr.
Suite 103
Beverly Hills, CA 90210
(310) 277-3050

Aris Entertainment

This company offers several sets of CD-ROMs for Windows, MAC and PCs that contain a combination of sound effects, full-color photographs and/or video clips. Under the trade name of MediaClips the following sets illustrate the Aris offerings: Worldview: space images and sounds; Wild Places: North American photos and audio clips; Majestic Places: nature photos and audio clips; Business Background: photos, audio clips and sound effects.

Aris Entertainment, Inc.
4444 Via Marina, Suite 811
Marina del Rey, CA 90292
(310) 821-0234
(800) 228-2747

Digital Zone

Digital Zone hires professional photographers to take stunning photos. The photos are then stored on Kodak's Photo CD and free to use for purchasers of one of the collections.

Digital Zone Inc.
P.O. Box 5562
Bellevue, WA 98006
(800) 538-3113

Archive Films/Archive Photos

This collection contains thousands of hours of historical and entertainment footage and stills produced from 1894 until the present. Includes: Albert Einstein, Jacob Astor, Hollywood, presidents, kings, the Depression.

Archive New Media
530 West 25th St.
NY, NY 10001
(212) 620-3980

CBS News Archives

CBS
524 West 57 St.
New York, NY 10019
(212) 975-2875

Buyout Music Library

Musi-Q
P.O. Box 451147
Sunrise, FL
(305) 572-9276

Station Break

40 Glen Street
Suite 1
Glen Cove, NY 11542
(800)-ON-AIR-99

Video Tape Library

This collection offers news clips such as LA Riot, Gang shootings, sports.

VTL
1509 N. Crescent Heights Blvd.
Suite 2
Los Angles, CA 90046
(213) 656-4330

PhotoDisc

Each CD contains 336 multipurpose images from award-winning photographers of landscapes, rain forests, deserts, animals, etc. Arranged in a user friendly slide show.

PhotoDisc
2013 4th Ave.
Seattle, WA 98121
(206) 441-9355

Clipper

A monthly clip art subscription service. You have choice of medium: paper, floppy or CD-ROM.

Dynamic Graphics Inc.
6000 N. Forest Park Dr.
P.O. Box 1901
Peoria, IL 61656
(800) 255-8800

Masterclips

Masterclips, Inc.
5201 Ravenswood Rd.
Suite 111
Ft. Lauderdale, Florida 33312
(800) 292-2547

References

(1) Briggs, Allan. *"Digital Editing — The Key to Digital Production,"* The Ultimate Sourcebook of Multimedia, J. Keyes, ed. McGraw-Hill. 1997.
(2) Hendrix, Josh and Alton Christensen. *"Digital Video a la Carte,"* The Ultimate Sourcebook of Multimedia, J. Keyes, ed. McGraw-Hill. 1997.
(3) Whiteside, Mary F. and J. Allan Whiteside. *"Using Audio in Multimedia Applications,"* The Ultimate Sourcebook of Multimedia , J. Keyes, ed.McGraw-Hill. 1997.

Index

#D modeling software, 264
@home, 11
3D, 197
3WB, 26

ActiveX Streaming Format, 70
ActiveX, 68
ActivMedia, 1
adaptive rendering, 196
Adobe Premiere, 77, 160
Adobe, 263
AIFF, 179
Alpha channel, 259
AlphaServer, 68
American Telemedicine Association, 4
Amiga, 262
answering machine, 173
anti-aliasing, 259
artifacts, 125
ASF Editor, 71, 81
ASF, 70
ASX, 72
AT&T, 5
ATM, 42
AU, 100, 179
audio codecs, 179
audio conferencing, 173, 179
audio considerations, 261, 261
audio encoding, 136
audio hints, 269
audio source file, 123
Audio Tuning Wizard, 88
audiocast, 51
AudioNet, 99
Authorware, 232
AVI, 49, 68, 153, 156, 164

back-channel, 49
bandwidth negotiation, 106, 139

bandwidth scalability, 147, 158
bandwidth, 12
BeZerk, 29
Bluestone, 2
BMP, 77
Bosnia, 9
Brainworks Net, 29
broadcast quality software, 259
broadcast, 36
Broadway, 225
broken image, 168
Buchanan, Leigh, 7

cable, 252
CAD, 253
CameraMan, 22
capturing VDOLive video, 54
Carpoint, 93
cellular systems, 245
centering the wave, 124
Cerf, Vint, 252
CGI, 22
ChannelWorks, 254
chat tool, 173, 175, 234
CineWeb, 202
Cisco, 148
Citibank, 4
ClearFusion, 202
ClearVideo Decoder, 226
clipping, 123
CNBC, 8
Cogger, Dick, 228
collaboration, 234
collaborative learning, 254
CommerceNet, 2
compression codecs, 185
compression, 67, 79, 100, 125, 148, 228
    lossy, 100
    video, 148
CompUSA, 48
CONNEXIONS, 228

convergence, 8
converting:
    analog to video, 153
    video to audio 162
Cool Edit, 100
CoolTalk, 171
creating a plug-in, 166
Crescendo Plus, 202
Cuba Memorial Hospital, 3
CU-SeeMe, 227

DAT, 100
data compression, 12
Data Translation, 225
Dateline, 9
DC offset, 124
desktop video broadcasting, 141
Desktop Video, 10
DIB, 77
Dickinson, Sarah, 6
digital editing, 262
digitizing, 258
Director Studio, 232
Director, 232
DirectX, 214
distance learning, 30
Dorcey, Tom, 228
DVE, 259
DVMRP, 40, 43

Echospeech, 203
ECnet, 253
e-mail, 3
embed tag, 110
embed, 166
embedded video, 164
encoding:
    MPEG, 225
    RealAudio, 104
equalization, 126
Ethernet multicast addresses, 40
Ethernet, 41

FDDI, 41
Federal Internet Exchange, 52
Ferris, David, 3
Film Scouts, 23
Financial News Network, 8
Financial Times, 18
firewall, 66
FIX, 52
Flashware, 203

Frame Relay, 42
frames, 121
Freehand, 232
FutureSplash plug-in, 96
FutureWave, 96
FX, 264

Georgia Institute of Technology, 4
Gerlach, Ken, 30
GII, 246
graphics formats, 177
groupware, 2
GSM, 179

H.261, 59
H.323, 85
Hambrecht & Quist, 1
Hardie, Mark, 4
Hawaii Public Schools, 254
HDTV, 239
HDTV, 61
headend, 253
Hewlett-Packard, 30
HFC, 252
HTML authoring, 178
HTML, 9
    RealAudio, 115
    VDO links, 164
HTTP_USER_AGENT, 168
Huntington Bancshares, 5
hybrid fiber coax, 252

IBM, 5, 15
IIEEE-802, 40
IETF 1058, 43
IETF, 35
    RFC 1075, 42
    RFC 1112, 42
    RFC 1584, 42
    RFC 1889, 41
IGMP, 39
IIG, 50
illustrated audio, 69
Image Multicast Client, 58
imagemap, 30
InBox Direct, 178
InPerson 59
input levels, 123
INRIA Videoconferencing System, 59
InSoft, 171
Intel intercast, 45
Intel, 6

interactive games, 240
intercast, 10, 15, 45
Internet Engineering Task Force, 2, 35
Internet Group Management Protocol, 39
Internet Multicast backbone, 36
Internet Society, 2
InterVU, 203, 220
intranets, 66
IP multicast, 65
IS411 server, 173
Iterated, 226
ITV Net, 18
ivs, 59

jaggies, 259
Java, 15, 179
JavaScript, 179
Jellyvision, 29
Jeopardy, 29
JPG, 77

LAM, 181
Lie, Cheat and Steal, 9
Lingo scripts, 232
live audio encoding, 138
Live Bamba, 15
LIVE Share, 6
live stream, 102
Live3D, 196
LiveAudio, 27, 189
LiveConnect, 192, 229
LiveFiles, 217
LiveMedia, 179
LiveVideo, 193
LMSP, 181
loss tolerant JPEG, 79
Lotus Notes, 3
Lycos, 2

Ma and Pa Bell, 243
Macintosh, 85
Macromedia Shockwave, 231
MacZilla, 203
Marimba, 13
Massachussets General Hospital, 4
Mbone   13, 36, 51, 147
    mailing lists, 55
    software, 53
MCI device driver, 156
Media Converter, 185
Media Server installation, 181
Media Server, 179, 180

Meet the Press, 9
MetaVoice coding, 229
microphone gain, 261
Microsoft Network, 9, 95
Microsoft, 8, 65, 141
MIDI, 179
MIDPLUG, 204
mime configuration, 110
mime:
    Netscape Media Server, 182
    RealAudio, 133
    VDOLive, 164
    VIVO, 209
mixing boards, 126
mmcc, 60
morphs, 264
MOSPF, 40, 43
MOV, 78
MovieStar, 204
MPEG Plaza, 225
MPEG, 68, 78, 216
mrouted, 43
MSNBC, 9
multicast islands, 36
multicast routing protocols, 40
multicasting problems, 60
multimedia across networks, 37
Multimedia Conference Control tool, 60
multimedia, 66
Multipoint Appication Sharing, 91
Mungo Park, 95
music, 265
    selecting, 267

narration, 265
NASA, 37, 58
NBC Interactive Media, 9
NBC, 7, 148
NBC.com, 9
NetCam, 15
NetMeeting, 85, 171
Netscape:
    Communicator, 178
    Conference, 179
    Media Server, 171
    multimedia plug-ins, 201
    sound converter, 181
NetShow, 65
    Live server, 84
    Live, 76
    On-Demand, 76
Network Video, 59
Network Voice Terminal, 59
nevot, 59

Nielsen Media, 1
noise gating, 125
nonlinear editing, 258
normalization, 127
nv, 59
NYSERNet, 228

OmniBox, 7
Oracle Media Server, 7
Oracle, 11
Party Girl, 229

PBS, 148
PC Card Camera, 7
PCI bus, 49
PCM, 100
PCM, 59
PCMCIA, 7
Pearl, Amy, 6
performance issues, RealAudio, 134
Photoshop, 259
PictureTel, 6, 208
PictureWindow, 59
PIM, 40, 43
plug-in:
    creation, 166
    video, 166
    RealAudio, 110
pnserver, 129
PointCast, 13
power companies, 245
Presentation Assistant, 82
Preston, Dr. Jane, 4
Progressive Networks, 99, 180
ProShare, 6
proxy server, 76
pseudo-streaming, 220
push technology, 13

QuickTime, 23, 68, 193, 202

RA, 100
racut, 105
Radio Free Vat, 58
RAE, 120
RAID, 69
RAM, 107
rapaste, 105
RapidTransit, 204
RBOC, 243
Real Magic Producer, 225

real time transport protocol, 35
RealAudio Encoder, 100
RealAudio, 17, 99, 141, 180, 204, 269
    Hosting Service, 133
    Live, 138
    platforms, 130
    Player Plus, 99
    pricing, 128
    Server, 100, 127
    service providers, 140

reflector, 227
rendezvous point, 44
resource guide, 273
resource reservation protocol, 35
reverse path forwarding. 43
RFC 1889/1890, 84
RFC1112, 54
Rifff, 95
Rolling Stones, 37
route pruning, 54
routers, 37
Royal Bank of Canada, 5
RPM, 107
RSVP, 35, 179
RT29HQ codec, 230
RTP, 35, 41, 179
RTSP, 180

Sansers, Dr. Jay, 4
Sci-Fi channel, 21
SDK, 70
SDP, 38
server clustering, 133
serverless streaming video, 209
service providers, RealAudio, 140
Session Directory, 38, 57
shared whiteboard tool, 60
ShowMe, 59
SIGGRAPH, 58
Silicon Graphics, 262
Simulated Live Transfer Agent, 116
simulcast, 141
Site Developer's Conference, 141
SMDS, 42
sound effects, 265
sound effects, selecting, 267
sound quality, 122
speech, 265
    developing, 266
streaming, 11, 65
StreamWorks Transmitter, 219
StreamWorks, 18, 26, 216
subpixel positioning, 259

Sun Microsystems, 6
SuperNet, 9
Surround Video 92
synchronized audio, 180
synchronized multimedia, 120
synchronizing video playback, 222

T.120, 85
Talker, 204
TCI, 11
TCP, 61
TCP/IP, 35, 41, 65, 117
technology, VDOnet, 147
Tedesco, Dr. Francis, 4
telecom, 237
telecommunications, 237
telecommuting, 251
tele-education, 251
telemedicine, 3
television, 238
timeline syncrhonization, 70
Token Ring, 41
Toler, James, 4
Toolvox, 205, 229
Tower Group, 4
training, 7
TrueSpeech, 205
tunneling, 36
tunnels, 52

UDP, 69
UDP-based audio, 61
Ulead Media Studio, 161, 263
UltraThrob Online, 17
UnderWire, 95
unicast, 36, 41
universal in-box, 249
University Video Communications, 27
URL flipping, 78
User Location Server, 86

vat, 59
VDO:
    Capture, 153
    Clip, 153, 156
    file creation, 165
    Personal Server, 148
    Server, 149
    tools, 153
    VDOLive, 19, 30, 141, 205
VDOnet, 141

VDOVast Center for Multicasting, 148
VDOWave algorithm, 158
VHS, 258
video acceleration card, 263
video capture card, 153
video capture, 210
video compression, 156
video conferencing, 3, 5, 253
video malls, 239
video on demand, 239
video server log, 152
video server, 49
video telephony, 148
Videoconf, 6
videoconferencing, 51, 227
VidtoASF, 72
ViewMovie, 205
Virtual Film Festival, 25
Visicalc, 2
Visual Audio Tool, 59
Vitec Multimedia, 225
VIVO, 209, 260
VivoActive Producer, 209
VivoActive, 205, 208
VLSI Vision Ltd., 7
voice shadowing, 127
VoiceFonts, 230
Vosaic, 214
VOX file, 230
Voxware, 229
VRML, 198

WAV, 68, 77, 100, 137, 156, 179
WAVTOASF, 77
wb, 60
webcrawler, 1
WebMaster Magazine, 7
White Pine, 228
whiteboard, 15, 91, 173, 175, 253
Win32API, 69
Windows NT, 68
wireless communications, 243
Worldwide TV, 19

Xing, 18, 216
XingMPEG Encoder, 218

Yahoo, 1
Yon, Bruce, 7
You Don't Know Jack, 28
Yudkovitz, Martin, 9

ABOUT THE AUTHOR

Jessica Keyes is president of New Art Inc., a high-technology consultancy. Keyes has given seminars for such prestigious universities as Carnegie Mellon, Boston University, University of Illinois, James Madison University and San Francisco State University. She is a frequent keynote speaker on the topics of competitive strategy using information technology and marketing on the information superhighway. She is an advisor for DataPro, McGraw-Hill's computer research arm as well as a member of the Sprint Business Council. Keyes is also a founding Board of Director member of the New York Software Industry Association. She has recently been appointed to a two-year term to the Mayor of New York City's Small Business Advisory Council.

Prior to founding New Art, Keyes was Managing Director of R&D for the New York Stock Exchange and has been an officer with Swiss Bank Co. and Banker's Trust, both in New York City. She holds a Masters from New York University where she did her research in the area of artificial intelligence.

A noted columnist and correspondent with over 150 articles published, Keyes is also the author of nine books:

The New Intelligence: AI in Financial Services, HarperBusiness, 1990
The Handbook of Expert Systems in Manufacturing, McGraw-Hill, 1991
Infotrends: The Competitive Use of Information, McGraw-Hill, 1992
The Software Engineering Productivity Handbook, McGraw-Hill, 1993
The Handbook of Multimedia, McGraw-Hill, 1994
The Productivity Paradox, McGraw-Hill, 1994
Technology Trendlines, Van Nostrand Reinhold ,1995
The Ultimate Sourcebook on Multimedia, McGraw-Hill, January 1997
The Internet Consultant's Handbook, McGraw-Hill, November 1996

Infotrends was selected as one of the best business books of 1992 by the Library Journal. The Software Engineering Productivity Handbook was the main selection for the Newbridge book club for computer professionals. The McGraw-Hill Multimedia Handbook is now in its second reprint and has been translated into Chinese and Japanese.